Dis-History

Uses of the Past at
Walt Disney's Worlds

Jason S. Lantzer

Theme Park Press
The Happiest Books on Earth
www.ThemeParkPress.com

© 2017 Jason S. Lantzer

No part of this publication may be reproduced, distributed, or transmitted in any form or by any means, including photocopying, recording, or other electronic or mechanical methods, without the prior written permission of the publisher, except for brief quotations embodied in critical reviews and certain other non-commercial uses permitted by copyright law.

Although every precaution has been taken to verify the accuracy of the information contained herein, no responsibility is assumed for any errors or omissions, and no liability is assumed for damages that may result from the use of this information.

Theme Park Press is not associated with the Walt Disney Company.

The views expressed in this book are those of the author and do not necessarily reflect the views of Theme Park Press.

Theme Park Press publishes its books in a variety of print and electronic formats. Some content that appears in one format may not appear in another.

Editor: Bob McLain
Layout: Artisanal Text

ISBN 978-1-68390-077-1
Printed in the United States of America

Theme Park Press | www.ThemeParkPress.com
Address queries to bob@themeparkpress.com

Contents

A Preface of Acknowledgements   *v*
Introduction: Once Upon a Time   *ix*

CHAPTER ONE   **1**
Mickey Mouse and the Creation of Dis-History

CHAPTER TWO   **21**
A Whole New World:
The Creation of the Walt Disney Mythos

CHAPTER THREE   **55**
Main Street, U.S.A.

CHAPTER FOUR   **81**
A Small World of Fantasy(land)

CHAPTER FIVE   **103**
Give Me Liberty (Square)!

CHAPTER SIX   **131**
Dis-History's Mythic Frontier Adventure

CHAPTER SEVEN   **159**
A Great Big Beautiful Tomorrow(land)

CHAPTER EIGHT   **181**
A Dis-Historic Showcase at Home and Abroad

Happily Ever After: A Dis-Historic Conclusion   *213*

About the Author   *227*
About the Publisher   *229*

A Preface of Acknowledgements

Experience Disney's Contemporary Resort

Opened in 1971, the Contemporary Resort's history offers a first glimpse at Dis-History. Announced as one of several themed hotels Disney planned to operate on its own as part of its second park, the Contemporary was to be sleek and modern, a sort of "Tomorrowland" of hotels. The central elevator shaft was bracketed by steel A-frames, with rooms built modularly (and completely furnished) off site and then slid into place. The park's monorail line runs directly through the hotel itself, and a nearly ten-story tall mosaic tile mural flanks three sides of the concourse, making them "must see" parts of the structure for any visitor to the Magic Kingdom.[1] It is also the resort I stayed at during my first visit to Walt Disney World.

I have, in many ways, not just grown up with Disney, but at Walt Disney World. I first journeyed to Florida as a child of three, as part of a large Lantzer family vacation that included my grandparents, parents, aunts, and uncles. My memories are fuzzy, but I do recall the thrill of riding the monorail, the fun of getting Mickey ears and my very own Mickey Mouse, and the joy of eating breakfast with Chip and Dale. I next encountered Disney while I was in college, some eighteen years later. In the twelve years that I have been a parent, my wife and I have taken our children to a Disney park eleven times. On every visit new memories are created and my (and our) attachment to Disney grows. We are living proof of Disney's cross-generational appeal and pull.[2]

In between the trips, of course, were the movies, television shows, music, and books. To grow up in the United States in the second half

---

1 "Contemporary Resort Mural," disneycontemporary.com/content/contemporary-resort-mural, 16 August 2016; "Histories of Disney's Contemporary and Polynesian Resorts," https://disneyparks.disney.go.com/blog/2011/09/histories-of-disneys-contemporary-and-polynesian-resorts/, 16 August 2016.
2 Gary Cross, *Consumed Nostalgia: Memory in the Age of Fast Capitalism* (New York: Columbia University Press, 2015), 210–11.

of the twentieth century, whether one realized it or not, was to grow up with Disney. And though Walt[3] himself was dead before I ever set foot in Florida, the company which bears his name has achieved what few corporations can ever hope for: near ubiquity with their target audience, generation to generation.

Yet, Disney never entered my professional life. Oh, sure, there might be pictures shared with students at the start of the semester (though my children, more than Disney, was the focus), or stories about a vacation told to co-workers, but never—despite my own interest in American culture—did Disney appear on my periodic idea lists for my next project. All that changed in the fall of 2013, when, while talking about our upcoming Thanksgiving trip, my colleague Cathy Holland said, "You should do a book on Disney."

What would I do, exactly? There were and are plenty of books and articles (good and otherwise) about Walt Disney the man, about Disney the corporation (cast in both positive and negative lights), about the subtexts of movies, and Disney's influence on the animation process. The list seemed endless, and if not conclusive, at least somewhat exhaustive.[4] That is, until I started to think about how Disney uses, and in some ways forges out of, the American past a usable (for them) culture to display in their parks.

Working on this project has left me indebted to many. My academic home is at Butler University in Indianapolis, Indiana, and it was there that this book was conceived and nurtured. The first person I want to thank is Cathy Holland, who suggested I write something about Disney. I am also thankful to Judi Morrel, Rusty Jones, Melissa Friedman, and Dacia Charlesworth, my other colleagues in the CHASE office, for putting up with piles of books on my desk, Disney anecdotes, and trips to the library. Speaking of which, I cannot thank Susan Berger and Sarah Damery of the Butler University Library enough, as they once again facilitated my many interlibrary loan requests. I am thankful to my colleague Mindy Dunn, an expert on fairy-tale literature, for her insights, and am indebted to Gary Edgerton, the dean of the College of Communication, who has also written about Disney and was willing to share his knowledge with me, and to Rebecca DeGrazia for making sure Disney was a part of the Faculty Brownbag Series. In addition, I would be remiss if I did not also thank our former associate

---

3 Throughout the manuscript I have attempted to differentiate the man, as Walt, and the company he founded, as Disney, to avoid whenever possible confusion by the continual use and reference to Walt Disney.

4 Michael Barrier, *The Animated Man: A Life of Walt Disney* (Los Angeles: University of California Press, 2007), 324.

provost, Mary Ramsbottom, for her support. But mostly I wish to thank my former students, in particular Emelia (who, despite being busy working on her doctorate at the University of Michigan, read an early version of the manuscript), Cayla, Miley, Lainey, Gina, Rachel, Kalie, Ashley, Rachel, Rachael, Katie, Robert, Rebecca, Shelby, Olivia, and Mallory for their Disney perspectives, as well as all the others (especially those who took my honors seminar on Disney) who heard stories about Lantzer family vacations that turned into research trips.

Professionally, I am indebted to Kelly Baker and Brent Plate. It was over a conversation on Twitter about getting the DVD of *Frozen* for our respective children that I first officially mentioned the idea of this book to Kelly. She quickly put me in touch with Brent, who was kind enough to add me to a panel he was putting together for the American Academy of Religion's 2014 annual conference. As a result, I got an early opportunity to take my jumble of ideas and start creating a narrative—that grew and grew as I went along. Additionally, my undergraduate friend-turned-professional-colleague, Jason VanHorn of Calvin College, provided some excellent insights into the geographic undertakings of Disney, and connected me with one of his colleagues, Becca McBride. Another undergraduate friend, Josh Cogswell (as well as his mother Michelle and brother Clayton—my West Coast family), also deserve thanks for giving me my first glimpse at the inner workings of Hollywood, as well as introducing me to the story of his great grandfather, Billy Bletcher, who gave voice to several Disney characters. I am also thankful for the staff at Indiana University's Lilly Library for their help in tracking down Walt's correspondence with Upton Sinclair and John Ford. As always, I wish to thank James Madison, of Indiana University, who continues to offer assistance and advice to me now just as he has since I became one of his graduate advisees over fifteen years ago.

I also wish to thank the staff at the Walt Disney Archives, in particular Kevin Kern. Not everyone who writes about Disney gets the opportunity to spend time in the archives, and I was lucky enough to do so. Kevin made the entire process easy, and my time on the studio grounds a true professional pleasure. And even if it was only a taxi, it was a thrill to get to use the executive entrance when I departed.

Of course, I am deeply thankful to Theme Park Press. Publisher Bob McLain made the process an easy and joyful one, from start to finish. His encouraging words about the manuscript arrived, magically enough, while I was at Epcot in March of 2017. In addition, they could not have come at a better time in terms of my own thinking about this project.

Personally, I owe thanks to my grandparents, John and Margaret Lantzer, for helping make possible my very first Disney trip when I was three. When I told my grandmother about this project, she wrote me a note recalling our trip and her memories of it.[5] I am also thankful to my own parents, Jack and Juanita Lantzer, who have not only provided me with love and support over the years, but also came with my family on one of our vacations to Walt Disney World in 2012. I am grateful for and to my two sets of in-laws: once again, I was blessed to do some of my writing at the lake cottage of James and Kathy Heuer, who in addition to opening their home to their son-in-law, also made sure I was well fed and their grandchildren well entertained. As with my other writing projects, Susan and Bill Hebert again provided clutch babysitting and support for me at crucial moments during the writing process. I should also thank my sister-in-law, Anne, who welcomed us into her home in California over Christmas 2014 and again in April 2016, which allowed me to visit "Walt's park" firsthand, as well as some other important Disney related sights, not to mention, via her wedding, providing a reason to go to Disneyland Paris!

Lastly I wish to thank my daughter Kate (who dubbed herself my "research helper") and son Nick (who patiently went through Liberty Square with me on a hot July morning) for their enthusiastic—though perhaps, considering the topic, not unexpected—support and insights into the wonderful world of Disney. However, this book, ultimately, is a gift to my wife, Erin. When we were in college, she, some friends, and I spent a few days in Orlando during spring break, one of which was spent at the Magic Kingdom. While standing in line, I told her, "This is my happy place." What went unsaid at the time was that as magical as it was, I was truly happy there only because I was with her. Therefore, thank you, my darling dearest, for helping make all of my dreams come true.

---

5 My grandmother wrote in part, "When I think about Disney, the biggest thing I remember is Space Mountain and how glad I was when it was over, and how I looked in that big mirror and my hair was standing straight up. But, it was a wonderful vacation."

INTRODUCTION

Once Upon a Time

Experience Walt Disney's Firehouse Apartment

As guests enter Disneyland, Walt Disney's first theme park, and stroll down Main Street, they literally walk in the footsteps of both a man and a mouse. They will see them both, soon enough, as standing before Sleeping Beauty Castle is a statue of Walt and Mickey Mouse. However, if they pause and turn their gaze toward one of Main Street's buildings, they will find the Disneyland Fire Department. In a second-story window, there is a light turned on. If guests could see past the curtains, their view would be of Walt Disney's private apartment, built so he could spend nights in the park (especially to oversee its construction). The light was turned on to let people know Walt was there. It is left on today to remind guests that though Walt is dead, his spirit remains.[1]

Since *Steamboat Willie* debuted in movie theaters in 1928, a mouse named Mickey, as well as the man and the company that brought him to life, has captivated the world: Walt Disney. Over the next few decades, Disney became both a representation and a molder of American culture. This was largely by design, as Walt hoped to forge a broad culture for all Americans. Doing so entailed not only standardizing folk and fairy tales, but also drawing inspiration from literature and history. While this process is seen in their movies, Disney brought the concept of Dis-History (shorthand for Disney's version of history) alive in its parks.

Dis-History[2] is a manufactured version of the past, but it is also something much more than just tapping into nostalgia. It is a theoretical praxis and an organizing principle for the parks, which gives

---

1 "Virtual Tour of Walt Disney's Apartment," disneyparks.disney.go.com/blog/2010/12/virtual-tour-of-walt-disneys-apartment/, 22 November 2016.

2 What I call Dis-History was inspired as a term by Stephen Fjellman's work, though he used the term "Distory." Others, such as Kevin Sandler, have opted for "Disneyfication" of either history or culture.

them a narrative thread and helps guests to navigate the parks, while also serving as a means to talk of the past and future. And, perhaps just as important, Dis-History is an accurate (so far as Disney is concerned) version of history that helps form a common, popular, cultural narrative for guests, allowing them to "create" personal history, or memories, for themselves and their families that binds them to others and events much more momentous than a mere vacation. In short, it is an interpretative framework, working on multiple levels, which helps the past "sell" Disney's version of American culture.

To Disney, the concept works because the public likes it and has an interest in it, even if historical knowledge is not as deep as academic historians might like. Thus, it is a "hook" to get people to come and enjoy the Disney parks.[3] However, it is more than that. Walt Disney was explicit (as has the company in the years since) that he was drawing from history (and fantasy) as he built his park.[4] As Michael Wallace noted, Walt was "a passionate historian" and his parks influence how people "perceive ... the past" in very real ways.[5]

The relationship between history and culture in the mind of both Walt and his company is both real and important. Culture is often discussed in terms of high (what the elite and wealthy enjoy) and low (what most people enjoy, and what might be considered as popular culture). Because Walt hoped to forge a common American culture based in Dis-History, this meant finding ways to bridge the divide between the two subsets. Perhaps the best example of this in films came with *Fantasia*, where Disney married classical music to animation—whether or not it fit the theme of the composer. Walt hoped that the film would both expose to a popular audience the kinds of things high culture routinely regaled in.[6] Broad cultural formation also had a practical business angle as well. Walt wanted as many people as possible to to see his films because that is how the company made a good deal of its money. His films were already popular with the public, so one might argue that *Fantasia* and such efforts were also about convincing members of high culture to better appreciate what he was doing, not

---

3 Douglas Greenberg, "History is a Luxury: Mrs. Thatcher, Mr. Disney, and (Public) History," *Reviews in American History,* 26(March 1998), 303.

4 Richard Francaviglia, "Walt Disney's Frontierland as an Allegorical Map of the American West, "The *Western Historical Quarterly,* 30(Summer 1999), 157.

5 Warren Leon and Roy Rosenzweig, editors, *History Museums in the United States: A Critical Assessment* (Chicago: University of Illinois Press, 1989), xxiii, 158.

6 Richard Schickel, *The Disney Version: The Life, Times, Art and Commerce of Walt Disney, Third Edition* (Chicago: Ivan R. Dee Publisher, 1997), 182–183.

from an industry or technological standpoint, but by coming to the theater to enjoy an animated film.[7] However, *Fantasia* also showed the kind of backlash Disney could expect from this cultural merging. Many within high-cultural bastions saw Disney's work (even more so once Disneyland was constructed) of broad cultural creation as anathema.[8] Ultimately, Walt wanted to entertain people and believed he was "making pictures for the great public and not for a certain select few."[9] Disney artist Floyd Norman believed Walt never sought "adulation from the crowd" or "acceptance from the intellectuals and critics." He just wanted to construct his vision of what culture might be.[10]

American audiences have long been familiar with great works of literature and art, even when they have not read them or seen them for themselves, and these works have been enjoyed by both popular and elite audiences. Walt came of age at precisely the time when artists like Shakespeare were being transformed from something that Americans, regardless of class, might enjoy together, to that which only certain audiences were exposed. The Bard went from someone whose works were shown across the nation during the nineteenth century to one that cultural critics believed could only be truly appreciated by audiences of a certain societal status. Elites decided, according to Lawrence Levine, that certain arts and types of artists belonged to them, not to the masses. Popular forms of art had to be regulated to second-class status.[11] Walt sought to rectify this development.

Culture is a product of the past interacting with the present. At the time that Walt was starting to forge a broad culture, there was a prevailing notion that America had yet to create a culture of its own—a process made more difficult by migration and immigration. Highbrow culture was less about setting a standard that others might reach for and increasingly about preserving from the "unwashed masses" that which only the social betters could appreciate. Only in the second half

---

7   Wasko, *Understanding Disney*, 13; Christopher Finch, *Walt Disney's America* (New York: Abbeville Press, 1978), 118-119; Watts, *The Magic Kingdom*, 350, 358.

8   Schickel, *The Disney Version*, 280–281; Watts, *The Magic Kingdom*, 79, 102, 122-123, 130, 408-409; Thomas, *Walt Disney*, 125, 133; Gabler, *Walt Disney*, 614.

9   Watts, *The Magic Kingdom*, 350, 358; Jackson, editor, *Walt Disney: Conversations*, 110.

10   "My Review of the Walt Disney Documentary—Mr. Fun's Journal," http://floydnormancom.squarespace.com/blog/2015/9/17/my-review-of-the-walt-disney-documentary, 17 September 2015.

11   Lawrence W. Levine, *Highbrow/Lowbrow: The Emergence of Cultural Hierarchy in America* (Cambridge: Harvard University Press, 1990), 13, 18–19, 30–31, 56, 71, 86, 100–101, 115, 136, 149, 197.

of the twentieth century did the lines again begin to blur.¹² While there are many reasons for this, it is hard to miss that the shift began about the same time that Disneyland opened.

Walt understood that American culture was shaped differently than culture had been in the past. In our democratic-republic, the rich and poor alike have access to a wealth of information, artistic representations, and education unprecedented in world history.¹³ What he believed was needed was a standardized, easy-to-digest narrative that gave Americans a common starting point. The result was Dis-History. In creating this standard American culture, Walt was wedding both Disney itself and the concept of Dis-History to the forces of Americanization, which swept over the globe as the twentieth century advanced.¹⁴ These forces, some said, were led by Mickey Mouse himself.

Indeed, Walt became "a spokesman for the American way of life" and the culture he constructed via Dis-History was heavily influenced by his own "taste and morality," which Richard Schickel labeled as being "comfortably reflected … of those of the middle-class American majority."¹⁵ We should not be surprised that the times in which he lived, indeed, that contemporary concerns, influenced Walt's use of Dis-History. In the 1950s, Disney was able to present a problem-free history, which reflected Dwight Eisenhower being in the White House and the United States as an ascendant super power. Power and post-war prosperity had their own issues, however. Abroad, America faced a rival in the form of the Soviet Union, which seemed to be its antithesis. Its Cold War struggle, many feared, would end in a nuclear war. At home, suburban dislocation and emerging societal challenges to the consensus domestic order called into question the stability and tranquility Americans had already started to take for granted. In an uncertain world, it is nice to have something to hold on to, and Disney offered that to America, defining the nation's "Cold War self-image" by offering itself as "a community of memory" for Americans to draw strength from.¹⁶

---

12 Levine, *Highbrow/Lowbrow*, 33, 214–219, 228, 234, 244–249.

13 Steven Watts, *The Magic Kingdom: Walt Disney and the America Way of Life* (New York: Houghton Mifflin Company, 1997), 162.

14 "How the World Was Won: The Americanization of Everywhere review—a brilliant essay," https://www.theguardian.com/books/2014/nov/02/how-the-world-was-won-americanization-of-everywhere-review-peter-conrad, 27 July 2016.

15 Watts, *The Magic Kingdom*, 163; Richard Schickel, "Walt Disney: Myth and Reality," http://www.americanheritage.com/content/walt-disney-myth-and-reality, 2 June 2014.

16 Carr, *What is History?*, 51; Stephen F. Fjellman, *Vinyl Leaves: Walt Disney*

Much of this cultural creation was a reaction to changes caused by modernism and had earlier precedents. The late nineteenth and early twentieth centuries were full of technological, philosophical, artistic, scientific, and political changes that not only helped shape the modern world, but also fashion modernism, a school of thought that challenged traditional norms, beliefs, and assumptions. While that led to innovations and ideas, modernism had a disdain for tradition and had produced destructive and disruptive conflicts.[17] Some, like Henry Ford (and eventually Walt as well), came to believe that the only way to combat these trends was by embracing the past.

In Ford's case, the industrialist grew frustrated with changes that were occurring in the United States, and waged (in the words of Steven Watts) "a larger cultural campaign to reclaim and defend American values and practices from an earlier day,"[18] To do so, he attempted to outsource production of his cars to village-based factories, that could allow his workers to also work as farmers. In places like Iron Mountain, Michigan, or his "Emersonian arcadia" Fordlandia (located in the jungles of Brazil), Ford attempted to bring the past and present literally into coexistence with each other. His war on modernism also extended to the employment of history itself. Near Detroit, Ford built Greenfield Village, a museum that was an ode to both the past and the advances that science and industry had made over time.[19]

Walt wanted to do more than just display the past, however. While he drew inspiration from both Ford and John D. Rockefeller, Jr. (who spent millions of dollars saving and restoring Colonial Williamsburg in Virginia), he had little interest in some sort of living history park. Likewise, Walt did not want to use the past, as his fellow park owner and fellow Californian Walter Knott did, as mere window dressing. Dis-History is an attempt to create a usable, coherent, broad or middle-brow culture for all Americans. It was not an attempt to "make America great again," but rather to demonstrate what made America great already. While critics might find in this echoes of Cold War conformity

---

World and America (Boulder: Westview Press, 1992), 36–37, 57, 61; Watts, *The Magic Kingdom*, 325; Greg Grandin, *Fordlandia: The Rise and Fall of Henry Ford's Forgotten Jungle City* (New York: Picador, 2009), 370.

17 "History of Modernism," https://www.mdc.edu/wolfson/Academic/ArtsLetters/art_philosophy/Humanities/history_of_modernism.htm, 21 November 2016; Grandin, *Fordlandia*, 54.

18 Grandin, *Fordlandia*, 16, 286; Steven Watts, *The People's Tycoon: Henry Ford and the American Century* (New York: Vintage, 2006).

19 Grandin, *Fordlandia*, 58–65, 251–257, 372.

and solace for 1950s era "white-flight" suburbanites,[20] Walt always intended more from both the concept and from his company.

The parks, then, are full of "populist political emblems that further reinforced an American way of life" in an "unproblematic" way. Indeed, Dis-History shapes guest interactions virtually from the moment they enter the parks. Here, Disney created a space for visitors to reconnect with, even rediscover, the past, and experience it (even if vicariously) for themselves. Being exposed to Dis-History helped Americans "define who they were by depicting where they had been and where they were going," and to do so collectively as a people. As such, Disney became one of the chief arbiters of American culture[21] and an "overwhelming presence" when it comes to American cultural formation and its diffusion throughout the world. Its animated films and their wholesome image, both of which are amplified by the parks, drive much of this. Disney has not only helped define America culture, but has come to see that culture as a commodity and is in the business of designing, packaging, and selling it.[22]

We need to take Disney's passion seriously, as we look at how Dis-History is used to build culture and memory.[23] Doing so requires understanding not just American history (in both its academic and popular representations), but also a good dose of Disney history in all its forms as well. As Steven Watts notes, "both the man and his enterprise emerged [by the 1930s] as reassuring symbols of the American way of life."[24] That they continue to do so deserves scholarly attention. To do so we must understand two terms from the Disney lexicon. They are

---

20 See, for example, Eric Avila, *Popular Culture in the Age of White Flight: Fear and Fantasy in Suburban Los Angeles* (Los Angeles: University of California Press, 2004).

21 Watts, *The Magic Kingdom*, 392; Kuenz, Klugman, Waldrep, and Willis, editors, *Inside the Mouse*, 161; Richard Francaviglia, "Walt Disney's Frontierland as an Allegorical Map of the American West, " *The Western Historical Quarterly*, 30(Summer 1999), 158; Richard Francaviglia, "History after Disney: The Significance of 'Imagineered' Historical Places," *The Public Historian*, 17(Autumn 1995), 72.

22 Giroux, *The Mouse that Roared*, 11, 84–85; Elting E. Morison, "What Went Wrong with Disney's Worlds Fair," http://www.americanheritage.com, 2 June 2014; Fjellman, *Vinyl Leaves:*, 16; Douglas Brode, *Multiculturalism and the Mouse: Race and Sex in Disney Entertainment* (Austin: University of Texas Press, 2005), 5; Schickel, *The Disney Version*, 209–210.

23 Otis L. Graham, Jr., "Editor's Corner: Learning Together: Disney and the Historians," *The Public Historian*, 16(Autumn, 1994), 5.

24 Watts, *The Magic Kingdom*, 143.

"synergy"[25] and "experience." While it can be amusing and useful to know that Disney corporate culture defines its employees as "cast members," and all visitors to its parks as "guests," it is important to appreciate these other two words if Dis-History is going to be truly appreciated.

When Disney speaks of "synergy" the company is talking about ways its stories and characters can be/are used in its parks, motion pictures, publishing, merchandising, licensing, and the like. Synergy has been part of the company nearly since the beginning and is necessitated by its diversified nature. To achieve synergy, then, is to have as seamless as possible use of, say, Donald Duck or Cinderella in all the company's outputs. Indeed, Disney is perhaps the epitome of a corporation that understands and utilizes the concept.[26] For an historian, what Disney calls synergy, we might call narrative flow, for what Disney is doing is constructing a story for its guests that is the same wherever and whenever it is encountered.[27]

Our other watchword is "experience," and here Disney is not just thinking about a particular guest's visit to one of their parks (and it should be noted that "experience" seems to be a buzzword associated chiefly, if not exclusively, to the theme parks).[28] Rather, that said visit contains at least some "Disney magic," whether it is a sticker for being "honorary princess of the day" as the first guest for breakfast at Cinderella Castle is bestowed, an impromptu family picture as part of helping open one of a resort hotel's stores, or a free drink upgrade to a collector's cup. "Experiences" are those special little things that make for lasting memories. If synergy is about narrative, experience is about forging personal, historic bonds with and through Disney.

Corporate jargon aside, Dis-History actually employs the past in multiple ways. First, it directly pulls from the historic past for inspiration for aspects of its entertainment business—whether films or parks. The result is an "ideal vision of American history" that plays on the nostalgia of its guests[29] and which drives the company's vision.

---

25 Fjellman, *Vinyl Leaves*, 151.

26 Janet Wasko, *Understanding Disney: The Manufacture of Fantasy* (Cambridge: Polity Press, 2001), 70–71, 82–83, 157–158; Andi Stein, *Why We Love Disney: The Power of the Disney Brand* (New York: Peter Lang, 2011), 216–217; Benjamin R. Barber, *Jihad vs. McWorld* (New York: Ballantine Books, 1996), 65.

27 Hayden White, *The Content of Form* (Baltimore: Johns Hopkins University Press, 1987), 1.

28 John Taylor, *Storming the Magic Kingdom: Wall Street, the Raiders, and the Battle for Disney* (New York: Alfred A. Knopf, 1987), 26.

29 Judith A. Adams, *The American Amusement Park Industry: A History of Technology and Thrills* (Boston: Twayne Publishers, 1991), 87.

But we need to understand that Disney uses not only the history of the United States but also the (now Americanized) myths, folk tales, and history of other parts of Western civilization, and increasingly beyond it as well to make not just its stories but to form its theme parks. The second way Disney uses the past is by drawing on its own creations to reissue or inspire new adventures for its established characters. The third way Disney makes use of the past is by drawing upon the memories that guests and cast members make together via the experiences of being at the park. This latter usage is perhaps the most important forge in creating attachment, not just nostalgia, for Disney. Lastly, there is simply the history of the company itself, which is shaped by and helps to form these uses of history. All told, Dis-History is a complex historical undertaking, not just a narrative slogan.

Dis-History, then, is how Disney goes about its work as an entertainment company. The idea of corporate synergy perhaps makes more sense to readers than the idea of creating experiences; however, both are intrinsically important to the understanding of Dis-History. As anthropologist Alexander Moore noted, "to visit Walt Disney World is to enter a ritual threshold,"[30] crossing it takes us to a different place than where we came from. The experiences one has at Disney's parks are both real and mythic at the same time, made up of "fantasy and dreams" (to borrow from Henry Giroux) becoming "more powerful when played out against a broader American landscape in which cynicism has become a permanent fixture."[31] At Disney parks, as William Arnal pointed out, an "ideal world" is created by separating the "fantastic" from everyday life. Thus, it is only at Disney that magic happens, and once a guest leaves the parks, they return to a life bare of such experiences.[32]

The assertions by Moore, Giroux, and Arnal speak to the power of history that Disney has harnessed. As David Snow has commented, the experiences its guests encounter are "a triumph of historical imagination."[33] Ultimately, Dis-History is about constructing culture by creating myths, for it is only "through historical myth," Will Wright argues, "which establish an analogy between past and present" that

---

30 Alexander Moore, "Walt Disney World: Bounded Ritual Space and the Playful Pilgrimage Center," *Anthropological Quarterly*, 53(October 1980), 208.

31 Giroux, *The Mouse that Roared*, 6; Virginia A. Salamone and Frank A. Salamone, "Images of Main Street: Disney World and the American Adventure," *Journal of American Culture*, digital edition, 85.

32 William Arnal, "The Segregation of Social Desire: 'Religion' and Disney World," *Journal of the American Academy of Religion* 69(March 2001), 5.

33 Francaviglia, "History after Disney, 70.

people can make sense of both.³⁴ As such, Dis-History is a mass-mediated culture that defines the United States in very real ways that are immediate, pervasive, and open to anyone and everyone. Thanks to the scope of the Disney undertaking, Dis-History is not confined to the United States alone. According to Michael R. Real, the company's "specific values and ideology [have spread] internationally,"³⁵ making Dis-History a force of Americanization as well as its product.

Central to Dis-History's success is working off what people already know about the past, and even more importantly, what they "know." The first, of course is actual facts about the past. The second has more to do with how people remember, interpret, and blend facts and memories into encounters with the past that meet their expectations.³⁶ What Dis-History does, then, is display the tension between realities (historic facts) versus memories (historic recollection).³⁷ Dis-History is also at odds with an interpretation that Disneyland was just a place where Walt brought cinematic themes to a park, where genres were brought to life for guests. Such an argument ignores both Walt's personal interest in history as well as the realities that inspired the genres to begin with. Thus, Disney taps into both nostalgia and larger themes of American history, utilizing "social memory" more than "historical reconstruction," creating experiences people both enjoy and return to repeatedly.³⁸

Much of Dis-History operates on nostalgia of the known. As Walt put it, "I love the nostalgic myself. I hope we never lose some of the things of the past."³⁹ Historian Gary Cross takes such sentiment and argues that nostalgia-based "personal experience" does not seek to challenge audiences, but calls upon (often childhood) memories of a comfortable past to feed our present understanding. Disney, Cross argues, has

---

34 Will Wright, *Six Guns and Society: A Structural Study of the Western* (Los Angeles: University of California Press, 1975), 208–210.

35 Michael R. Real, *Mass-Mediated Culture* (Englewood Cliffs, New Jersey: Prentice-Hall, 1977), x, 3–4. Real defines such an occurrence on page viii as "...culture in the form of widespread symbols, rhythms, beliefs, and practices available through media in the form of television, radio, records, films, books, periodicals and other means of communication that transmit in a mass manner from a single source...."

36 *The Imagineering Field Guide to the Magic Kingdom at Walt Disney World: An Imagineer's Eye Tour* (New York: Disney Editions, 2005), 23.

37 *The Imagineering Field Guide to Disneyland: An Imagineer's Eye Tour* (New York: Disney Editions, 2008), 25.

38 Paul Connerton, *How Societies Remember* (New York: Cambridge University Press, 1989), 13.

39 Dave Smith, *The Quotable Walt Disney* (New York: Disney Editions, 2001), 253.

tapped into this stratum of nostalgia and helped transform Americans into a nation of "nostalgiacs."[40] However, Cross also acknowledges that Dis-History has its origins in the Victorian notion of "rational re-creation," where re-creation was not just about fun or amusement but about learning or appreciating something. While intellectuals often do not appreciate this kind of nostalgia wedded to re-creation, the public does, despite the wishes of professional historians.[41]

Though history is intrinsic to what Disney does, it is, however, a straw man to think that Walt Disney intended his parks to be history museums or living history sites. Nor do people expect them to be. Institutions such as Colonial Williamsburg have noted from surveys and focus groups that the public that goes to both theme parks and museums understands (perhaps better than professional historians care to admit) that there are different levels of historical interpretation and adjust their expectations accordingly.[42] Disney is a company that seeks to make money.[43] It uses the past to its own ends. Thus, the experiences at the parks might not be "authentic" in a professional, historical sense,[44] but they are real to the people who have them on a personal, historical level. Moreover, the interplay between these types of history are at the heart of Dis-History.[45] The parks need people in them; otherwise, their purpose is not served. Walt knew that to get people into the parks required a story. Dis-History was forged to provide that story.

Dis-History, though it is source material created by a corporation, does have intrinsic educational value to what is produced. As Alvin H. Rosenfeld noted, "The historian's role is and will remain crucial to uncovering the past, yet historical memory broadly conceived may depend less on the record of events drawn up by scholars than on the projection of these events by writers, filmmakers, artists, and others."[46] Rosenfeld wrote those words about the Holocaust, a topic that seems the polar opposite of the happiest place on earth. Yet, if they

---

40 Gary Cross, *Consumed Nostalgia: Memory in the Age of Fast Capitalism* (New York: Columbia University Press, 2015), 2, 6, 200.

41 Cross, *Consumed Nostalgia*, 12–14, 174.

42 Cary Carson, "Mirror, Mirror, on the Wall, Whose History is the Fairest of Them All?" *The Public Historian*, 17(Autumn 1995), 64–65.

43 Cher Krause Knight, *Power and Paradise in Walt Disney's World* (Gainesville: University Press of Florida, 2014), 147.

44 Stephen F. Mills, "Disney and the Promotions of Synthetic Worlds," *American Studies International*, 28(October 1990), 73–74.

45 Knight, *Power and Paradise in Walt Disney's World*, 28–29.

46 Alvin H. Rosenfeld, *The End of the Holocaust* (Indianapolis: Indiana University Press, 2011), 2.

are true of the greatest crime of the twentieth century, how much more are they true to other historical events and representations of the past? Furthermore, Douglas Greenberg has argued that Americans believe history to be public property, not just the preserve of experts.[47] What Disney does is present a copy of reality, or a simulacrum, where the real world is placed into a synthetic universe. Thus, one can get "ethnic food" without having to deal with actual "ethnics," or see "representations" of actual sites that allow for the "experience" of "being there," with the only requirement being a journey to a Disney park rather than around the globe.[48] While some critics might balk, such simulations and replicas have real value in enticing and enriching guests' appreciation for the stories they encounter.[49]

Walt Disney knew that his work, including Dis-History, would be studied and interpreted.[50] He told *Time* magazine in 1937 that "we just try to make a good picture. And then the professors come along and tell us what we do."[51] It is my hope that this professor will be able to add to the discussion of where Disney—the man, the company, and the culture they helped forge—fits historically in twenty-first century America.[52] My book is an attempt to do that by using Walt Disney World (though the company's other parks will also be considered) in a "city as text" manner.[53] In a place like Disney World, and perhaps only there, we see not the attempt to remake or re-create the past, but a merging of popular and academic historical trends to fashion a usable past in the midst of the present and the future. It is a laboratory of sorts for the real world beyond both the ivory tower and suburban hedges.

As historian Simon Schama noted, historians need to find "a sense of place" by "using the archive of the feet," not just books, letters, and

---

47 Greenberg, "History is a Luxury", 301.

48 Arnal, "The Segregation of Social Desire: 'Religion' and Disney World," 8-9; William A. Covino, "Walt Disney Meets Mary Daly: Invention, Imagination, and the Construction of Community," *JAC* 20(Winter 2000), 153. This is based off Jean Baudrillard's work.

49 Knight, *Power and Paradise in Walt Disney's World*, 97.

50 Elizabeth Bell, Lynda Haas, and Laura Sells, editors, *From Mouse to Mermaid: The Politics of Film, Gender, and Culture* (Indianapolis: Indiana University Press, 1995), 1.

51 Quoted in Watts, *The Magic Kingdom*, v.

52 Watts, *The Magic Kingdom*, viii; Denis E. Cosgrove, *Social Formation and Symbolic Landscape* (Madison: The University of Wisconsin Press, 1998), xiii.

53 Real, *Mass-Mediated Culture*, 239. For more on the notion of a "readable city," see Rachel Bowlby, "Readable City," *PMLA*, Vol. 122, No.1, Special Topic: Cities (January 2007), 306–309.

artifacts to fully appreciate the past.[54] Being on the ground allows us to see the "past" being created before us.[55] Visiting the parks are central to understanding Dis-History. To those ends, I (and my willing family) have traveled to Walt Disney World in 2012, twice in 2013, once in 2014, twice in 2015, twice in 2016, and once in 2017, along with trips to Disneyland in 2014, 2016, and 2017, as well as Disneyland Paris in 2015. I have intertwined observations made on those trips into my narrative, alongside archival and secondary sources.

Whether it is a guest's first visit or their one hundredth, the parks, even as they change, remain constant. They are renewed (cleaned) every night, so that they are fresh each morning. It has to be that way—in order to make sure that every guest has a wonderful experience. It may not be a clean slate, exactly, but it is a renewed one, and so it allows a consistent venue for study. By being there, we can begin to appreciate not just the scope of the undertaking Disney has attempted and accomplished, but also how important memories are to the construction of the past. So, let us venture to a place where "dreams come true," "experiences" happen, and Walt Disney created an American mythology.[56] Let us go to Walt Disney World.

---

54   Simon Schama, *Landscape and Memory* (New York: Vintage Books, 1995), 24.

55   Steven Feld and Keith H. Basso, editors, *Senses of Place* (Santa Fe, New Mexico: School of American Research Press, 1996), 17, 24–27; Denis E. Cosgrove, *Social Formation and Symbolic Landscape* (Madison: The University of Wisconsin Press, 1998), 1, 13; Yi-Fu Tuan, *Space and Place: The Perspective of Experience* (Minneapolis: University of Minnesota Press, 1977), 3–4.

56   Watts, *The Magic Kingdom*, 145.

CHAPTER ONE

Mickey Mouse and the Creation of Dis-History

Experience Epcot's Spaceship Earth

When guests of Walt Disney World arrive at Epcot, their gaze is instantly drawn to "the ball." Disney describes it as "the iconic geosphere," though to most people at first glance, it looks much more like a large silver golf ball. However, it is much more than either a gimmick or wonder of engineering. The ball is home to an attraction, Spaceship Earth. Like many who pass through Epcot's gates, our journey into Dis-History (or Disney's version of history) starts here.

As both the symbol of and gateway to the park, Spaceship Earth serves as the potential introduction for Disney guests to the Future World portion of Epcot, if not to Walt Disney World itself. Officially, the attraction tells the story of human communication, from prehistoric times to the present (while also allowing guests to get a glimpse at what their future may look like as well). The ride reminds guests that "the future was invented, one step at a time," and the entire historical journey is narrated by famed actress and Oscar-winner Judi Dench, who is accompanied by a musical score that "features styles and instruments appropriate to the era, transitioning seamlessly into the next." The story arc is based on an original script (since modified) by author Ray Bradbury.[12]

---

1 "Spaceship Earth," https://disneyworld.disney.go.com/attractions/epcot/spaceship-earth/, 4 June 2014; *USA Today*, 7 June 2012. As Marty Sklar notes, Ray Bradbury's initial script was married to research done by Disney staff on key historic moments. In actually building the attraction, Disney discovered that despite its size, the dome did not lend itself to easy storytelling pacing. See, Marty Sklar, *Dream It! Do It!: My Half-Century Creating Disney's Magic Kingdoms* (New York: Disney Editions, 2013), 195-196.
2 Spaceship Earth file, Walt Disney World Eyes and Ears, 1/20/83, Walt Disney

From a Dis-History perspective, the story that unfolds is less about communications (and a future brought to you in part by Siemens, the attraction's current corporate sponsor (though they notified Disney in 2017 that they would not be renewing their lease), and more about the historical drama of Western civilization—guests receive a glimpse of history in the making and though seated, are active participants to its creation. They witness cave-dwelling hunters painting pictures of their kills on walls, Egyptians creating papyrus, the Phoenicians devising an alphabet, the Greeks and Romans spreading their culture, ideas inspiring the Renaissance, monks copying books by hand, and Johannes Gutenberg operating his printing press followed by newspapers announcing the end of the Civil War, the advent of the telegraph and telephone, the creation of computers and the televised landing on the moon[3]—all before being asked to ponder the wonders of what the future might hold. It is a concise historic overview with an uplifting (and fun) finish. It is very much in the Whig school of historic interpretation (where one can chart the historic progress of a civilization, from the state of nature to the present) but also one in which technology is seen to undergird progress as well (a recurring Disney motif).

For an academic historian, Spaceship Earth represents both the best and worst aspects of Dis-History, all in a single experience. On the positive side, in a few short minutes, riders are given a sweeping demonstration of human history and Western civilization. On the negative side, as critics such as William F. Van Wert are quick to point out, the scenes are largely void of historical context. For all the painstaking details one can see as they pass by, there are also missing (or "suppressed" and "compressed") historical details as well.[4] For example, painting on caves was fine, so long as people stayed near those particular caves. Egyptian papyrus is given preference here over Sumerian cuneiform. Phoenicians, Greeks, and Romans are all mentioned, but not the creation of the Hellenistic empire, the collapse of Rome, nor the sectarian wars pitting Christians and Muslims against one another. Indeed, while Islamic and Jewish scholars are mentioned directly, Christianity is not referred to by name at all—merely "monks." Guttenberg is seen in the midst of the Renascence (but not

---

Studio Archives, Burbank, California.

3 "Spaceship Earth," https://disneyworld.disney.go.com/attractions/epcot/spaceship-earth/, 4 June 2014.

4 William F. Van Wert, "Disney World and Posthistory," *Cultural Critique*, 32(Winter, 1995-1996), 200–201; Janet Wasko, *Understanding Disney: The Manufacture of Fantasy* (Cambridge: Polity Press, 2001), 176; Alan Bryman, *Disney and His Worlds* (New York: Routledge, 1995; ebook version), 163.

the Reformation his printing press helped to fuel), and the painting of the Sistine Chapel is viewed with little commentary. Newspapers mention the Civil War, radio talks about Amelia Earhart, there is a film reel showing Jesse Owens' triumph at the 1936 Olympics, and Walter Cronkite's broadcast of the Apollo 11 moon landing, but nothing about what those events meant at that time or since. Indeed, much of this history is likely lost upon younger and increasingly "older" (those born since the 1980s) guests as well. We might understand, to a degree, the lack of specificity, because of the pacing of the ride, and appreciate that though each scene is detail rich and of museum quality, this is not a museum. But since guests cannot stop the ride to soak it all in, Disney critics allege the company is missing out on an opportunity to educate, either by some name dropping or simply by more context on the scenes themselves.

Or, is it? Spaceship Earth asks its riders several questions throughout the course of their journey, which despite what critics might believe; have a surprising staying power even with young riders: Who are we? Where have we come from? Where are we going? While some critics find these questions "trite," and merely a means to an end, they are also important questions that have been asked for millennia and are key to unlocking how Disney uses history. At its core, Dis-History is an attempt by Disney to create a cultural narrative that both entertains and informs its guests. Disney gives us one version of American (as part of wider Western civilization) culture, pulled from history. And while critics argue that Dis-History is a place where contrary points of view are not heard or are silenced, with examples pulled from their historic, literary, and geographic contexts in order to serve Disney's ends, the fact remains that Dis-History is a powerful and popular force that does offer some redeeming educational value and must be understood on its own terms, rather than dismissed out of hand.[5]

Dis-History, as conceived by Walt Disney, fashioned a cultural mythos for Americans, which helps them make sense of the world and their place in it. In a multicultural society, where not all groups share a common story and yet live in the same nation state, this mythos is important.[6] As an arbiter of culture (both in the United States and globally), Disney's decision to utilize Dis-History is important and has wide-ranging affects. As Jean Baudrillard once said, "History is our lost referential, that is to say our myth," and that the "decline" of such referentials is

---

5 Stephen F. Fjellman, *Vinyl Leaves: Walt Disney World and America* (Boulder: Westview Press, 1992), 30–32, 88–90.

6 Fjellman, *Vinyl Leaves*, 25.

a danger to society.⁷ "A myth," as film historian Will Wright once noted, "is a communication from a society to its members: the social concepts and attitudes determined by the history and institutions of a society are communicated to its members through its myths." Wright was heavily influenced by Claude Levi-Strauss, the famed anthropologist who argued that the differences between historical and mythical thought lie primarily in the modes of explanation, not in their accuracy."⁸ Whether Walt ever read Levi-Strauss or not, he made the same argument via the development of Dis-History, sensing that Americans needed some sort of common cultural grounding as the twentieth century progressed.

Mickey Mouse's Dis-History and Its Discontents

Epcot's Spaceship Earth is but one attraction at Walt Disney World in Florida, in one of its parks. In addition to Epcot, there is the Magic Kingdom (a larger version of Walt's beloved Disneyland and the chief source for much of our discussion); Disney's Hollywood Studios (formerly Disney-MGM Studios, whose main comparison is to Universal Studios' nearby park), conceived as a place where film came to life and where actual shows might be produced; and Disney's Animal Kingdom, a part zoo, part theme park, which was Disney's answer to Sea World and Busch Gardens—and a new direction for the company⁹). Taken together, these parks are the largest entertainment area on Earth. Collectively, they are Walt Disney World.

The Walt Disney World complex is just one of Disney's parks. The company's first theme park and its "second gate" are in California: Disneyland and the newer California Adventure. In Europe, there is Disneyland Paris (with a second gate, Walt Disney Studios Park). In Asia, three Disneyland-esque parks, in Tokyo (which also has a second gate, DisneySea), Hong Kong, and Shanghai, make up the physical manifestation of the company's entertainment empire. In addition to the parks of course, there are movies, music, books, websites, hotels, cruise ships, television programs, and channels, all of which keep the Disney brand before the entire world. All of it is because of a little mouse.

---

7   Jean Baudrillard, *Simulacra and Simulation* (Ann Arbor: The University of Michigan Press, 1994), 43, 49, 79.

8   Will Wright, *Six Guns and Society: A Structural Study of the Western* (Los Angeles: University of California Press, 1975), 16, 203, 206–207.

9   "Disney's Hollywood Studios," http://www.wdwinfo.com/wdwinfo/guides/mgm/st-overview.htm, 13 August 2014; Michael D. Eisner, *Work in Progress* (New York: Random House, 1998), 224–227, 232–233.

Mickey Mouse was born on the eve of the Great Depression, out of the dire necessity and desperation of Walt Disney. Walt, who had moved his fledgling animation studio from Kansas City to Los Angeles in 1923, worked long hours and late nights, slowly creating movie shorts and characters in the form of Alice (where he mixed live action, fairy-tale plots, and animation) and Oswald the Rabbit (the cartoon predecessor to Mickey Mouse) that, by 1926, had transformed a small motion-picture operation into Walt Disney Studios.[10] That success, however, was short lived. Walt watched as his distributor (Charles Mintz) took control of not just his films (through a contractual loophole) and characters, but also plundered his creative talent to create a rival studio. It was on the train ride from New York back to California, after learning of the situation, that Mickey Mouse was born.[11]

Mickey became the start of something new. In 1928, the studio released *Steamboat Willie*, the first animated "talkie" and starring the Mouse. Almost immediately, Walt had a revolutionary hit and an iconic figure on his hands. Despite the worst economic downturn in modern history, Mickey and his pals (the studio quickly added characters like Minnie Mouse, Donald Duck, Goofy, Pluto, and Pegleg Pete) provided a safe harbor and secure financial underpinning for the company. Indeed, as the Great Depression got worse, Disney's successes seemed only to grow, both in the United States and internationally, as people around the country and theworld flocked to theaters to see the mouse with a can-do spirit and his latest adventures.[12]

Once they had Mickey, Disney never again risked losing control of one of its creations.[13] As a studio, it survived by making sure it had

---

10 Timothy S. Susanin, *Walt Before Mickey: Disney's Early Years, 1919–1928* (Jackson: University Press of Mississippi, 2011), 79, 81, 88, 95, 130, 153; Leslie Iwerks and John Kenworthy, *The Hand Behind the Mouse: An Intimate Biography of the Man Walt Disney Classed "The Greatest Animator in the World,"* (New York: Disney Editions, 2001), 38-39, 50–51.

11 Susanin, *Walt Before Mickey*, 165–175; Iwerks and Kenworthy, *The Hand Behind the Mouse*, 54–55, 58–59; Joe Flower, *Prince of the Magic Kingdom: Michael Eisner and the Re-Making of Disney* (New York: John Wiley and Sons, Inc., 1991), 11; Alan Bryman, *Disney and His Worlds* (New York: Routledge, 1995; ebook version), 23; Janet Wasko, *Understanding Disney: The Manufacture of Fantasy* (Cambridge: Polity Press, 2001), 9.

12 Judith A. Adams, *The American Amusement Park Industry: A History of Technology and Thrills* (Boston: Twayne Publishers, 1991), 92; Steven Watts, *The Magic Kingdom: Walt Disney and the America Way of Life* (New York: Houghton Mifflin Company, 1997), 255; Wasko, *Understanding Disney*, 123.

13 Andi Stein, *Why We Love Disney: The Power of the Disney Brand* (New York:

distribution deals, "product differentiation," and merchandising.[14] As a small studio, Mickey's sustained success meant maximized profits that allowed it to grow alongside Hollywood. In the span of just a few years, the studio went from little more than a storefront operation, to a growing collection of buildings along Hyperion Avenue, ushering in a new era for Walt, his company, and the industry of which he was now an integral part.[15]

With a stable of characters and a studio structure coming into place, Walt sought stories to employ both the animated characters and the animators. Already he believed that capturing the spirit of a story was much more important than being faithful to every detail of the text.[16] Walt told an interviewer, "I just make what I like—warm and human stories, and ones about historic characters and events, and about animals."[17] While he pushed his animators for realism in their work (even when depicting something fanciful he wanted the depiction to be lifelike and realistic),[18] his philosophy was that their art should show the world as it ought to be.[19] Walt did not feel that he needed to add negativity or cynicism to the world. There was enough of both already.[20] This idea applied to the use of history as well.[21] From very early on, Dis-History's tenants included the ability to clean up and improve the history being presented.[22]

Using historical stories was hardly a business consideration alone. Walt had enjoyed learning about history since he was a little boy. As he grew into adulthood, his reading habits reflected it as

---

Peter Lang, 2011), 49; Wasko, *Understanding Disney*, 9.

14 Wasko, *Understanding Disney*, 12.

15 Watts, *The Magic Kingdom*, 64, 66, 80-81; Richard Schickel, *The Disney Version: The Life, Times, Art and Commerce of Walt Disney, Third Edition* (Chicago: Ivan R. Dee Publisher, 1997), 5.

16 Robin Allan, *Walt Disney and Europe: European Influences on the Animated Feature Films of Walt Disney* (Indianapolis: Indiana University Press, 1999), 213.

17 Kathy Merlock Jackson, editor, *Walt Disney: Conversations* (Jackson: University of Mississippi Press, 2006), 134.

18 Jane Kuenz, Karen Klugman, Shelton Waldrep, and Susan Willis, editors, *Inside the Mouse: Work and Play at Disney World* (Durham: Duke University Press, 1995), 81; Davis, Marc. Interviewed by Gabe Essoe, 1972, Walt Disney Studio Archives, Burbank, California.

19 Watts, *The Magic Kingdom*, 453.

20 Paul Jerome Croce, "A Clean and Separate Space: Walt Disney in Person and Production," *The Journal of Popular Culture*, 25 (Winter 1991), 94.

21 Bryman, *The Disneyization of Society*, 8.

22 Fjellman, *Vinyl Leaves*, 59, 63.

well—with shelves full of the latest books on the Founding Fathers, the Revolutionary War, and biographies of Thomas Jefferson and Abraham Lincoln—as did the conversation topics he seemed to enjoy the most. Perhaps just as important, he felt he had a duty to teach his fellow Americans, especially children, about their heritage.[23] Walt embraced the concept of popular history and likewise should be considered one of the first public historians (before academic historians adopted the term). He understood what many academic historians rarely like to admit, that rather than specialization, most people (and perhaps especially Americans) want to hear stories about the past rather than grand theories, and that they bristle at the notion that history is the preserve of experts who have a "monopoly on the past" and its stories.[24]

Walt's love for history, and the power of Dis-History, is clear in the Hollywood Studios attraction, Walt Disney: One Man's Dream. Here, in the midst of the Florida park's version of California's Hollywood studio system, guests can wander through a museum dedicated to Walt himself. The artifacts on display include such items as his second-grade desk (hard wood and basic), various audio and film clips, vintage toys, models for park attractions, the original audio-animatronic Abraham Lincoln from the 1964 World's Fair, and a host of other things tied to Disney's history and life. Similar touches of history abound in Disneyland's Great Moments with Mr. Lincoln, which includes the actual park bench that Walt sat on and where his inspiration for building a park came from.[25] These small museums are more than just shrines to the founder of the company, though they are that as well. They show various sides of Walt's sometimes complex personality, while also continuing the cultivation and protection of his

---

23 Watts, *The Magic Kingdom*, 347; Bob Thomas, *Walt Disney: An American Original* (New York: Disney Editions, 1994), 284; Patricia Mooney-Melvin, "Beyond the Book: Historians and the Interpretive Challenge," *The Public Historian*, 17(Autumn 1995), 78; Jackson, editor, *Walt Disney: Conversations*, 136; Stephen F. Mills, "Disney and the Promotions of Synthetic Worlds," *American Studies International*, 28(October 1990), 71; Karal Ann Marling, "Disneyland, 1955: Just Take the Santa Ana Freeway to the American Dream," *American Art*, 5(Winter-Spring, 1991), 191; Didier Ghez, editor, *Walt's People: Volume 6: Talking Disney with the Artists Who Knew Him* (New York: Xlibris Corporation, 2008), 142.

24 Patricia Mooney-Melvin, "Beyond the Book: Historians and the Interpretive Challenge," *The Public Historian*, 17(Autumn 1995), 77; Christopher Finch, *Walt Disney's America* (New York: Abbeville Press, 1978), 30, 179.

25 "Walt Disney: One Man's Dream," https://disneyworld.disney.go.com/attractions/hollywood-studios/walt-disney-one-mans-dream/, 19 February 2014; Fjellman, *Vinyl Leaves*, 403.

image.²⁶ They are also examples of how dependent Walt was, and his company remains, on history as a discipline.

Few guests who visit these museums will likely think about what Disney does with the past, and that is exactly the point. Dis-History is so seamlessly done, so integrated into what they do with the park, that guests see it only as part of the presentation. The museums are merely the most obvious example of how Disney grounds itself in the historical past. Indeed, the parks constantly tap into "collective cultural memory"²⁷—a concept Walt understood long before he was the centerpiece of a museum. He believed that by telling stories, and binding Americans together, he could help preserve and foster a common culture. Dis-History is wedded to American popular culture and seeks to capture and "replicate the essences of historic environments," according to Richard Francaviglia.²⁸ It is integral to "Disney reality," the way the company views and portrays itself to its guests.²⁹

Walt's inkling of what Dis-History might accomplish was shaped by being part of the motion-picture industry. Like historic events, movies are very democratic in the sense that anyone and everyone can experience them and draw their own conclusions from them.³⁰ Throughout the 1930s, everyone in America, it seemed, was going to see Mickey's movies and knew who the Mouse was, just as everyone

---

26 Neal Gabler, *Walt Disney: The Triumph of the American Imagination* (New York: Vintage Books, 2007), 567; Watts, *The Magic Kingdom*, xvi; Kevin S. Sandler, editor, *Reading the Rabbit: Explorations in Warner Brothers Animation* (New Brunswick, NJ: Rutgers University Press, 1998), 43; Eric Smoodin, *Animating Culture: Hollywood Cartoons from the Sound Era* (New Brunswick, NJ: Rutgers University Press, 1993), 96, 98; Didier Ghez, editor, *Walt's People: Volume 7: Talking Disney with the Artists Who Knew Him* (New York: Xlibris Corporation, 2008), 214–215.

27 Kathy Merlock Jackson and Mark I. West, editors, *Disneyland and Culture: Essays on the Parks and Their Influence* (Jefferson, NC: McFarland and Company, 2011), 17.

28 Sacred Matters, "Why I Still Love Disney, or, Imagineering Religion," https://scholarblogs.emory.edu/sacredmatters/2014/02/11/why-i-still-love-disney-or-imagineering-religion/, 5 March 2014; Richard Francaviglia, "Walt Disney's Frontierland as an Allegorical Map of the American West, " *The Western Historical Quarterly*, 30(Summer 1999), 168; Richard Francaviglia, "History after Disney: The Significance of 'Imagineered' Historical Places," *The Public Historian*, 17(Autumn 1995), 69.

29 Michael Wallace, *Mickey Mouse History and Other Essays on American Memory* (Philadelphia: Temple University Press, 1996), 255.

30 Levine, *Highbrow/Lowbrow: The Emergence of Cultural Hierarchy in America*, 1–8.

was experiencing the Great Depression. These common experiences forged Dis-History as a means to present a democratized version of the past to the American people in order to give them a common culture.

By the end of World War II, Walt saw himself more as a teacher than just an entertainer.[31] Writing in 1945, he expressed confidence that he could use films as a means of both education and entertainment. Noting that "the motion picture took a leading part in all phases of wartime education—propaganda and information as well as training," Walt saw no reason why that might not be continued in the post-war world. Animated features, in particular, offered the chance to "depict the birth of a continent, the rhythm of a stellar system, the structure of an atom or the anatomy of a microbe" because of the medium's "versatility."[32] Disney viewed such films (or other materials) merely as "a new tool for the educator's kit. There can be no presumption that a film can replace the textbook, the laboratory or even the lecture," he wrote.[33]

While the advent of a theme park (the eventual Disneyland) is often attributed to Walt's desire to take his children some place clean and create a place where families could have fun together, as well as a means by which he could tinker and create on a larger scale than just with film,[34] in those post-war writings another step has been taken in the direction of Dis-History: the use of culture to educate. In that same 1945 article for *The Public Opinion Quarterly*, we see the first attempt by both the man and company that bears his name to articulate Dis-History: "The educational film must be true, it must give a rounded view of the subject, or aspect of a subject, it must hold the interest of the student and finally it must impel the student to apply his new knowledge."[35] For a time, Walt sought a means to display "a Disney view of American history and culture" by creating a series of miniature exhibits that could travel the country by train.[36] But if Dis-History was good enough for the films he was making or for an exhibit, why not for the park as well? Dis-History, then, was to be a tool of educating Baby Boomers and the American public at large across Disney's corporate outputs.

Walt understood that history could help people understand

---

31 Kuenz, Klugman, Waldrep, and Willis, editors, *Inside the Mouse*, 221.

32 Walt Disney, "Mickey as Professor," *The Public Opinion Quarterly*, 9(Summer 1945), 119–120.

33 Disney, "Mickey as Professor," 122.

34 Marling, "Disneyland, 1955: Just Take the Santa Ana Freeway to the American Dream," 173, 175.

35 Disney, "Mickey as Professor," 121–122.

36 Jeff Kurtti, *Walt Disney's Imagineering Legends and the Genesis of the Disney Theme Park* (New York: Disney Editions, 2008), 3.

morality, power, and culture, through the lens of the present.[37] Indeed, as Paul Connerton argued, "Our experience of the present very largely depends upon our knowledge of the past."[38] Thus, the use of the past to not just inform, but also possibly entertain the present (and current questions and problems) was perfectly reasonable. As Stephen Fjellman noted, history is essentially "value neutral" and much of what people know about the past is shaped by popular history; thus, Disney's decision to construct Dis-History made perfect sense.[39] Of course this makes who is creating popular history important, because invoking the past, utilizing its images, legitimates society.[40] By the mid-twentieth century (and perhaps even more so by the twenty-first) the images were starting to dominate how people perceive the world around them.[41] Few organizations understood the power of images better than Disney did.[42]

Walt fused "entertainment and education" into a corporate force and his company became "a teaching machine" with broad-ranging influence. Hundreds of millions of people every year watch Disney movies (which are transgenerational in their audience, if not always their appeal) and television shows. Millions more listen to Disney music, and tens of millions visit Disney theme park. Every year. Disney has to be true and faithful to not just history, but to their own corporate history as well.[43] Dis-History plays that role in the parks. It is the "concentrated distillation of one version of the United States and its view of the world, a version both mythical and real," according to Fjellman.[44] Since Walt's time, the company had as its mission not just making money for its stockholders, as John Taylor relates it, but

---

37 E. H. Carr, *What is History?* (New York: Alfred A. Knopf, 1962), 28; Jackson and West, editors, *Disneyland and Culture*, 195.

38 Paul Connerton, *How Societies Remember* (New York: Cambridge University Press, 1989), 2.

39 Fjellman, *Vinyl Leaves*, 63.

40 Connerton, *How Societies Remember*, 3.

41 Eva T. H. Brann, *The World of the Imagination: Sum and Substance* (New York: Rowman & Littlefield Publishers, 1991), 9.

42 Brann, *The World of the Imagination*, 173.

43 Henry A. Giroux, *The Mouse that Roared: Disney and the End of Innocence* (New York: Rowman and Littlefield, 1999), 18–19; Fjellman, *Vinyl Leaves*, 157; Eleanor Byrne and Martin McQuillan, *Deconstructing Disney* (Sterling, Virginia: Pluto Press, 1999), 58–59; Kuenz, Klugman, Waldrep, and Willis, editors, *Inside the Mouse*, 51.

44 Fjellman, *Vinyl Leaves*, 21.

"to celebrate and nurture American values."[45] Disney believes that as a cultural force it can (and does) shape the course of history.[46]

There is an additional component of Dis-History. Disney does not just use history or shape its understanding; it is also in the business of making history. Not only does the company help its guests to create personal history (or memories), but it also shapes the history of the United States. Take Orlando as an example. Who can doubt that the creation of Walt Disney World radically altered the Orlando area's history forever? Think of how many jobs were created in the park's construction (and continued remodeling). What did those jobs mean to the workers, their families? What of the park guests? How was the very land itself (from the ecology to things like the transportation network that was created) changed and altered? What of all the people who moved to and created modern Orlando because of a Disney park simply being there? What did that mean to Florida? Asking and even attempting to answer these questions quickly demonstrates that a good deal of history, in and by a variety of means, has happened in the 43 square miles of Florida that is home to Walt Disney World.[47]

No person, no company, can use history and attempt to construct culture the way Disney does without attracting critics. Indeed, criticism has been a mainstay of Dis-History from the start. Intellectual critics questioned Walt's decision to try to create a broad American cultural experience through his films.[48] As the company formally created Dis-History, critics began to argue that Disney used the past for comedic effect or brushed over the more difficult aspects of the past altogether and thus distorted how the past is understood.[49] Dis-History, according to its critics, is a place where there is no conflict or strife, a place where nostalgia is used to sell merchandise.[50] As such, "Disney distorts real history for the sake of commercial gain" and tends to re-inscribe the stories it tells "with a typically American value system" no matter where their origination.[51] William F. Van

---

45   John Taylor, *Storming the Magic Kingdom: Wall Street, the Raiders, and the Battle for Disney* (New York: Alfred A. Knopf, 1987), viii.
46   Giroux, *The Mouse that Roared*, 28.
47   William F. Van Wert, "Disney World and Posthistory," *Cultural Critique*, 32(Winter, 1995-1996), 212; Fjellman, *Vinyl Leaves*, 185, 189–191.
48   Gabler, *Walt Disney*, xviii.
49   Bryman, *Disney and His Worlds*, 128, 134; Warren Leon and Roy Rosenzweig, editors, *History Museums in the United States: A Critical Assessment* (Chicago: University of Illinois Press, 1989), 173.
50   Giroux, *The Mouse that Roared*, 42–43.
51   Brenda Ayres, editor, *The Emperor's Old Groove: Decolonizing Disney's Magic*

Wert called Walt Disney World "an elaborate and highly successful blueprint of high modernism (and assembly-line capitalism)" as well as a place that "eradicated all sense of shame from history." Additionally, he argued that entering the park marks the moment of enslavement on the part of visitors to the skewed reality that Disney has created.[52] Van Wert has many allies, with critics alleging that guests walk around with "glazed eyes" in a "trancelike state" from one problematic (because of either theme or mechanical failure) attraction to another. Little more than zombies to the Mouse, guests ask no questions and receive no answers to the historic questions that Disney parks raise by their very existence raises, but never answer.[53]

Then there are the political critics. Conservative criticism argues that the once wholesome image Walt articulated was destroyed or altered by those now running the company.[54] Leftist criticism tends to be much more broadly constructed. Some attack the wholesome image conservatives claim Disney once represented,[55] while others blast Disney for "sexism, racism, conservatism, heterosexism, andro-centricism, imperialism (cultural), imperialism (economic), literary vandalism, jingoism, aberrant sexuality, censorship, propaganda, paranoia, homophobia, exploitation, ecological devastation, anti-union repression, FBI collaboration, corporate raiding, and stereotyping." For all these reasons Disney is, according to Eleanor Byrne and Martin McQuillan, "beyond the political pale."[56]

Still more critics focus on how Disney does business. According to this group, Disney engages in "the manipulation of memory," with Dis-History contributing to "historical forgetting." In addition, these critics

---

Kingdom (New York: Peter Lang, 2013), 94.

52 Van Wert, "Disney World and Posthistory," 187, 190. To his credit, at least Van Wert actually went to the park. He points out in the article, not all critics have even bothered to do that. See also, Kuenz, Klugman, Waldrep, and Willis, editors, *Inside the Mouse*, 1–4, 10, 27, 106

53 Adams, *The American Amusement Park Industry*, 146–147; Watts, *The Magic Kingdom*, 395.

54 Kuenz, Klugman, Waldrep, and Willis, editors, *Inside the Mouse*, 90; Elizabeth Bell, Lynda Haas, and Laura Sells, editors, *From Mouse to Mermaid: The Politics of Film, Gender, and Culture* (Indianapolis: Indiana University Press, 1995), 47; Charles Carson, "Whole New Worlds: Music in the Disney Theme Park Experience," *Ethnomusicology Forum*, 13(November 2004), 232.

55 Schickel, *The Disney Version*, 352–353; Watts, *The Magic Kingdom*, 451.

56 Giroux, *The Mouse that Roared* 85–86, 100, 164-167, 170; Eleanor Byrne and Martin McQuillan, *Deconstructing Disney* (Sterling, Virginia: Pluto Press, 1999), 1–2.

are dismayed by how heavy-handed Disney (and Disney in particular seems to generate most of the discussion on this front) is when the company takes control of artistic works for adaptation.[57] These stories become Walt Disney products, or versions, at times quite dissimilar to their authors' original intent or tone. The company, critics say, buys rights to books and stories cheaply, and thanks to the Disney machine, this version usually outsells and dominates the originals.[58] While Disney might talk of standardization and "artistic license," to critics Disney's transformation of literature into films is little more than a "debasement" of the original work. Francis Clark Sayers, for example, argued that Disney engaged in the "manipulation" of the original versions, did not understanding the power of folklore, and then created book versions of the films that provided even less content.[59]

The problem with many of these criticisms, as we will explore in the pages that follow, is that "condescension is not thinking." Disney created something that has to be dealt with in concrete ways, not with sneers.[60] For now, let us focus on one area in particular where criticisms mostly fall flat, Dis-History's use of nostalgia. In his book *Metahistory*, Hayden White talks of an "analysis of the deep structure of the historical imagination," asking readers "what does it mean to think historically?" Part of the answer is that to think historically requires people to select what they are going to remember and how they will remember it. Thinking about the past not only separates it from the present, but also implies methods of relating the present to the past in meaningful ways.[61] Furthermore, history thrives on the connection between memory and place, which is increasingly "disjointed" in the United States thanks to both social and physical mobility. By not grounding ourselves in the past (or a past), we risk entering the future with no sense of how we got there or being able to put down roots anywhere.[62]

---

57 Douglas Brode, *Multiculturalism and the Mouse: Race and Sex in Disney Entertainment* (Austin: University of Texas Press, 2005), 260.

58 Schickel, *The Disney Version*, 296-297, 344–345.

59 Peggy A. Russo, "Uncle Walt's Uncle Remus: Disney's Distortion of Harris's Hero," *The Southern Literary Journal*, 25(Fall, 1992), 21.

60 Karal Ann Marling, editor, *Designing Disney's Theme Parks: The Architecture of Reassurance* (New York: Flammarion, 1997), 202–207.

61 Hayden White, *Metahistory: The Historical Imagination in Nineteenth-Century Europe* (Baltimore: The Johns Hopkins University Press, 1985), 1, 5, 20–21, 109, 241, 403.

62 Dolores Hayden, *The Power of Place: Urban Landscapes as Public History* (Cambridge: The MIT Press, 1995), 45, 227; Janelle L. Wilson, *Nostalgia: Sanctuary of Meaning* (Lewisburg: Bucknell University Press, 2005), 93, 99.

Dis-History grounds the past (on multiple levels and in multiple ways) in an actual place. Nostalgia is an attractive tool for Disney (and others, including many in Hollywood) because it conforms to the modern concept of time as linear and unrepeatable. Through nostalgia, the past we imagine seems more clearly defined than our present and a means to recover some meaning from what has been lost to time.[63] Nostalgia is not about historic truth as much as it is how individuals make sense of the past personally. It is tied deeply to emotion and indulged in by people who have leisure time to devote to the recovery of a mythic past.[64] People remember things, but they also choose what to remember. They tend to remember the positive aspects of the past rather than the negative.[65] Such things form the basis for collective memory—events that many people experience and remember. These, in turn, form the basis for "transmitting memory" that binds a civilization together, according to Svetlana Boym.[66] Walt saw Dis-History as part of this process.

Still, like other businesses, Disney uses nostalgia because it works as a business technique.[67] The company's genius is selling "generational experiences" of the "always already nostalgic."[68] Walt recognized, perhaps before anyone else, that people enjoy going to new places, but they also like what they already know.[69] Since nostalgia is steeped in both personal and collective memory, these two forces are found hard at work within Dis-History and thus, in the parks. Within a pluralistic society like the United States, there are many subcultures, but that does not mean there is not also a dominant culture, or core, around which the others feed. Dis-History's goal was to construct that common culture.[70]

Culture is the means by which we connect to one another as a people. It is "the stories that people tell about themselves and their world."[71] Because Disney delves into popular, or mass, culture, and does so via

---

63 Boym, *The Future of Nostalgia*, xii–xiv, 3, 5, 8, 13, 38-39.

64 Wilson, *Nostalgia: Sanctuary of Meaning*, 7–8, 21–23, 27, 29, 31, 36, 46, 51, 160.

65 Wilson, *Nostalgia: Sanctuary of Meaning*, 48, 80.

66 Boyd, *The Future of Nostalgia*, 53, 293.

67 Wilson, *Nostalgia: Sanctuary of Meaning*, 26, 30, 32, 37.

68 Jason Sperb, *Disney's Most Notorious Film: Race, Convergence, and the Hidden Histories of Song of the South* (Austin: University of Texas Press, 2012), ix

69 Thomas Beller, "The Topographical Soul," http://www.theparisreview.org/blog/2012/03/05/the-topographical-soul/, 4 May 2015.

70 Wilson, *Nostalgia: Sanctuary of Meaning*, 38–43.

71 Eric Avila, *Popular Culture in the Age of White Flight: Fear and Fantasy in Suburban Los Angeles* (Los Angeles: University of California Press, 2004), xiii.

media methods, it is hardly surprising that it counts among its detractors many who find artistic merit only in what might be considered high or elite art. Disney, from Walt's time forward, has been interested in producing a product that most people will enjoy. That is, art for the masses. The problem for critics is that the more a mass-mediated culture spreads, the more it blurs the older understanding of what art is. It gives people what they want, expands access to culture, tends to be more innovative (and thus, open to new ideas and expressions), and has a wide variety of products for consumers to pick from.[72] That a corporation, with vast reach and influence, which can easily spread its version of culture, constructed Dis-History also worries many of Disney's critics,[73] who have charged that Disney is little more than a corrupter of "popular culture," with "vulgar," "crassly commercial" offerings. One critic went a step further, saying Disney was the "source" of the "heat of darkness" that was "mass culture."[74] Furthermore, mass-mediated culture can mask real problems in society (such as racism) under a veneer of myth.[75] And the culture that Disney has produced? According to its critics, it is full of "mass reproductions and controlled, repetitive behavior." It also appropriates holidays and traditions for its own use, with little care for their cultural or religious origins.[76]

The very existence of mass-mediated culture is how Dis-History sustains itself. Not only does it help create synergy (and thus the continuity to keep characters' stories straight from book to movie to park and back again), but it also makes the theme parks themselves manageable. The vast crowds that come to the Magic Kingdom are largely orderly, not just because they are there on vacation, but also because people "police themselves" if they all believe "the same stories."[77] In many ways, Walt Disney World is an imagined community. In addition, not everyone is comfortable with that, or with the community, and its use of history. Writer John Schultz said that Disney World's

---

72 Michael R. Real, *Mass-Mediated Culture* (Englewood Cliffs, New Jersey: Prentice-Hall, 1977), 6-8, 14, 22-23.

73 Giroux, *The Mouse that Roared* 78-79.

74 Taylor, *Storming the Magic Kingdom*, 25; Joe Flower, *Prince of the Magic Kingdom: Michael Eisner and the Re-Making of Disney* (New York: John Wiley and Sons, Inc., 1991), 18; Kuenz, Klugman, Waldrep, and Willis, editors, *Inside the Mouse*, 124-125.

75 Real, *Mass-Mediated Culture*, 20-24. Perhaps no place shows this more clearly in Dis-History than with how the company has dealt with *Song of the South*. See, Sandler, editor, *Reading the Rabbit*, 4-5.

76 Kuenz, Klugman, Waldrep, and Willis, editors, *Inside the Mouse*, 32-33.

77 Wasko, *Understanding Disney*, 29; Fjellman, *Vinyl Leaves*, 3.

"mythology [was] created almost entirely by its publicists and the oral testimony of its visitors." Upon his own visit, in the late 1980s, he saw no reason to cheer what Disney's Imagineers had created in what was once Florida swampland.[78]

Such criticisms have been around nearly since the start. When Disneyland opened, for example, it was blasted by *The New York Times* as "too Hollywood" and "slick, commercial, star-studded, [and] glitzy," not to mention so reverential as if it was a "national shrine." Then came the attacks over commercialization and consumerism (via retail sales).[79] Richard Schickel believed that Disneyland offered little more than a "sanitization of experience." The Disney theme parks, critics believe, are little more than places where "history and the wilderness and, yes, ideas [are] tamed." They are thus places where "stupefaction" occurs, leading their guests "easy prey for evil ideologues."[80]

Schickel and like-minded critics at least acknowledge that guests are experiencing something at the parks. Others are less sure. Because guests are engaging in the "fantastic"[81] (those things Tzvetan Todorov described as being in the space between the world we know and a world in which the supernatural—or things that do not normally occur—operates openly, where fiction and reality merge),[82] some critics decry the parks for being "unrealistic" and shortchanging guests by encouraging them to participate in a simulation instead of the real thing.[83] One critic lamented that people would be satisfied taking Disney's Jungle Cruise (full of "tawdry substitutes") over experiencing the real rivers of the world for themselves. In short, people were being placated by the false experiences conjured up by Disney (and their own imaginations) rather than having actual experiences for themselves.[84]

What really confounds the critics, as Umberto Eco notes, is that Disney is merely doing what most museums do daily. In order for every

---

78 John Schultz, "The Fabulous Presumption of Disney World: Magic Kingdom in the Wilderness," *The Georgia Review,* 42(Summer 1988), 275, 277.

79 Marling, "Disneyland, 1955: Just Take the Santa Ana Freeway to the American Dream," 170–172.

80 Schickel, *The Disney Version*, 6.

81 Umberto Eco, *Travels in Hyper Reality* (New York: Harcourt Brace and Company, 1986), 43.

82 Tzvetan Todorov, *The Fantastic: A Structural Approach to a Literary Genre* (Cleveland: The Press of Case Western Reserve University, 1973), 25, 34, 75.

83 Jean Baudrillard, *Simulacra and Simulation* (Ann Arbor: The University of Michigan Press, 1994), 1–5, 8–11.

84 Marling, "Disneyland, 1955: Just Take the Santa Ana Freeway to the American Dream," 172.

museum that wants a T-Rex skeleton to have one, for example, or an urn from ancient Rome, casts and replicas are widely used (with appropriate signage, of course). Most guests do not care if it is authentic or a replica, only that they get to see it (whatever it is) for themselves. Americans, in particular, according to Eco, "demand the real thing, and to attain it, must fabricate the absolute fake."[85] Or, in the case of the Jungle Cruise, it is more realistic for visitors to experience a ten-minute cruise of the world's greatest rivers than it is for those same people to actually travel around the globe and do it for real.

Many of Dis-History's more recent critics, then, are postmodernists who argue that because the past is presented everywhere, can be repeatedly encountered, and is out of its actual historical context (the Liberty Bell in Disney's Liberty Square, for example, is a reproduction sitting in Florida, not the original bell that resides in Philadelphia), the past in a Disney park loses all meaning. As such, Dis-History's attempt to forge a common culture via experiences is doomed to failure.[86] The postmodern critique, however, neglects to appreciate that Walt's Dis-History was itself a critique of modernism. For Walt, the past could be experienced on multiple levels and in multiple ways, all of which might engage guests when the idea of the past was itself invoked. As Michael Wallace notes, while Americans enjoy certain aspects of the past, and appreciate that there is a connection between it and the present, they also have a tendency to be ahistorical in their thinking. Walt's goal was to prompt them to engage the past, even if only for a few moments.

Such thinking is at the heart of the broad culture that Walt hoped to create via his films and eventually the parks, in the form of Dis-History. Critics often claim that guests do not want to draw conclusions from what their visits actually mean. Perhaps, or perhaps most guests simply disagree with the critics. It is incorrect to believe that visitors do not understand what is going on in a Disney park. Guests rarely seem to compare the park's Main Street to, say, their hometown, but rather to other amusement or theme parks.[87] Of course it is not real, even children know the difference between the real world and the fantasy one that Disney has created. However, that does not mean that the parks do not convey very real things. Sometimes it is worth asking if critics have ever actually been to a Disney park.

---

85 Eco, *Travels in Hyper Reality*, 7–15, 36–37.

86 Eric Smoodin, editor, *Disney Discourse: Producing the Magic Kingdom* (New York: Routledge, 1994), 9; Cher Krause Knight, *Power and Paradise in Walt Disney's World* (Gainesville: University Press of Florida, 2014), 21

87 Kuenz, Klugman, Waldrep, and Willis, editors, *Inside the Mouse*, 78, 111; Real, *Mass-Mediated Culture*, 72.

It is much easier for academics to attack Disney than not. Often those criticisms do not attempt to place Disney, its films or its parks, within the proper historical context.[88] Ultimately, critics and supporters all agree that Disney creates and shapes popular culture.[89] That is an important point. It means on some level that their criticisms are merely their opinion of that popular culture of which Disney is a part. As such, theirs need not be the final word on anything related to the subject (as substantive or petty as the various criticisms might be). It also means that the driving idea behind Disney's version of popular culture, what I refer to in this book as Dis-History, is even more important to understand than merely criticizing the products that Disney generates.

Attacking Dis-History for being inauthentic is a bit disingenuous. Disney does not claim to be in the business of promoting history, it largely uses history—stories—to promote itself and its corporate values. As Stephen Mills has noted, even the more historic areas of Disney parks are doing little different than what many museums, historical sites, and historical societies do in attempting to "re-create the past" they give to visitors as experiences, which no matter how well done, lack a sense of authenticity because the past never can be recaptured.[90] Indeed, how many museum exhibits on the past touch on the "hurtful history" that critics like Van Wert believe Disney avoids at all costs?[91] As for substituting the "tawdry" imagineered reality for "actual" experiences, critics tend to forget that it is much more in the budget of a family of whatever size to spend a week at Walt Disney World and Disney experiences than it is for them to travel around the globe and see all the cultures that one trip to Florida can give them a taste for.

Our reactions to Disney parks and movies have much to do with our perceptions of Dis-History. It is important to remember that we bring our own perspectives into viewing Disney. Most negative reactions toward Disney have a good dose of "elitist cultural attitudes" directed against a mass culture phenomenon like Disney.[92] Disney experiences, of course, vary. However, one study of guests found that less than one percent said they would never come back.[93] No matter how much

---

88 Brode, *Multiculturalism and the Mouse*, 6–11.

89 Schickel, *The Disney Version*, 10.

90 Stephen F. Mills, "Disney and the Promotions of Synthetic Worlds," *American Studies International*, 28(October 1990), 75–76.

91 Van Wert, "Disney World and Posthistory," 188.

92 Giroux, *The Mouse that Roared*, 7, 10; Bell, Haas, and Sells, editors, *From Mouse to Mermaid*, 97; Wasko, *Understanding Disney*, 210.

93 Giroux, *The Mouse that Roared*, 5-7; Real, *Mass-Mediated Culture*, 70.

some critics protest, it is difficult to get around the fact that going to a Disney park is fun and gives pleasure to its guests.[94]

For scholars, "critical observations" are just as important as applied academic theories.[95] Disney's parks offer a wonderful place to study mass culture. As Kathy Merlock Jackson and Mark I. West note, "Disney's egalitarian park celebrated the accomplishments and aspirations of the audience for whom it was designed—the American people."[96] The study of popular culture is incredibly important in America, since "popular culture made in Hollywood" crafts America's "national myths" that are then exported around the world. It provides "a sense of shared memory and a sense of identity." The popular culture Walt created is full of flaws, but they are flaws common to most Americans and their relationship to the past. It is steeped in both myth and history, and as Walt intended, Dis-History attempts to give meaning to the American past.[97] To do so, he drew upon historic stories from both American and Western culture. Inevitably, those tales were fused in the parks to the myths and legends that have grown up about the man and the company he created. It is to Walt Disney himself that we now turn.

---

94 Tison Pugh and Susan Aronstein, editors, *The Disney Middle Ages: A Fairy-Tale and Fantasy Past* (New York: Palgrave Macmillan, 2012), 1–2, 175.

95 Kuenz, Klugman, Waldrep, and Willis, editors, *Inside the Mouse*, 1.

96 Kuenz, Klugman, Waldrep, and Willis, editors, *Inside the Mouse*, 10; Jackson and West, editors, *Disneyland and Culture*, 8.

97 Wilson, *Nostalgia: Sanctuary of Meaning*, 30, 44; Schickel, *The Disney Version*, 12–13, 361; J. G. O'Boyle, "'Be Sure You're Right, then Go Ahead': The Early Disney Westerns," *Journal of Popular Film & Television*, Summer96, Vol. 24 Issue 2. Accessed on 25 September 2014; Flower, *Prince of the Magic Kingdom*, 5.

CHAPTER TWO

A Whole New World: The Creation of the Walt Disney Mythos

Experience: California Promenade

At Disney California Adventure, guests encounter Buena Vista Street. Disney bills this park gateway as "a salute to 1920s and 30s Los Angeles, around the time that Walt Disney arrived in California." Guests can "stroll the tree-lined street, do some shopping, grab a snack, or take in the period "streetmosphere" entertainment. Carthay Circle at the end of the block features a beautiful fountain and a replica of the Carthay Circle Theater, where the premiere of *Snow White and the Seven Dwarfs* was held back in 1937."[1] It is a stunning physical re-creation and a restrained entrance when compared to Epcot's Spaceship Earth that we encountered in the first chapter.

Then again, California Adventure is a different kind of park. It is a love letter to California. The theme is strong and well maintained. Beyond Buena Vista Street, there is Condor Flats (home to the popular Soarin' over California attraction), Grizzly Peak, Pacific Wharf, Paradise Pier, Cars Land, A Bug's Land, and Hollywood Land (which at present has a good deal of *Frozen* mania about it). At California Adventure, guests can actually take part in an animation class, which only strengthens the Dis-Historic bonding between them and Disney, as well as ride, eat, and shop. They are getting a taste of Disney's own past (both man and company) while being in the midst of the park's very real present.

Inventing new words ("streetmosphere") aside, the grounding of the park in an historic time and place is important. It looks like a normal

---

[1] "California Adventure Buena Vista Street, "http://www.wdwinfo.com/california-adventure/california-adventure-buena-vista-street.htm, 13 October 2014.

street; indeed, one might compare it to nearby Culver City. However, this is Disney's version of the California that gave the world Walt Disney. Here is where a little mouse gave birth to a giant corporation, where Dis-History propelled Walt to build his park. The California adventure of the early twentieth century that Walt undertook is important to understanding Dis-History. Walt arrived in California in 1923 from Kansas City.[2] It was here that the studio millions know was ultimately born. Its importance is such that the company later brought California to Florida for its Hollywood Studios park. Here, of course, the idea is to remind guests of the California that Walt Disney lived and worked in when the studio was taking off and becoming a cultural force.[3]

Neither California-themed park entrance has the emotional pull of Main Street, which we will encounter in the next chapter, perhaps because not everyone who visits has a mythic/historical tie to Hollywood the way they might to small-town Main Street, but the importance of it to Disney's own history is not lost on guests. The image presented is of "old Hollywood," or perhaps of a "Hollywood in the making." Like every Disney park, these Hollywood-inspired streets are always clean. Here, it takes on a new meaning. According to Richard Schickel, Walt's reputation (one that he helped to create and foster, and one that his company still fights to uphold) was that his films were "wholesome," indeed that he could be pointed to as the "clean" image of Hollywood itself (which even in the 1920s and 1930s had its fair share of scandals).[4] Hollywood Studios and California Adventure, though, do not depict the struggle Disney went through to survive in the Golden Age of Hollywood, rather they are representations of how he and the company remembered it after success had become commonplace.[5] It is a bit of corporate nostalgia in the midst of Dis-Historic theming.

In the Footsteps of Walt

We have already encountered Walt Disney as an historian, but it is also important to understand him as a person, businessman, and ultimately as the architect of the parks that embody the ideal of

---

2 John Taylor, *Storming the Magic Kingdom: Wall Street, the Raiders, and the Battle for Disney* (New York: Alfred A. Knopf, 1987), 7.

3 Stephen F. Fjellman, *Vinyl Leaves: Walt Disney World and America* (Boulder: Westview Press, 1992), 176–177.

4 Richard Schickel, *The Disney Version: The Life, Times, Art and Commerce of Walt Disney, Third Edition* (Chicago: Ivan R. Dee Publisher, 1997), 94–95.

5 Jason Sperb, *Disney's Most Notorious Film: Race, Convergence, and the Hidden Histories of Song of the South* (Austin: University of Texas Press, 2012), 27.

Dis-History. Walt was a dreamer. Unlike many dreamers, he made his dreams into reality, and did so by creating a business that became hugely successful.[6] While Walt said he wanted to "bring back happy memories for those who remember the carefree times," his own story, at least as it is often related in print, was far from idyllic.[7]

Walt was complicated. He was someone who could project a down-home image, that of "Uncle Walt," and was, according to his daughter Diane, a normal father who did not spoil his children. But he was also a very astute (if not ruthless, in the eyes of critics) businessman—someone who spent millions of dollars on the latest technology, but often paid his actors, artists, and the authors whose stories he told well below what they were worth. A man, according to one critic, who had a "nineteenth-century emotions in conflict with a twenty-first century brain." If we hope to better understand him, then we need a better understanding of where he came from.[8]

Walt was born on December 5, 1901, in Chicago. Before he turned five, his family moved to a small town in Missouri named Marceline. By his own account, the move as a boy from Chicago to Marceline left a "deep impression" on him. He later recalled looking out the train window as his family made their way south to their new home and soaking in every detail of the passing landscape. He spent his boyhood on a farm. Walt later reflected that those were the most important years of his childhood, calling them "the happiest days of my life."[9]

Of course, Walt only arrived in Marceline because his parents decided to move. His father, Elias Disney, was of Anglo-Irish decent and was born in Ontario, Canada, in 1859. Elias lived there until moving to the United States with his family around the age of 20, when the Disneys resettled in Kansas. The family's beef and wheat farm abutted

---

6   Schickel, *The Disney Version*, 42.

7   Warren Leon and Roy Rosenzweig, editors, *History Museums in the United States: A Critical Assessment* (Chicago: University of Illinois Press, 1989), 161.

8   Kathy Merlock Jackson, editor, *Walt Disney: Conversations* (Jackson: University of Mississippi Press, 2006), 126; Schickel, *The Disney Version*, 4; Paul Jerome Croce, "A Clean and Separate Space: Walt Disney in Person and Production," *The Journal of Popular Culture*, 25 (Winter 1991), 91; Bob Thomas, *Walt Disney: An American Original* (New York: Disney Editions, 1994), 4–5.

9   Bob Thomas, *Building a Company: Roy O. Disney and the Creation of an Entertainment Empire* (New York: Hyperion, 1998), 14; Schickel, *The Disney Version*, 45; Robin Allan, *Walt Disney and Europe: European Influences on the Animated Feature Films of Walt Disney* (Indianapolis: Indiana University Press, 1999), 2; Kathy Merlock Jackson, editor, *Walt Disney: Conversations* (Jackson: University of Mississippi Press, 2006), 10–11.

a railroad line, an important internal improvement for the American West. Walt's mother, Flora, "remains a more shadowy figure," though Walt credited her with giving him his sense of humor. Elias and Flora were married in 1888 and eventually had five children together.[10]

Elias spent his whole life working and trying to make it in America. He left Kansas for Florida, where he grew oranges for a time (in Kissimmee, near where Walt Disney World was later constructed). When his orange venture failed, he moved his young family to Chicago, where he finally made a decent living building housing for the World's Columbian Exposition.[11] Though actively engaged in the community, the family did not put down deep roots in the Windy City. Elias decided to move his family to the country after some neighbor boys were involved in a robbery and the death of a police officer. Elias looked at other places, but Marceline had the added advantage of nearby Disney family—his brother Robert owned a 500-acre farm in the community.[12]

Life for the family might be construed as difficult. Elias drove his sons hard, putting them to work in the fields. To complicate matters, he was not a very good farmer. The stress of relocating and watching the farm slowly fail contributed to a stern demeanor toward his children. Toys were not allowed in the house, a fact that Walt remembered for the rest of his life. Walt's older brother Roy felt their father was strict, but disagreed with portrayals (including some by Walt) that Elias was mean.[13] To his credit, Elias instilled in his son Walt the value of self-discipline and hard work. Walt later said of his childhood, "We always were self-sufficient, but we had no luxuries—had to earn everything we got, which is good for a boy growing up."[14]

---

10 Jackson, editor, *Walt Disney: Conversations*, 100; Schickel, *The Disney Version*, 45; Robin Allan, *Walt Disney and Europe: European Influences on the Animated Feature Films of Walt Disney* (Indianapolis: Indiana University Press, 1999), 2; Steven Watts, *The Magic Kingdom: Walt Disney and the America Way of Life* (New York: Houghton Mifflin Company, 1997), 14, 17.

11 Thomas, *Building a Company*, 7, 12–13; Judith A. Adams, *The American Amusement Park Industry: A History of Technology and Thrills* (Boston: Twayne Publishers, 1991), 88; Lawrence Culver, *The Frontier of Leisure: Southern California and the Shaping of Modern America* (New York: Oxford University Press, 2010), 134.

12 Thomas, *Walt Disney*, 25; Michael Barrier, *The Animated Man: A Life of Walt Disney* (Los Angeles: University of California Press, 2007), 10; Thomas, *Building a Company*, 17.

13 Adams, *The American Amusement Park Industry*, 89; Thomas, *Building a Company*, 14–15, 22–23; Richard Snow, "Disney: Coast to Coast," http://www.americanheritage.com/content/disney-coast-coast, 2 June 2014.

14 Jackson, editor, *Walt Disney: Conversations*, 136.

Walt had three older brothers, Herbert, Raymond, and Roy, and a younger sister, Ruth. The Disney family had only been in Marceline a few months when the two oldest Disney boys, Herbert and Raymond, left the farm and went back to Chicago.[15] This fact is perhaps more significant than others who have looked at the family have given it credit for. What it meant in the short term was that work on the farm was going to be more difficult for the Disneys than it might otherwise have been, or more to the point, the remaining family would have to work harder to make ends meet. It likely accentuated and exacerbated any stressful times the family faced in trying to get the farm to run properly (and perhaps led Elias to have even less use or time for frivolity). In the long term, this disrupted family life may have left a deep impression on Walt—one that eventually led to the creation of films and then a park system where families could spend time together just having fun, with no need to worry about work.

Though the family was far from perfect, it was from within his family that Walt received his biggest asset, his older brother Roy. It was during these farm years that the two brothers bonded. While eight years older than Walt, Roy tried to look out for his younger brother. Perhaps it was because of their upbringing that neither brother ever seemed to let the money they eventually made really change who they were. Roy and Walt were brothers and they were business partners. Both of those things meant that they would not always see eye-to-eye. Those things also meant they had an incredible bond. They might disagree, they might even argue, but they were always a team. Their time together was really only interrupted when Roy served in the Navy during World War I.[16]

In many ways, Marceline gave the world Walt Disney. Walt had few memories of being a boy in Chicago, but he never forgot the farm. Nearby there was a Civil War veteran, Erastus Taylor, who told Walt stories of his war experiences. Perhaps it was from him that Walt learned the possibilities of history in narrative form. It was also as a boy that Walt discovered that the liked to draw. More importantly, there were people around (an aunt, a local doctor) who encouraged his artistic talents.[17] Like many of us, Walt Disney remembered the good about his past. When he returned to Marceline in 1956, he told his audience that he felt sorry for people who only knew living in the city. Granted, he spent only a few years there and spent the rest of his life

---

15   Schickel, *The Disney Version*, 47; Barrier, *The Animated Man*, 14; Thomas, *Building a Company*, 24–25.

16   Schickel, *The Disney Version*, 34, 56–57; Barrier, *The Animated Man*, 15; Thomas, *Building a Company*, ix, 4–5, 36–37.

17   Thomas, *Walt Disney*, 26, 29; Schickel, *The Disney Version*, 54.

living in urban environments, but obviously, those years left a deep, lasting, happy impression on him.[18]

The work only grew when Elias sold the farm and moved the family to Kansas City. In Walt's memory, this is when problems for the family truly developed. Elias seemed to be unsure if his place was in the countryside where he was born or in the growing cities. When he moved his family to Kansas City, it was to buy a paper route as the family's primary source of income. Roy and Walt were expected to work the route, rising early each morning and delivering newspapers regardless of the weather. While the other boys who worked alongside them were paid, the Disney boys were not, as Elias kept their money to help pay the family's expenses. Working for his father taught Walt hard work and it made him miss being a child in many respects. However, living in Kansas City also opened up for Walt new ways of seeing the world.[19]

These years gave Walt exposure to work on both a rural farm and the streets of a city and they provided him with all the formal education he ever acquired. According to Richard Schickel, his education was basic (if not "poor"), and his home life was one that "no objective observer could possibly describe as happy," leaving Walt "essentially an untutored man."[20] However, Schickel's depiction is hardly fair. Walt's education was actually typical of his time, place, and even of America in the early twentieth century. Many children only had an eighth-grade education, and far fewer actually went on to college than in the twenty-first century. Walt himself remembered enjoying spelling, arithmetic, and history.[21] The education he did receive served him well.

At the age of eighteen, Walt sought out employment as an artist "because it was easier to get a job" as one than at the local newspaper. He became a commercial artist, rather than going to art school. As

---

18 Christopher Finch, *Walt Disney's America* (New York: Abbeville Press, 1978), 64; Watts, *The Magic Kingdom*, 3–5.

19 Richard Francaviglia, "History after Disney: The Significance of 'Imagineered' Historical Places," *The Public Historian*, 17(Autumn 1995), 70; Schickel, *The Disney Version*, 46, 55; Neal Gabler, *Walt Disney: The Triumph of the American Imagination* (New York: Vintage Books, 2007), 21; Finch, *Walt Disney's America*, 48. In the movie *Saving Mr. Banks*, the actor Tom Hanks, portraying Walt Disney, in his quest to win the rights to make a movie about Mary Poppins, says of his childhood and his relationship with his father, "I am tired of remembering it that way."

20 Schickel, *The Disney Version*, 5; Richard Schickel, "Walt Disney: Myth and Reality," http://www.americanheritage.com/content/walt-disney-myth-and-reality, 2 June 2014

21 Jackson, editor, *Walt Disney: Conversations*, 136.

such, he got to be very creative. He picked up all sorts of tips from those he worked with, including Ubbe Iwerks, who became one of his first collaborators. Walt's skill was never truly as an artist, it was in seeing the possibilities of taking an art form to a new level. He eventually stopped working as an animator, took more control over content (what others were drawing), began creating story ideas, and launched his own business. In the early 1920s, Walt founded first Kaycee Studios and then Laugh-O-Gram Studio. It was in these early years that Walt worked most as an artist, experimented with animation and live action, and realized that fairy tales offered a great amount of source material. Both of these early studios also failed for lack of business.[22]

Walt knew what he was doing. While Disney eventually sentimentalized his boyhood and what the Midwest was like when he was growing up there, he also developed the necessary drive and skills he needed to later transform his industry and even American culture. His youth fostered his immense imagination and willingness to innovate,[23] as well as making him quite "practical." Schickel argues that this practicality was unassuming, that Midwesterners like Walt asked plenty of "how" questions, but never asked many "why" questions about things or events. Perhaps this explains both Walt's curiosity as well as some of the criticism his work eventually received. To Schickel and other critics, Midwestern assumptions about being "real Americans" are a detriment that deep thinkers fled from (such as Ernest Hemingway).[24] In Disney's case, he seemed to become a missionary for those ideas and qualities once he left for Los Angeles, akin (in some ways) to Kurt Vonnegut, rather than Hemingway. Rather than be ashamed of such values, or try to overthrow them, Walt hoped to display them in new ways.[25] Unlike his critics, Walt never seemed ashamed of who he was or where he came from.[26]

---

22 Finch, *Walt Disney's America*, 43; Leslie Iwerks and John Kenworthy, *The Hand Behind the Mouse: An Intimate Biography of the Man Walt Disney Classed "The Greatest Animator in the World,"* (New York: Disney Editions, 2001), 4–5; Barrier, *The Animated Man*, 47; Timothy S. Susanin, *Walt Before Mickey: Disney's Early Years, 1919–1928* (Jackson: University Press of Mississippi, 2011), 3, 7, 16, 29, 55, 73.

23 Elting E. Morison, "What Went Wrong with Disney's World's Fair," http://www.americanheritage.com, 2 June 2014; Barrier, *The Animated Man*, ix; Neal Gabler, *Walt Disney: The Triumph of the American Imagination* (New York: Vintage Books, 2007), 41, 205.

24 Schickel, *The Disney Version*, 70–73.

25 Steven Watts, *The Magic Kingdom: Walt Disney and the America Way of Life* (New York: Houghton Mifflin Company, 1997), 23.

26 Schickel, *The Disney Version*, 40-41; Thomas, *Walt Disney*, 13.

In 1923, Walt moved to California. He had no real reason to think he would do any better in California than he had in Kansas City, where he had been successful enough to make enough money to eat and live, if just barely.[27] He soaked in Hollywood, and with the help of his Uncle Robert (who rented space in his garage to Walt and Roy), the two founded the Disney Brothers Studio.[28] Their venture was different from the outset. They were Midwesterners, at a time when most Hollywood studios were run by New Yorkers and immigrants from Europe. However, the California of the 1920s and 1930s was full of Midwesterners like the Disney brothers and the rapidly changing nation they were a part of was open to the films they were about to make.[29]

While Walt handled the creative side of the ever-growing company that soon bore his name alone, Roy was largely in charge of taking care of the financial side of the business. Walt was an artist and an entrepreneur who was willing to take risks. Roy was a risk-averse, consensus-building businessman. Together, they created a very beneficial and lucrative familial business relationship for some forty years, one that made the brothers (and their own families) incredibly wealthy. Their siblings, though often the recipients of stock, never joined the company. Nor did their parents fully appreciate what their middle children were able to accomplish. Tragedy hit the family in 1938, after Roy and Walt moved their parents to California and into a home the brothers had had built for them. That November, due to a faulty furnace, Flora Disney died when gas, instead of fresh air, was recirculated into the house. Elias, who seemed lost without her, died a few years later.[30]

Animation quickly became the bedrock upon which the Disney studio stood. Equally as fast, Walt seemed to find and set the tone for what animation became. Such statements are also only true because of the company's ultimate success. At the outset, there was no proof it was going to work. What Walt did was combine things in new ways, including the industrial output of his films. Sergei Eisenstein argued that Disney's work was a "revolt" against bland culture. Animation became a means to understand the United States, with cartoons a reflection

---

27 Schickel, *The Disney Version*, 85.

28 Andi Stein, *Why We Love Disney: The Power of the Disney Brand* (New York: Peter Lang, 2011), 15.

29 Thomas, *Building a Company*, 1; Eric Avila, *Popular Culture in the Age of White Flight: Fear and Fantasy in Suburban Los Angeles* (Los Angeles: University of California Press, 2004), 115.

30 Thomas, *Building a Company*, 2–3, 124–126, 233–235; Taylor, *Storming the Magic Kingdom*, 10–11; Didier Ghez, editor, *Walt's People: Volume 6: Talking Disney with the Artists Who Knew Him* (New York: Xlibris Corporation, 2008), 160.

of current events (even if delayed by the production process).[31] [32] As it turned out, it was the right combination at exactly the right time.

While starting out in short cartoons (starring Mickey and his pals), Disney eventually turned to feature films as a business consideration. The Disney shorts were popular, but if they brought people into a theater, ultimately it was the feature presentation that benefited from the extra traffic. *Snow White*, the company's first attempt at a full-length animated feature, opened at the Carthay Theater in December 1937. It was a runaway hit transforming the studio's finances in just a few short months. A new studio complex, made possible by *Snow White*, also changed the nature of the company. It went from being a close-knit operation to a large concern, where Walt was no longer "one of the boys." That transition continued after World War II, when Disney made his foray into major "adult" live-action movies. To the end, and despite the diversification of the company, Walt remained as engaged as he could in every creative facet the Disney brand was a part of.[33]

The successes that started with the creation of Mickey Mouse and Snow White gave Walt a sense of intellectual freedom that his critics did not always appreciate. It was not just financial security (as there were constant business strains); it was the ability to dream. Far from being done taking risks, as moving to Los Angeles had been, Walt found himself able to think about doing more than just making movies. By the late 1940s, he wanted more. Walt wanted to build a park.[34]

The Parks

The official version of the genesis of Disney's parks is that it was all because of his daughters. As Walt put it, "It came about when my daughters were very young. ... I felt there should be something built. Some kind of amusement enterprise, where the parents and the children could have fun together."[35] Walt had married Lillian Bounds (an inker

---

31 Paul Wells, *Animation and America* (Manchester: Edinburgh University Press, 2002), 1, 9, 26, 28, 39, 40, 45, 65, 118–119, 123.

32 Davis, Marc. Interviewed by Bob Thomas, 1973, Lectures and Transcripts, Walt Disney Studio Archives, Burbank, California.

33 Barrier, *The Animated Man*, 101, 125, 131, 241, 280; Thomas, *Walt Disney*, 167; Gabler, *Walt Disney*, 323–324.

34 Avila, *Popular Culture in the Age of White Flight*, 117; Paul Wells, *Animation and America* (Manchester: Edinburgh University Press, 2002), 48; Didier Ghez, editor, *Walt's People: Volume 1: Talking Disney with the Artists Who Knew Him* (Theme Park Press, 2014), 152; Watts, *The Magic Kingdom*, 402.

35 Dave Smith, *The Quotable Walt Disney* (New York: Disney Editions, 2001), 51.

at his studio) in 1925. The couple had one daughter, Diane, and adopted another, Sharon. By virtually every account, Walt was a "doting parent." Each weekend, he took his girls to little parks on "Daddy's day." There he noticed parents got bored watching their children play, the parks themselves were often not very clean, and at times, rather neglected. Walt came to realize that amusement parks could be a show in and of themselves. Guests could progress through a story, like a movie, and meet characters along the way. It took Disney about fifteen years, from the time his girls were little until Disneyland was a reality.[36]

Of course, building a park was never just about taking his daughters some place nice to have fun. There were other reasons to build one. Walt thought people who came out to Hollywood were ultimately disappointed with the experience. Even on studio tours, the public were offered little to see and even less to do. An amusement or theme park could change this and, Walt believed, make its owner money.[37] So, whenever he visited an amusement or theme park, or even a circus, Walt studied what was there and how things worked to garner ideas for himself.[38] He became friends with park owners. He tried to learn from them about how to handle lines and how to achieve park capacity.[39]

Constructing an amusement park was not a new idea, either in America or in southern California. The United States had some 2000 amusement parks in the early twentieth century. However, they harbored a reliance on the electric trolley, both as a means to get patrons to them and for their very existence, as many of the parks were built and owned by the trolley companies. Without the trolleys, the parks could not exist and that reliance proved their undoing with the advent of the automobile. Amusement parks declined further in the 1940s and early 1950s. By the time Walt started taking his girls to them,

---

36 Barrier, *The Animated Man*, 191; Watts, *The Magic Kingdom*, 355; John Hench with Peggy Van Pelt, *Designing Disney: Imagineering and the Art of the Show* (New York: Disney Editions, 2008), 2; Thomas, *Walt Disney*, 11; Ghez, editor, *Walt's People: Volume 6*, 174–175; Didier Ghez, editor, *Walt's People: Volume 3: Talking Disney with the Artists Who Knew Him* (New York: Xlibris Corporation, 2006), 130.

37 Janet Wasko, *Understanding Disney: The Manufacture of Fantasy* (Cambridge: Polity Press, 2001), 155; Thomas, *Walt Disney*, 218.

38 Barrier, *The Animated Man*, 235; Thomas, *Walt Disney*, 241; Paul Jerome Croce, "A Clean and Separate Space: Walt Disney in Person and Production," *The Journal of Popular Culture*, 25 (Winter 1991), 94.

39 Irvine, Dick. "Disney Biography: Bob Thomas' Interview with Dick Irvine 1968", Lectures and Transcripts, Walt Disney Studio Archives, Burbank, California.

there were just some 300 left.⁴⁰ Walt was looking for a way to avoid the pitfalls of amusement parks (which middle-class Americans had started to shun because they were dirty, noisy, and often urban) while also offering something that was "refined but still fun." He found it by embracing the past.⁴¹

In creating his park idea, Disney was merely building upon and surpassing the older concepts of world fairs and international exhibitions.⁴² In many ways, Disney was merging these with existing amusement parks.⁴³ Indeed, Disneyland owes a great deal to Walt's visit to the 1948 Chicago Railroad Fair, where he not only got to see all sorts of railroad equipment from the past, present, and projected future, but witnessed (and even participated in) the various "lands" that the exhibitors had put together in order to showcase different parts of America that could be visited by rail.⁴⁴

The trip to Chicago was only one catalyst. His experiences taking his daughters to parks were reinforced as he began inspecting the surviving amusement parks around the country. He found many of them, including New York's famed Coney Island, to be ill-planned and almost manic in nature. He planned to counter that with order and theming at his park. The urban nature of Coney Island also bothered Walt, because it relied, as other parks before had, on public transportation to guarantee guests would be able to easily get there. It was some place that allowed diverse New Yorkers (many of whom were immigrants during the park's heyday) to get out of their ethnic neighborhoods and experience something else.⁴⁵ Walt was quickly concluding that his future park might find a home in the suburbs, not the city itself.

In addition, he was also influenced by something that happened before he was born, the 1893 Chicago World's Fair and Columbian Exposition. During the six months the fair was open, one in four

---

40   Christopher Finch, *Walt Disney's America* (New York: Abbeville Press, 1978), 51; Judith A. Adams, *The American Amusement Park Industry: A History of Technology and Thrills* (Boston: Twayne Publishers, 1991), xiii, 57, 66–67, 164; Avila, *Popular Culture in the Age of White Flight*, 106; Wasko, *Understanding Disney*, 154.

41   Gary Cross, *Consumed Nostalgia: Memory in the Age of Fast Capitalism* (New York: Columbia University Press, 2015), 204–207.

42   Stephen F. Mills, "Disney and the Promotions of Synthetic Worlds," *American Studies International*, 28(October 1990), 70.

43   Avila, *Popular Culture in the Age of White Flight*, 130–131, 227.

44   Karal Ann Marling, "Disneyland, 1955: Just Take the Santa Ana Freeway to the American Dream," *American Art*, 5(Winter-Spring, 1991), 185.

45   Avila, *Popular Culture in the Age of White Flight*, 8, 106–110, 118.

Americans visited its attractions. Granted, the White City that was a part of Chicago's fair "had its darker, shadowed side," and it was very "elitist" and "ignored the realities of urban poverty and the treatment of nonwhite races."[46] Though Walt's park eventually was accused of the same things, elitism is hardly one of them. If he took anything away from learning about the fair his father helped to build, it was that planning was key and openness to all was paramount.[47] Trends within cultural and historic parks during the 1950s also influenced Disney. Colonial Williamsburg and Greenfield Village, which were both showcases of the past, crafted and championed by very powerful captains of industry, much like himself, served as further proof that the past could be democratized in a park environment.[48]

Walt began planning a park of some kind in earnest in 1953. He even created a separate company, Walt Disney, Incorporated (later changed to WED Enterprises, which eventually became the Imagineering division of the Walt Disney Company, once Roy convinced Walt that it looked bad to have employees working for two different, yet obviously related, companies), to handle the early stages of what became Disneyland. He pulled the people he needed (animators, directors) away from the studio to work directly for him. His Imagineers knew little about parks per se, but did know how to tell a Disney story.[49] Among them were men like Harper Goff and Herbert Ryman, who had shared life experiences with Walt, in that they had also came from small towns to California, had been born in the early twentieth century, and had witnessed changes to the country.[50] Collectively, the Imagineers' job became not just to design and build something that wasn't a typical amusement park of the time, but also to make it a Disney product with details, story, and humor. Unsurprisingly, they

---

46 Elting E. Morison, "What Went Wrong with Disney's World's Fair," http://www.americanheritage.com, 2 June 2014; Adams, *The American Amusement Park Industry*, 19–20, 28–29.

47 Adams, *The American Amusement Park Industry*, 35–39.

48 Warren Leon and Roy Rosenzweig, editors, *History Museums in the United States: A Critical Assessment* (Chicago: University of Illinois Press, 1989), 159; Adams, *The American Amusement Park Industry*, 93; James Howard Kunstler, *The Geography of Nowhere: The Rise and Decline of America's Man-Made Landscape* (New York: Touchstone Book, 1993), 198–199. Greenfield Village celebrates Henry Ford and Thomas Edison.

49 Jeff Kurtti, *Walt Disney's Imagineering Legends and the Genesis of the Disney Theme Park* (New York: Disney Editions, 2008), v; Thomas, *Building a Company*, 237–239, 254–255, 260–262.

50 Kurtti, *Walt Disney's Imagineering Legends and the Genesis of the Disney*

drew heavily from the films they had worked on.[51] It was their early work that won Roy over to the whole idea of a park and that morphed it from a small studio attraction into something much more.[52]

Beyond an idea and Imagineers, Walt had something else going for him: reputation. People knew the Disney name and they trusted it. He knew that better than anyone else did. Walt was sure he could build a park that people would want to visit. He wanted to make a place that could be enjoyed by both adults and children. Walt stressed that the park should be more about fun than about the "thrills" that dominated most amusement parks. Dis-History would give guests something else to interact with instead: themed stories. He hoped that the park would promote "happiness" by giving guests a "pleasant experience."[53]

Creating a place for leisure and entertainment at the same time, especially for the common person, was a new development.[54] Walt believed that "liking the guests" was imperative and charged his Imagineers with thinking about the park from the guests' perspective. This guiding principle meant that everything that went into an amusement park had to be reimagined and thought about in terms of how it would fit into Disney's themed park. Each attraction, each park in the Disney system has and invokes a certain mood or ambiance to guests. Every aspect, right down to the rest rooms, were designed with the guest experience in mind. Nothing, not even color selection or when and where guests meet characters, was left to chance.[55] However, before any of these ideas could become a reality, Walt first had to find the money to actually build his park.

The Birth of Disneyland

Building a park became Walt's dream and he was prepared to go to great lengths to achieve it. He sold the concept of Disneyland personally.

Theme Park, 4, 12, 34, 40.

51 Ghez, editor, *Walt's People: Volume 6*, 201, 202; *Marc Davis: Walt Disney's Renaissance Man* (New York: Disney Editions, 2014), 7, 109–110.

52 Thomas, *Building a Company*, 180–182; Thomas Hine, *Populuxe* (New York: Alfred A. Knopf, 1986), 151.

53 Thomas, *Walt Disney*, 279; Gabler, *Walt Disney*, 535; Alan Bryman, *The Disneyization of Society* (Thousand Oaks, California: Sage, 2004), 21; Michael R. Real, *Mass-Mediated Culture* (Englewood Cliffs, New Jersey: Prentice-Hall, 1977), 50–51; Avila, *Popular Culture in the Age of White Flight*, 138.

54 James Duncan and David Ley, editors, *Place/Culture/Representation* (New York: Routledge, 1994), 173.

55 Hench with Van Pelt, *Designing Disney*, 20–22, 30–32, 56, 96, 106–107.

Roy had to reign Walt in with the park idea when it first came up. The company simply did not have the money. Walt was not interested in limitations. He wanted to know what could be done. Roy noted that Walt "always strives for something that has not been done before. That sort of policy, of course, is always costly." Still, Roy was never quite as against the idea as he sometimes made others think he was. Walt made the rounds to bankers, sometimes without Roy knowing about it. Many banks saw real potential in the park and once Roy learned that his brother was cashing in a life-insurance policy in order to help fund development, the elder Disney got on board and began earnestly working the banks along with Walt.[56]

Ultimately, funding arrived not from a bank but from a partnership between Disney and the upstart technology of television. The 1950s were a time of transition for Hollywood. The studio system that had held sway since the Golden Age was falling apart, prompted in large part by the advent of the democratic medium of television. Despite his desire, Walt did not have an easy time finding a partner. There was animosity between the two systems, and not everyone embraced the idea of working with Disney. CBS passed on a partnership. NBC showed some initial interest, but negotiations stalled. Roy eventually found willing partners with ABC. Not only did ABC get a programming deal (which helped them grow their market share), but Disney got an infusion of cash to start building the park. The Disney-ABC partnership, which was lucrative to both companies, lasted until 1957. Walt would use and need every penny he could get his hands on to realize his dream.[57]

The potential marketing power television had is what convinced Walt to enter into a partnership to build his park. He realized that with television, he could speak directly to the people in their homes because television was a truly democratic medium that met people where they lived. The deal with ABC meant that Disney programming could generate the necessary revenue to fund construction costs. Walt had toyed with the new medium as early as 1950–1951, when the company began making collections of short cartoons which could be easily broken up for broadcast. Walt later said that whenever he

---

56 Thomas, *Walt Disney*, 219, 244; Michael D. Eisner, *Work in Progress* (New York: Random House, 1998), 203; Joe Flower, *Prince of the Magic Kingdom: Michael Eisner and the Re-Making of Disney* (New York: John Wiley and Sons, Inc., 1991; Theme Park Press, 2017), 26; Gabler, *Walt Disney*, 501-502; Barrier, *The Animated Man*, 68; Thomas, *Building a Company*, 96; "Disneyland History," http://www.disneydreamer.com/history/disneyland.htm, 9 December 2014.

57 Flower, *Prince of the Magic Kingdom*, 16; Thomas, *Building a Company*, 183–193, 204–205; Avila, *Popular Culture in the Age of White Flight*, 129.

thought of getting involved in television, he thought of the park. Unlike many of his contemporaries, Walt saw television as an ally to filmmakers, not their foe. It was a way to promote products, whether the studio's latest movie or even Disneyland itself. Television was a means to an end when it came to the park.[58] Television allowed Walt to make the case directly to viewers that his creation was not going be just another amusement park. It was going to be a Disney product.[59]

The Disney brand was important. The park's success or failure was predicated on getting people to it. Walt's television appearances (the show was structured around Walt introducing the show of the week, which all happened to correspond with one of the proposed lands of Disneyland) helped cement the notion that Disney was pro-family and thus his park would be a good place for families to visit. As the park idea progressed, the studio (which had long nourished the idea that it was family friendly) now began making more films that uplifted the family as a quintessential part of the American way of life. This included defending the family as an institution from outside attack by the forces of the modern world. One of the company's first shows, the *Mickey Mouse Club*, became a standard-bearer for family values.[60] In addition to promoting the park and the family, television helped sell more Disney themed merchandise: from Mickey Mouse Club memberships to Davy Crockett coonskin hats.

Diversification was not new for the company, even if television was. Disney always pushed to use different platforms and media to widen its market share.[61] The company began licensing character likenesses in the 1930s. That decision had helped keep the company going during

---

58 T.D. Allman, "The Theme-Parking, Megachurching, Franchising, Exurbing, McMansioning of America," *National Geographic* 211 (March 2007), 96–115; Scott Bukatman, "There's Always Tomorrowland: Disney and the Hypercinematic Experience," *October* (Summer, 1991), 61; Avila, *Popular Culture in the Age of White Flight*, 127; Thomas, *Walt Disney*, 244–245; Tom Stempel, *Storytellers to the Nation: A History of American Television Writing* (New York: Continuum, 1992), 62; Eric Smoodin, *Animating Culture: Hollywood Cartoons from the Sound Era* (New Brunswick, NJ: Rutgers University Press, 1993), 104–105; Kathy Merlock Jackson and Mark I. West, editors, *Disneyland and Culture: Essays on the Parks and Their Influence* (Jefferson, NC: McFarland and Company, 2011), 22; Barrier, *The Animated Man*, 228–229, 242–245; Paul Wells, *Animation and America* (Manchester: Edinburgh University Press, 2002), 76.

59 Marty Sklar, *Dream It! Do It!: My Half-Century Creating Disney's Magic Kingdoms* (New York: Disney Editions, 2013), 88.

60 Watts, *The Magic Kingdom*, 325–345.

61 Sperb, *Disney's Most Notorious Film*, 25–26.

the Depression. The parks offered an opportunity for even more retail sales; indeed, they were the culmination of Disney's diversification of its business.[62] As Walt put it, "We do television; we do the theatrical things, and again my park, the Disneyland park. I use the same talents to develop the different attractions at the park that I do to make my cartoons and make my other films here." To pull off this synergistic approach, the company created a production pipeline and began rolling out enough movies each year that if one of them failed, the others would cover the losses. They also began, in 1953, to be in charge of their own film distribution, making them independent and more profitable.[63] It was this unified vision that allowed Walt to build Disneyland.[64]

Initially, Walt hoped to build the park close to his studio, either as a back-lot attraction or as a sixteen-acre amusement park. However, Burbank officials could not get past the idea that the park might end up being like Coney Island, despite Disney's assurances to the contrary. Walt wanted to avoid the ocean/coastal area because he didn't want people to think of it as a pier amusement park.[65] Largely for these reasons, along with the desire for more land, Walt turned his attention to Orange County. Here, amongst groves of orange and walnut trees, he got to "reimagine" the amusement park.[66] Finding enough land

---

62 Richard E. Foglesong, *Married to the Mouse: Walt Disney World and Orlando* (New Haven: Yale University Press, 2001), 35; Thomas, *Building a Company*, 70; Eric Smoodin, editor, *Disney Discourse: Producing the Magic Kingdom* (New York: Routledge, 1994), 3, 117. Smoodin argues that Disney is best understood as akin to Henry Ford and Thomas Edison, as an innovator in his own right but also someone who created a "technological system" that was a fully functioning horizontally and vertically integrated business.

63 Bryman, *The Disneyization of Society*, 84; Wasko, *Understanding Disney*, 49; Schickel, *The Disney Version*, 308–309; Kathy Merlock Jackson, editor, *Walt Disney: Conversations* (Jackson: University of Mississippi Press, 2006), 78; Alan Bryman, *Disney and His Worlds* (New York: Routledge, 1995; ebook version), 11; Robin Allan, *Walt Disney and Europe: European Influences on the Animated Feature Films of Walt Disney* (Indianapolis: Indiana University Press, 1999), 1; Andi Stein, *Why We Love Disney: The Power of the Disney Brand* (New York: Peter Lang, 2011), 72–73; Thomas, *Building a Company*, 160; Watts, *The Magic Kingdom*, 370–371.

64 Watts, *The Magic Kingdom*, 384–385.

65 Irvine, Dick. "Disney Biography: Bob Thomas' Interview with Dick Irvine 1968", Lectures and Transcripts, Walt Disney Studio Archives, Burbank, California.

66 Avila, *Popular Culture in the Age of White Flight*, 120-122; Dolores Hayden, *The Power of Place: Urban Landscapes as Public History* (Cambridge: The MIT Press, 1995), 109. See as well, Carol S. Jeffers, "In A Cultural Vortex: Theme Parks, Experience, and Opportunities for Art Education," *Studies in Art Education*, 45(Spring 2004), 221–233.

was problematic, however.[67] Disney employed the Stanford Research Institute to help them, but even then, the effort was cash strapped, faced reluctant owners, and very real competition (and rising prices) as news leaked out about what the company was up to.[68]

Eventually, Disney was only able to buy 270 acres before they ran out of money. The first orange trees were cleared in August 1954, under the supervision of Admiral Joseph Fowler, the man Disney entrusted with overseeing the construction of Disneyland. Fowler had helped design U.S. Navy ships during World War II. In 1954, Disney hired him to build the park. Fowler grasped intuitively that the parks (he eventually oversaw construction of the Magic Kingdom in Florida as well) needed to be able to handle, not just accommodate, large crowds.[69]

The reason Fowler was brought in was that no sooner had ground been broken than the company realized that the entire park could not be completed in time for the opening. This point became abundantly clear as construction delays hit the park, ranging from union issues, to plumbers who did not finish all the toilets, to Teamsters who wanted to put guests on and off attractions. But between Walt's earnestness, Fowler's organizational skills, and the work of C.V. Wood (an engineer who had previously worked for the Stanford Research Institute and had helped select Anaheim as the location for Disneyland, as well as helped supervise its construction), the park slowly took shape.[70]

As trees met the bulldozer, it became clear that Disney was creating a "total environment," with nearly no trace of what had once been there remaining.[71] Walt was giving his guests the chance to view not just different "lands" but completely different landscapes, with various areas rolling out before them—almost as if they were stepping into a movie, or at least the set of a film.[72] Yet Walt's idea for a park was different from anything that previously existed.[73] There were all sorts of reasons

---

67 Harrison Price, *Walt's Revolution! By the Numbers* (Orlando: Ripley Entertainment Incorporated, 2004), 27.

68 Pierce, *Three Years in Wonderland*, 52, 58, 162.

69 *New York Times*, 14 December 1993.

70 Ghez, editor, *Walt's People: Volume 1*, 228–229.

71 Thomas, *Building a Company*, 187-189; Watts, *The Magic Kingdom*, 386; Jane Kuenz, Karen Klugman, Shelton Waldrep, and Susan Willis, editors, *Inside the Mouse: Work and Play at Disney World* (Durham: Duke University Press, 1995), 166.

72 Gabler, *Walt Disney*, 534; Christopher Finch, *Walt Disney's America* (New York: Abbeville Press, 1978), 75; Stein, *Why We Love Disney*, 25; Hench with Van Pelt, *Designing Disney*, 23, 68.

73 Harrison Price, *Walt's Revolution! By the Numbers* (Orlando: Ripley Entertainment Incorporated, 2004), 26.

not to build the park the way he was doing it. Putting in lots of details did not make any money. Something like the proposed castle was not going to make any revenue (it was a showpiece after all, not a ride).[74] But in creating an "emotional environment," Walt was giving guests places where the look, feel, sounds, and smells invoked feelings and memories that seemed correct and authentic; Disney was tapping into things much larger than the thrill of rides.[75] The "storybook realism" the Imagineers were designing aimed to transport guests out of their daily world entirely.[76] The theming ideas behind Disneyland linked every design element, from architecture to the colors chosen, as a means to get away from conceptual contradictions, which produces competition in the minds of guests. Museums suffer from this as well, because the mind goes from one exhibit to another and guests cannot take it all in.[77] Such theories were soon tested by very real guests of all ages. Their reactions would be the proof of whether Walt was right or not.

Ultimately, Walt was the "chief strategist" of the park. Despite the work of Fowler and Wood, as well as others, in many ways he personally oversaw the construction Disneyland. Seemingly, all Walt did was think about Disneyland. His focus was on the park, and his interest in the movies (both animated and live action) lessened. Walt wanted everything to be perfect. He expected the best and he expected that people would appreciate it and come to his park. After his apartment was finished over the firehouse, Walt often surprised workers by

---

74 Price, *Walt's Revolution!*, 30-31; Irvine, Dick. "Disney Biography: Bob Thomas' Interview with Dick Irvine 1968", Lectures and Transcripts, Walt Disney Studio Archives, Burbank, California.

75 Josef Chytry, "Walt Disney and the Creation of Emotional Environments: Interpreting Walt Disney's oeuvre from the Disney Studios to Disneyland, CalArts, and the Experimental Prototype Community of Tomorrow (EPCOT), *Rethinking History: The Journal of Theory and Practice*, published on line, 25 May 2012; Sharon Zukin, *Landscapes of Power: From Detroit to Disney World* (Los Angeles: University of California Press, 1993), 223, 230; Thomas Hine, *Populuxe* (New York: Alfred A. Knopf, 1986), 152; Charles Carson, "Whole New Worlds: Music in the Disney Theme Park Experience," *Ethnomusicology Forum*, 13(November 2004), 228; Jeff Kurtti, *Walt Disney's Imagineering Legends and the Genesis of the Disney Theme Park* (New York: Disney Editions, 2008), 138-139; Didier Ghez, editor, *Walt's People: Volume 2: Talking Disney with the Artists Who Knew Him* (Theme Park Press, 2015), 140-142; Christian Moran, *Great Big Beautiful Tomorrow: Walt Disney and Technology* (Theme Park Press, 2015),.

76 Beth Dunlop, *Building a Dream: The Art of Disney Architecture* (New York: Harry N. Abrams, 1996), 14; Kurtti, *Walt Disney's Imagineering Legends*, viii.

77 Hench, John (1). "Interviewed by Gabe Essoe 1972," Lectures and Transcripts, Walt Disney Studio Archives, Burbank, California.

coming down in his bathrobe and talking with them in the morning. From the food to the rides, he inspected every facet and made recommendations that resulted in changes. Walt's involvement in the day-to-day construction of Disneyland meant it was as near as it could be to exactly what he wanted.[78]

Disneyland opened on July 17, 1955, as a lavish televised Hollywood production, which was nearly a fiasco. There were problems with the grand opening, most of which had to do with the fast-paced construction to be ready for opening day. Not all the drinking fountains worked, food stands ran out of items, some stores had nothing in them, there was even a small gas leak, and additionally not all the lands were actually finished. However, the biggest problem was the turnout. More than double the number of guests came to the park that first day than had been planned for, prompting congested roads and long lines for attractions and available food, water, and bathrooms. A few days later, temperatures soared, making some people reluctant to go. Critics doubted if Disneyland would survive or perhaps even destroy the company. Even though the opening of park was not perfect (the company handled the public relations spin perfectly), Walt was quite pleased that he had pulled it off, and that his vision of a park was now a reality. Once the "kinks were worked out" (and that was done very quickly) it became quite clear just how awesome Walt's idea was. Simply put, people kept coming.[79]

On opening day, Walt said, "Disneyland is dedicated to the ideals, the dreams, and the hard facts that have created America."[80] Here, according to Walt, Dis-Historic edutainment would become manifest. "The idea of Disneyland," he said, "is a simple one. It will be a place for

---

[78] Thomas, *Walt Disney*, 273; Gabler, *Walt Disney*, 523, 565; Barrier, *The Animated Man*, 259; Didier Ghez, editor, *Walt's People: Volume 5: Talking Disney with the Artists Who Knew Him* (New York: Xlibris Corporation, 2007), 51; Didier Ghez, editor, *Walt's People: Volume 7: Talking Disney with the Artists Who Knew Him* (New York: Xlibris Corporation, 2008), 54.

[79] Barrier, *The Animated Man*, 254; Judith A. Adams, *The American Amusement Park Industry: A History of Technology and Thrills* (Boston: Twayne Publishers, 1991), 95; Thomas, *Walt Disney*, 14–15; Thomas, *Building a Company*, 196–197; Watts, *The Magic Kingdom*, 387; Stein, *Why We Love Disney*, 110–111; Gabler, *Walt Disney*, 526–533; Sharon Zukin, *Landscapes of Power: From Detroit to Disney World* (Los Angeles: University of California Press, 1993), 223; Sklar, *Dream It! Do It!*, 74–75; 1955-News from Disneyland folder, Walt Disney Studio Archives, Burbank, California.

[80] Dave Smith, *The Quotable Walt Disney* (New York: Disney Editions, 2001), 52.

people to find happiness and knowledge. It will be a place for parents and children to share pleasant times in one another's company; a place for teachers and pupils to discover greater ways of understanding and education. Here the older generation can recapture the nostalgia of days gone by, and the younger generation can savor the challenge of the future."[81] As Walt put it, "Disneyland will be the essence of America as we know it, the nostalgia of the past with the exciting glimpses into the future."[82]

The steady stream of guests made others realize what Disney had accomplished. Disney wanted the park to be a "fully self-contained world." Thus, at the park's entrance a sign echoes Walt's opening day words: "Here you leave today and enter the world of yesterday, tomorrow, and fantasy." Disneyland produced its own reality, which shielded guests from the outside world, if only for a few hours, by making them active participants in the lands Disney had created.[83] As Walt's friend and supporter Ray Bradbury put it, "Walt Disney's Disneyland liberates men to be their better selves. ... The great thing is to walk around at Disneyland and see smiling people."[84] The park was a success, and to the end of his life, Walt's love and enthusiasm for it never wavered.[85]

Millions of Americans, for over sixty years, have proven to be equally enthusiastic. The big question was whether people really wanted to vacation at Walt's park. The answer, as opening day (even with all of its problems) showed, was yes. What Disney was tapping into was the relatively new phenomenon of leisure. The success of Disneyland (and eventually Walt Disney World) helped create the idea of a destination family vacation. Walt had the good fortune to open his park at the "peak of the baby boom" and it quickly became a "vacation mecca" for families. A place that people could come to and stay at, and as a result, spend more time and money.[86] The park's organization, its cleanliness and its polite staff, as well as the newness of the park itself, coupled with the familiarity of Disney's characters and the "safety"

---

81 Smith, *The Quotable Walt Disney*, 55.

82 Smith, *The Quotable Walt Disney*, 56.

83 Avila, *Popular Culture in the Age of White Flight*, 225; Michael D. Eisner, *Work in Progress* (New York: Random House, 1998), 204; Michael Steiner, "Frontierland as Tommorowland: Walt Disney and the Architectural Packaging of the Mythic West," *Montana: The Magazine of Western History*, 48(Spring 1998), 3.

84 *USA Today*, 7 June 2012.

85 Flower, *Prince of the Magic Kingdom*, 19; Barrier, *The Animated Man*, 288.

86 Ken Roberts, *The Leisure Industries* (New York: Palgrave Macmillan, 2004), 14; Mark Gottdiener, *The Theming of America: Dreams, Visions, and Commercial Spaces* (New York: Westview Press, 1997), 109.

factor of being in the park—both physically and psychologically—all played roles in both its initial and continued success.[87]

Almost immediately, Disneyland became "a key symbol of contemporary American culture."[88] The success of Disneyland sparked a revolution in themed parks across the nation, and was part of a larger theming of American society and of urban designers seeking to copy its "form follows function" ideal.[89] In revolutionizing the theme park, Disney was also changing how Americans lived, worked, and played—and even who they did those things with. Thus, Walt transformed the corporate world and how it dealt with people in fundamental ways. If McDonalds was promising its customers that they were guaranteed the same food whenever and wherever they visited one of its stores, Walt was offering guests a similar experience when they came to his park. The attractions and shows were consistent and repetitive, and thus one guest's experience did not vary from either a different guest's experience, nor from visit to visit. That kind of dependable guest experience helped drive people to the parks: they knew what to expect.[90] It is difficult to overrate the importance of consistency to people living during a period of population growth and a booming economy that was shifting where people lived and worked (not to mention Cold War fears).

Even when it was finished, and money started flowing into Disney's coffers from the parks, the bills continued. Walt was never finished tweaking it and always looking for ways to make the park better: from adding attractions, to improving the views for shows, to making sure that customer service was a top priority (like moving away from purchasing tickets for specific attractions to a single admittance fee—which cut operating costs), to making sure that the illusion of the park was never shattered for guests.[91] All these things cost money, but they

---

87   Avila, *Popular Culture in the Age of White Flight*, 123–124; Gabler, *Walt Disney*, 613.

88   Karal Ann Marling, editor, *Designing Disney's Theme Parks: The Architecture of Reassurance* (New York: Flammarion, 1997), 9.

89   Gottdiener, *The Theming of America: Dreams, Visions, and Commercial Spaces*, 3–4; Price, *Walt's Revolution!*, 83; Sklar, *Dream It! Do It!*, 63–64.

90   Marling, editor, *Designing Disney's Theme Parks*, 31; Kathy Merlock Jackson and Mark I. West, editors, *Disneyland and Culture: Essays on the Parks and Their Influence* (Jefferson, NC: McFarland and Company, 2011), 1; Watts, *The Magic Kingdom*, 394; Bryman, *The Disneyization of Society*, 4, 168; Barrier, *The Animated Man*, 257; Avila, *Popular Culture in the Age of White Flight*, 125.

91   Thomas, *Walt Disney*, 288–290; Michael R. Real, *Mass-Mediated Culture* (Englewood Cliffs, New Jersey: Prentice-Hall, 1977), 52; Adams, *The American*

were also good reinvestments that made the park even more profitable.

Highways and automobiles made Disneyland's success possible. Indeed, the park quickly became a model for how to handle cars and crowds. The reliance on cars required careful space planning. Yet, there was an almost instant understanding that despite talking about transportation, progress, and the like, once guests arrived at Disneyland, cars themselves were to be abandoned in parking lots and largely not encountered within the park itself. Indeed, as the park took off, Walt came to dislike cars, at least what they did to his park as other developers snatched up land nearby and drew his guests (and the cars that brought them to Disneyland) to their hotels, restaurants, and shops.[92]

At the same time, automobiles were important to Walt for another reason. They were part of the belief of many living in California in the mid-twentieth century that the Golden State was some sort of utopia. Automobiles promised unlimited freedom, from place.[93] However, they also created a desire for people to find something permanent to latch on to. As such, there are some who argue that Walt was creating Disneyland, at its opening, as a "city on a hill" in an homage to both John Winthrop's speech as well as the California dream. Disneyland was giving newly minted suburban dwellers a place to go to, that reflected their (largely in the 1950s) Euro-American "traditions, values, and practices." In very real ways, Disneyland was marketing (while also affirming) small-town values in the midst of urban sprawl, a cultural center to help guests make sense of the modern world.[94]

Walt's angst about automobiles and the sprawl they helped produce caused yet another kind of reaction. Walt knew he would never be done with the park. He also knew he needed more land than he could now buy in California to come close to realizing his dreams.[95] Just as

---

Amusement Park Industry, 96; Price, *Walt's Revolution!*, 110.

92 Kevin Starr, *Golden Dreams: California in an Age of Abundance, 1950-1963* (New York: Oxford University Press, 2009), 160; Avila, *Popular Culture in the Age of White Flight*, 121, 174, 203; "Luis Marin: Disneyland as Degenerate Utopia," http://lmc.gatech.edu/~broglio/1101/marin.html, 23 September 2014; Thomas, *Walt Disney*, 333; James Howard Kunstler, *The Geography of Nowhere: The Rise and Decline of America's Man-Made Landscape* (New York: Touchstone Book, 1993), 218; *The Imagineering Field Guide to the Magic Kingdom at Walt Disney World: An Imagineer's Eye Tour* (New York: Disney Editions, 2005), 16.

93 Kunstler, *The Geography of Nowhere*, 86.

94 Avila, *Popular Culture in the Age of White Flight*, 16, 63, 107; Starr, *Golden Dreams*, 12-16; Stephen E. Weil, *Rethinking the Museum and Other Meditations* (Washington: Smithsonian Institution Press, 1990), 4.

95 Thomas, *Building a Company*, 250.

he wanted distance from the sprawl, he also wanted guests to not be distracted by the outside world.[96] To overcome those problems, Disney looked to Florida.

The Florida Project

No sooner was the paint finally dry at Disneyland than Walt faced demand for another park by both public officials and the public.[97] Walt knew almost immediately that they needed more land. If you ask people to come to a park, you have to supply their needs. Where will they sleep? Where will they eat? Where will they get their haircut?[98] As he began thinking about "an Eastern Disneyland," Walt concluded that amusement and theme parks in the United States were primed for a "Disneyland revolution," in the words of one interviewer.[99] One of the key takeaways from Disneyland's construction was the importance of land and space to the success of the park. Disney wanted visitors to his parks to leave the world they knew behind and be immersed in the world (or land) that he created via Dis-History. The key to achieving that immersive experience was having enough room to grow but also to effectively exclude the outside world.[100] Obviously, as many commentators have pointed out, this meant the modern world, the work world; indeed, the normal life guests were living and escaping from via a vacation. However, on some other level Walt wanted his parks to echo what his guests already knew. That is where Dis-History came in.

Doing this cost money and to do it right meant having more money on hand than Walt had when building Disneyland. As it turned out, Disneyland itself became the answer. The profits were large, even with reinvestment. It took Walt six years of running Disneyland to buy out his initial partners (ABC and Western Printing and Lithograph Company), but he did just that. Now with sole ownership, park revenue

---

96 Thomas, *Walt Disney*, 17, 292; Stein, *Why We Love Disney*, 27-28; Paul Jerome Croce, "A Clean and Separate Space: Walt Disney in Person and Production," *The Journal of Popular Culture*, 25 (Winter 1991), 95.

97 Gabler, *Walt Disney*, 603.

98 Hench, John (1). December 1974 Interview, Lectures and Transcripts, Walt Disney Studio Archives, Burbank, California.

99 Jackson, editor, *Walt Disney: Conversations*, 83.

100 John Schultz, "The Fabulous Presumption of Disney World: Magic Kingdom in the Wilderness," *The Georgia Review*, 42(Summer 1988), 276, 279-280; Sacred Matters, "Why I Still Love Disney, or, Imagineering Religion," https://scholarblogs.emory.edu/sacredmatters/2014/02/11/why-i-still-love-disney-or-imagineering-religion/, 5 March 2014.

coupled with merchandise, movies, and a new television deal with NBC allowed Walt to start looking for a location for a second park.[101]

Walt picked Orlando over St. Louis, Baltimore, and the Niagara Falls area of upstate New York. Some backers had even tried to persuade Walt to build the park in New York City (on the site of the 1964 World's Fair). Disney's planners argued that any Disneyland East needed to be in a warmer climate, where it could operate year round.[102] The land southwest of Orlando might be a swampy "wasteland," "where alligators outnumbered people," but it also was where the people were willing to sell land "dirt cheap," and near two highways in central Florida. The decision was a strategic move more than it was a gamble. Walt truly believed that this time, he had enough "wilderness" to solve all his problems.[103]

Disney began secretly buying up land in Florida in April 1964, engaging "in a far-ranging conspiracy" to purchase as much acreage as possible. Walt benefited from the proximity of Cape Canaveral, as many people believed the federal government was actually buying land, and rumors swirled about major construction and perhaps as many as 5000 new jobs for the area. Still, speculation usually included Disney in the list of possible purchasers. On average, the company was able to buy land at $200 an acre (the price jumped to $75,000 an acre once Disney was the confirmed buyer). Emily Bavar, a reporter for the *Orlando Sentinel*, broke the story of Disney's second park coming to Florida when Walt protested a bit too much about why Orlando would never be a good spot for a park in an interview. Her story came just days before a planned announcement by state and company officials.[104]

Scrambling, Florida Governor Haydon Burns was forced to confirm the report on October 25, 1965. A few weeks later, on November 15,

---

101   Cher Krause Knight, *Power and Paradise in Walt Disney's World* (Gainesville: University Press of Florida, 2014), 11; Ghez, editor, *Walt's People: Volume 3*, 54.

102   Price, *Walt's Revolution!*, 38.

103   Barrier, *The Animated Man*, 301; Marling, editor, *Designing Disney's Theme Parks*, 148; T.D. Allman, "The Theme-Parking, Megachurching, Franchising, Exurbing, McMansioning of America," *National Geographic* 211 (March 2007), 96–115; Sklar, *Dream It! Do It!*, 123; *The Imagineering Field Guide to the Magic Kingdom at Walt Disney World: An Imagineer's Eye Tour* (New York: Disney Editions, 2005), 19.

104   Fjellman, *Vinyl Leaves*, 111; T.D. Allman, *Finding Florida: The True History of the Sunshine State* (New York: Atlantic Monthly Press, 2013), 371-372; Adams, *The American Amusement Park Industry*, 137–138; Leonard E. Zehnder, *Florida's Disney World: Promises and Problems* (Tallahassee: The Peninsular Publishing Company, 1975), 5–9, 12–13, 20–21, 24–25, 188, 191, 243; Sklar, *Dream It! Do It!*, 126–127.

Walt and Roy held a press conference with the governor. Even after press packets were distributed, the actual plans for Disney World were kept vague on purpose.[105] While the Disneys highlighted the wide range of jobs that were about to be created, in a feat of construction that was destined to transform central Florida, the company still had not finalized all the particulars about actually creating their second park. Disney worked Florida politicians hard in order to get what it wanted, which was near complete legal control over its land and the construction that was to take place on it. There were no real codes for what they were doing.[106] Even so, it was not hard to sell Florida politicians in the mid-1960s that this was a good deal, and that they should give Disney everything it wanted. Disney would get the land to build its park, and vast amounts of local control over two counties, and the state was set to reap jobs, name recognition as a vacation destination, and tourists. All of which meant increased tax revenues in local and state coffers.[107]

Interestingly, when Disney World was announced, no one had really ever considered what tourism might do to an area like Orlando. Supporters of the park believed it would draw people to central Florida. While there were negative consequences to the park and development, things were never as bad as critics alleged they would be. Disney was a "fuse" that caused an explosion of growth and change to Orlando. The parks created jobs, both in terms of construction and obvious park employees, but also in related service economies (both owned and auxiliary to Disney), such as hotel staff, cooks, and security guards as well as other positions. There were more jobs than there were people to take them during the construction phase. All those jobs pulled other people to the area to live and work. In the span of a few short years, the

---

105 Sklar, *Dream It! Do It!*, 12; Dave Smith and Steven Clark, *Disney: The First 100 Years* (New York: Hyperion, 1999), 97.

106 Hench, John (1). December 1974 Interview, Lectures and Transcripts, Walt Disney Studio Archives, Burbank, California.

107 Zehnder, *Florida's Disney World*, 4–5, 28–31, 38, 66–67, 80, 100–101; Allman, *Finding Florida*, 380; Henry A. Giroux, *The Mouse that Roared: Disney and the End of Innocence* (New York: Rowman and Littlefield, 1999), 38; Fjellman, *Vinyl Leaves*, 113; Barrier, *The Animated Man*, 311; Thomas, *Walt Disney*, 334; Richard E. Foglesong, *Married to the Mouse: Walt Disney World and Orlando* (New Haven: Yale University Press, 2001), 3–5, 15, 58. As Foglesong relates it, St. Louis was about to close the deal to land Disney's next park until a member of the city's delegation made a snide comment (which Walt overheard) about Disney's anti-alcohol policy within its parks. As a result, Walt backed out of the deal right before the paperwork was ready to be signed (1–2).

Orlando area went from swampland to one of the most technologically advanced and developed areas in the entire world.[108]

Like Disneyland, Disney World became a "vacation kingdom." It is over 27,400 acres in size and is completely dedicated to the business of and controlled by the Walt Disney Company.[109] Walt wanted his guests isolated not only from other rivals for their entertainment dollars, but also from the world. Here there was enough land to ensure that Disneyland's problems did not afflict Disney World. Indeed, all the lessons learned in California were about to be applied in Florida. Though critics doubted that Disney would be able to make its attendance estimates in its second park (pointing out that Disneyland relied on a large local population in California and was not dependent on tourists), once again Walt's vision proved them wrong. By 2014, it was estimated that Walt Disney World drew 19 million visitors a year.[110]

Walt did not live to see any of it come to fruition. By the mid-1960s, as his health started to decline, he pushed himself to work even harder. In November 1966, Disney went to the hospital. He had smoked for decades and doctors discovered lung cancer, prompting almost immediate surgery to remove one of his lungs. Upon his release, he told virtually no one how ill he was, worried that if news got out the company's stock price would drop. He was soon back in the hospital. As he lay on his deathbed, Walt talked about the Florida project. He died on December 15, just shy of his sixty-fifth birthday.[111]

Despite plans to retire, Roy stayed on to run the company, in order to make sure that Disney World was built. The parks were an economic moneymaker for the company, and Roy did not want that jeopardized in any way. He was right in his assessment. There was a consensus within the company that if Roy had not been in charge, Disney World would have never happened. As one associate, Jack Lindquist, put it, "It took a Disney to do it, and that was Roy." In short, Roy made

---

108 Zukin, *Landscapes of Power*, 265; Zehnder, *Florida's Disney World*, iii, 41, 151–152, 252–253, 258–261, 270–271, 349.

109 Fjellman, *Vinyl Leaves*, 10–11; Stein, *Why We Love Disney*, 115.

110 Giroux, *The Mouse that Roared*, 37; Zehnder, *Florida's Disney World*, 347; Adams, *The American Amusement Park Industry*, 111; Fjellman, *Vinyl Leaves*, 22–23, 200; "Disney CEO Iger's Empire of Tech," http://fortune.com/2014/12/29/disney-ceo-bob-iger-empire-of-tech/, 12 January 2015.

111 Barrier, *The Animated Man*, 306, 315; Timothy S. Susanin, *Walt Before Mickey: Disney's Early Years, 1919–1928* (Jackson: University Press of Mississippi, 2011), 180; Michael D. Eisner, *Work in Progress* (New York: Random House, 1998), 206. As a Disneyland cast member related to my family in April 2016, the clock inside Sleeping Beauty Castle is set at 4pm, the hour of Walt's death.

Walt's Disney World a reality, even deciding that the Florida Project was going to be renamed Walt Disney World in honor of his brother.[112]

Roy turned much of the day-to-day details of building Disney World over to Admiral Joe Fowler and General Joe Potter (both of whom, because of their military backgrounds, believed that any task could be accomplished and done so on time). Potter was a former major general in the Army Corps of Engineers and governor of the Panama Canal Zone, who had helped plan the invasion of Europe during World War II. He had recently joined Disney after helping pull off the World's Fair in New York. Potter "directed construction of the infrastructure" at Disney World. He worked very hard to bridge the gap between the company and Orlando.[113] Disney believed they needed someone with diplomatic skills and someone who knew about waterways and swamps. Potter was the obvious choice in that regard. However, construction in Florida was never as disciplined as Disneyland's, because there was no Walt to oversee every aspect of it.[114]

The Florida park gave Disney the opportunity to capitalize on lessons learned from Disneyland. In Disney World, the park was built on top of the infrastructure needed to run it. Guests are not in a tropical paradise, they are walking on top of a control center. Building the park was a massive engineering and construction undertaking. Dirt from the digging of the vast lagoon was placed over the control buildings, elevating the park further above sea level. A vast underground city and tunnel complex is the heart of the park, making the labor involved in operating it all but disappear. Also largely unseen by guests, the massive drainage system needed to transform swampland not just into dry land, but also into lakes and canals to keep it so.[115]

Walt had told the press that it would take Disney three years to build the park, which would cost around $100 million. By 1967, the company was estimating the cost at $600 million, with a four-to-five year construction timeline.[116] Roy believed it possible to open Disney World largely debt free. To do so, the elder Disney also started the process by which Disney owned its own hotels. While they were expensive to build (and Disney had much to learn about that and about

---

112 Thomas, *Building a Company*, 310, 316–317; Thomas, *Walt Disney*, 357.

113 *Los Angeles Times*, 8 December 1988; Beth Dunlop, *Building a Dream: The Art of Disney Architecture* (New York: Harry N. Abrams, 1996), 107.

114 Thomas, *Building a Company*, 308–309, 315, 318; Zehnder, *Florida's Disney World*, 39–40.

115 Allman, *Finding Florida*, 370–371; Kuenz, Klugman, Waldrep, and Willis, editors, *Inside the Mouse*, 157; Adams, *The American Amusement Park Industry*, 138–142.

116 Zehnder, *Florida's Disney World*, 80.

running them), having guests staying longer in Disney-owned hotels meant more money for the company.[117] Indeed, this was one of the Disneyland lessons learned that the company brought to Florida.[118]

Walt Disney World opened on October 1, 1971, at a price tag of $400 million. The event was strategic. October was a low tourist month in Florida. Additionally, the day was Friday, a traditionally slow one at theme parks. Picking the date gave the company time to work out any kinks that might develop before large numbers of tourists arrived. That, however, did not take long. By Thanksgiving, it was obvious that the park was an overwhelming success. In the first year, an estimated 11 million people came to the Magic Kingdom.[119]

The Florida park, almost from its opening, was a destination resort. People now came to Florida to go to parks, not (just) beaches.[120] In that sense, it was transformative. While of course an artificial creation, Walt Disney World's Magic Kingdom has an "intimacy of scale and richness of texture" in its construction that is simply "grander" than Disneyland, and because of the vast wilderness surrounding it, even more of "a utopian version of America" than its predecessor.[121] As much as he loved Disneyland, Ray Bradbury cherished Walt Disney World even more. As he put it, "Can one man dream and build one city and change world history? One man could. One man did. Walt Disney. And you all know the city: Walt Disney World." Bradbury saw it as a place to be inspired by—whether you were a guest, a student, a city planner, an urban redeveloper, an architect, or a builder.[122] Far more than just a copy of the California original, Walt Disney World is a place of inspiration and maybe just a little bit of magic.

---

117 Thomas, *Building a Company*, 306, 320; Zehnder, *Florida's Disney World*, 195; Janet Wasko, *Understanding Disney: The Manufacture of Fantasy* (Cambridge: Polity Press, 2001), 158.

118 Michael R. Real, *Mass-Mediated Culture* (Englewood Cliffs, New Jersey: Prentice-Hall, 1977), 79.

119 Eisner, *Work in Progress*, 207; Thomas, *Building a Company*, 327, 332; Adams, *The American Amusement Park Industry*, 141.

120 Eisner, *Work in Progress*, 202; Allman, *Finding Florida*, 381.

121 Adams, *The American Amusement Park Industry*, 127, 144; Finch, *Walt Disney's America*, 190; Paul Wells, *Animation and America* (Manchester: Edinburgh University Press, 2002), 136.

122 *USA Today*, 7 June 2012.

Living with the Parks

Millions of people, every year since they opened, have made an inspired pilgrimage to one of the Disney parks. Today they are the most visited attractions in the world.[123] Disney has figured out how to reach both children and adults, just as Walt intended.[124] Journeying to a park makes what people have read, seen, and heard real in a sense. Guests are engaged by Disney at every one of the sensory levels, creating a "collective fantasy" that builds "the narrative that characterizes utopia," according to one commentator.[125] Which park, whether in California, Florida, Japan, France, Hong Kong, or China, does not matter. A guest is "in Disney" regardless of geographic location. They come not because they have been tricked or lured, but because they want to be there. The parks are safe spaces in the best sense, and offer guests reassurance about life and about how life can be.[126]

Dis-History is a large part of how the parks accomplish this mission for Disney. Walt's park concept not only revolutionized theme and amusement parks, but also helped to foster "collective memory" by invoking things and events from the past as present experiences, all the while being accessible for guests. Thus, on a fundamental level, the Disney parks are based on "history, material culture, visual culture, built environment, and nostalgia."[127] For Americans, the parks have become a means to teach "common codes" toward sustaining a "national community" in the wake of modernity.[128] The parks

---

123 Wasko, *Understanding Disney*, 56.

124 Charles Carson, "Whole New Worlds: Music in the Disney Theme Park Experience, "Ethnomusicology *Forum*, 13(November 2004), 229; Thomas, *Walt Disney*, 11.

125 Real, *Mass-Mediated Culture*, 46-47; Andrew Lainsbury, *Once Upon an American Dream: The Story of Euro Disneyland* (Lawrence: University Press of Kansas, 2000), 196; Tison Pugh and Susan Aronstein, editors, *The Disney Middle Ages: A Fairy-Tale and Fantasy Past* (New York: Palgrave Macmillan, 2012), 59; Adams, *The American Amusement Park Industry*, 155 ; "Luis Marin: Disneyland as Degenerate Utopia," http://lmc.gatech.edu/~broglio/1101/marin.html, 23 September 2014.

126 Lainsbury, *Once Upon an American Dream*, 5; Pugh and Aronstein, editors, *The Disney Middle Ages*, 21.

127 Adams, *The American Amusement Park Industry*, xiv, 97; Zukin, *Landscapes of Power*, 221-222; Kathy Merlock Jackson and Mark I. West, editors, *Disneyland and Culture: Essays on the Parks and Their Influence* (Jefferson, NC: McFarland and Company, 2011), 119, 205.

128 Paul Jerome Croce, "A Clean and Separate Space: Walt Disney in Person and Production," *The Journal of Popular Culture*, 25 (Winter 1991), 95.

are national touchstones, secular shrines to the American Dream. As Benedict Anderson noted in his writings on "political museumizing," there is a sense of prestige on the part of builders, in the mere construction of something. Keeping monuments viable and accessible passes that prestige on to successive generations and those who might come to see what was built. Doing this kind of construction is important for creating national identity.[129] Walt hoped his parks, via Dis-History, would play that role for the United States.

What Walt accomplished was visionary. As artist and longtime Imagineer John Hench put it, "He introduced people to a new way of experiencing a planned environment." A place "designed so that every element contributes to telling a story."[130] The doubts within the amusement park industry were real, but they did not take into account that Disneyland was different.[131] Disney parks are an "imagined community," to borrow again from Anderson. People who visit the parks will never know everyone who is there, and yet are in "communion" with them at the same time. We have seen this in Spaceship Earth already. Media, such as the newspapers and book publishing, help create community and nations, as did the Reformation, which owed much to the revolution in media (in particular printing).[132] Though Disney was about realism—Walt strove for it, and pushed those who worked for him to do the same—the parks create a sort of hyper reality, where over time, it becomes increasingly difficult to tell what is and what is not real, and where the present and past (purged of the bad things in life) merge into very real experiences for those who are there.[133] This common culture for Americans is the founding principle behind Dis-History.

Of course, there are critics both of the construction and the culture that Walt attempted in the parks. According to some, Dis-History in the

---

129 Benedict Anderson, *Imagined Communities: Reflections on the Origin and Spread of Nationalism* (New York: Verso Press, 1998), 181–183.

130 Hench with Van Pelt, *Designing Disney*, 1.

131 Hench, John (1). December 1974 Interview, Lectures and Transcripts, Walt Disney Studio Archives, Burbank, California.

132 Anderson, *Imagined Communities*, 6, 33-34, 39.

133 Gabler, *Walt Disney*, 176–177, 187; Wasko, *Understanding Disney*, 177; Robin Allan, *Walt Disney and Europe: European Influences on the Animated Feature Films of Walt Disney* (Indianapolis: Indiana University Press, 1999), 228; Jackson and West, editors, *Disneyland and Culture*, 2, 11–12; Eric Smoodin, editor, *Disney Discourse: Producing the Magic Kingdom* (New York: Routledge, 1994), 186–188; Michael Steiner, "Frontierland as Tommorowland: Walt Disney and the Architectural Packaging of the Mythic West," *Montana: The Magazine of Western History*, 48(Spring 1998), 7.

parks is little more than the "dominant groups of American society" crafting a place where their "real conditions" meshed with the "real history" of the nation, which was not, out of hand, what was really happening outside the boundaries of the park itself. Thus, Dis-History is little more than "the reactionary nature of Disney's WASP orientation." As for the parks, critics allege that a guest there is little more than "a rat in a maze," with Disney's theming turning them into "mindless robots" blindly following a map from attraction to attraction, having surrendered their agency to the House of Mouse the moment they entered through the gates.[134] Places of temporary escape at best, the parks conceal an "aura of dread" beneath all of their fun.[135] Others claim, such as Michael Barrier, that the parks' influence and importance are exaggerated. The "economic and demographic trends" they represent and Disney helped give shape, he argues, were going to happen with or without the creation of Disneyland and the subsequent other parks.[136]

However, such claims, even if they have some merit, miss the point. The technological revolution that Disney unleashed on amusement and theme parks cannot be discounted. Nor can the popularity of what Disney has done. By 1989, according to one study, it was estimated that 70 percent of all Americans had visited a Disney park.[137] Furthermore, Disney's reliance on the past should not be underestimated. Walt saw Disneyland as a place of "happiness and knowledge."[138] He wanted the park to "be the essence of America as we know it, the nostalgia of the past with exciting glimpses of the future. It will give meaning to the pleasure of children—and pleasure to the experience of adults. ... It will be a place for the people to find happiness and knowledge."[139] Dis-History and the park experience "will be based upon and dedicated to the ideals, the dreams, and hard facts that have created America."[140] *Popular Science* described Disneyland as Walt created it as "a miniature historic America."[141] As Stephen Mills put it, the park was designed

---

134   Wasko, *Understanding Disney*, 166–169; "Luis Marin: Disneyland as Degenerate Utopia," lmc.gatech.edu/~broglio/1101/marin.html, 23 September 2014; Paul Wells, *Animation and America* (Manchester: Edinburgh University Press, 2002), 103.
135   James Howard Kunstler, *The Geography of Nowhere: The Rise and Decline of America's Man-Made Landscape* (New York: Touchstone Book, 1993), 217.
136   Barrier, *The Animated Man*, ix–x.
137   Schickel, *The Disney Version*, 6; Wasko, *Understanding Disney*, 162.
138   Barrier, *The Animated Man*, 243.
139   Finch, *Walt Disney's America*, 61.
140   Thomas, *Walt Disney*, 246.
141   Barrier, *The Animated Man*, 232.

to "help people re-create their trust in the past as a series of glorious adventures safely behind them, to be bettered only by the prospects offered by technology in an approaching future."[142]

It is important to note that Disney, in infusing the parks with Dis-History, is not misusing history per se. It is not (though we will discuss ways and times in which it is) usually in the business of acting as an historian. The word "business" is key in this analysis, because ultimately, Disney is a company in search of turning a profit. None of the parks, even when directly invoking history, is attempting to be a living history center like Colonial Williamsburg. Nor are the parks (primarily) an educational enterprise like the History Channel. In both of those places, guests or viewers expect historical accuracy. Disney is a business that sees history as a resource to be used because Disney's entire business model is built around telling stories.

That is not to say that Disney is unmindful of history. One of the reasons the company uses history is because it is full of stories. The company does not look for what people do not know, because they are not generally seeking to educate. They seek out that which is familiar. Walt, after all, sought to affirm what people knew and knew to be true in a popular, historical sense. History is a source that can be repeatedly drawn from. Disney on some level cherishes and revers history because it needs it to tell the stories it wants to tell. At the same time, Disney also constructs history and is even constrained by it. To reinvent or to change a ride or extend a story can be problematic—let alone contending with historical accuracy. Both of these examples, these dalliances with history, can spark backlashes by fans and experts alike.

The fact of the matter is that, like most things, understanding Disney is a complex undertaking.[143] The central tension of Dis-History, one that the parks illustrate clearly, is what happens when the actual past come in touch with and at times in conflict with the manufactured past that is existing as the present. What does that mean for a company that works with nostalgia and creates experiences (a past to draw on) for their guests? These are some of the questions one encounters when you begin exploring Dis-History. However, where to do so? Disneyland is important from an historic sense, but Walt Disney

---

142 Stephen F. Mills, "Disney and the Promotions of Synthetic Worlds," *American Studies International*, 28(October 1990), 72.

143 Douglas Brode, *Multiculturalism and the Mouse: Race and Sex in Disney Entertainment* (Austin: University of Texas Press, 2005), 140. Brode goes even further, arguing that Walt's movies during the 1950s set the stage for the counte-culture of the 1960s. See, Douglas Brode, *From Walt to Woodstock: How Disney Created the Counterculture* (Austin: University of Texas Press, 2004).

World is central to understanding Dis-History. Most studies tend to focus on Disneyland, but Walt Disney World tells so much more about the culture-building concept behind the parks.[144]

The company's second park is larger than Disneyland (even after the inclusion of the California Adventure second gate)—Walt Disney World is actually four parks. The Magic Kingdom, Epcot, Hollywood Studios, and Animal Kingdom, along with a wide variety of themed hotels, campgrounds, water parks, and entertainment venues (such as Disney Springs, the former Downtown Disney, which is full of shops and restaurants that are not all directly themed by Disney). All these things are venues that travelers know and expect when they vacation.[145] While each park is different, and each was crafted at a different time from the others (and have been remade countless times in big and small ways), it is in Florida that we can best grasp from the outside not just the multiple uses of history that Disney employs (and how they have evolved and been revised), but also the corporate synergy that binds these parks (and the company that they represent) together. This is perhaps especially true since "Project X" was not completed until after Walt's death. Dis-History, thus, helped bind it all together as a source of continuity for both the public and the company. Now it is time to enter the Magic Kingdom, and while you can get there many ways, the only entrance to the park itself is along Main Street.

---

144 Kuenz, Klugman, Waldrep, and Willis, editors, *Inside the Mouse*, 89.
145 Tom Gaughan, "Manifest Destiny at Disney World," *American Libraries* 26(January 1995), 82.

CHAPTER THREE

Main Street, U.S.A.

Experience Walking Down Main Street

Beyond the parking lots, the lagoon, the ticket counters and the bag check lines awaits the entry to the Magic Kingdom: Main Street, U.S.A. Guests, though they do not actually enter the park by train, still pass through a train station. Perhaps it is a bit grand, the historian among them, might think, for a small town of "Main Street, U.S.A.'s" size, but perhaps like many small towns that "got" the railroad in the late nineteenth century, it was optimistic about future. Surely, after you exit the station area into the "town" itself, you get a sense of grandeur—not just because it is a theme park—but because of the buildings that stand before you. Even if this is simply a one street town, it seems to be prospering. There are, of course, all sorts of shops and restaurants (this being a Disney park, there are not just places to shop, but also plenty of themed eating options as well). Perhaps most notable is the Crystal Palace, on the fringe of Main Street, which invokes a park-like setting causing guests to think of themselves as high society or perhaps even at the Great White City of the Chicago World's Fair (or maybe the historic Crystal Palace in London, since you are within sight of a castle) which mixed high and popular culture in its exhibits.[1] Though you know you are in a park, the façades of most of the buildings still call to mind a real town. On one side of the street, there is City Hall. On the other, the Town Square Theater. There is a fire station and a barbershop as well. The street itself runs straight and true, with only one real side street (which is more a cul-de-sac). Everything about this entryway invokes a "small town home."[2]

---

[1] "The Crystal Palace," http://www.archdaily.com/397949/ad-classic-the-crystal-palace-joseph-paxton/, 13 October 2015; Lawrence W. Levine, *Highbrow/Lowbrow: The Emergence of Cultural Hierarchy in America* (Cambridge: Harvard University Press, 1990), 208.

[2] Michael R. Real, *Mass-Mediated Culture* (Englewood Cliffs, New Jersey: Prentice-Hall, 1977), 53.

A visit to Main Street can be inspiring.[3] As my then nine-year-old daughter put it, once you step foot on Main Street, U.S.A., all you can think is "wow, this is going to be a fun day!"[4] There is a sense of energy along Main Street, the idea of which is that it is a place full of excitement.[5] That makes it perfect as the gateway to the park and something that must be experienced more than once to truly appreciate what Disney accomplished with its construction.[6] To understand both Disney and Dis-History, one must understand its importance.[7]

Main Street is the "axis" around which the park's narrative was built.[8] It is, on its surface, the epitome of the Victorian small town of the American Midwest that Walt Disney grew up in.[9] First constructed for Disneyland, it has set the tone for every park entrance that followed.[10] Cities reveal a good deal about people and the nation they live in. They are "theaters of memory." Walt's films rarely had much good to say about city living, and in Dis-Historic terms, Main Street became the way things ought to have been, mixing quite clearly "fantasy and reality."[11]

---

3   Richard Snow, "Disney: Coast to Coast, "http://www.americanheritage.com/content/disney-coast-coast, 2 June 2014; *The Imagineering Field Guide to the Magic Kingdom at Walt Disney World: An Imagineer's Eye Tour* (New York: Disney Editions, 2005), 21.

4   Kate Lantzer, as told to the author, during our July 2014 trip.

5   *The Imagineering Field Guide to the Magic Kingdom at Walt Disney World: An Imagineer's Eye Tour* (New York: Disney Editions, 2005), 29.

6   Stephen F. Fjellman, *Vinyl Leaves: Walt Disney World and America* (Boulder: Westview Press, 1992), 169-171, 203.

7   Kathy Merlock Jackson and Mark I. West, editors, *Disneyland and Culture: Essays on the Parks and Their Influence* (Jefferson, NC: McFarland and Company, 2011), 38; Karal Ann Marling, "Disneyland, 1955: Just Take the Santa Ana Freeway to the American Dream," *American Art*, 5(Winter-Spring, 1991), 201.

8   "Luis Marin: Disneyland as Degenerate Utopia," http://lmc.gatech.edu/~broglio/1101/marin.html, 23 September 2014; Karal Ann Marling, editor, *Designing Disney's Theme Parks: The Architecture of Reassurance* (New York: Flammarion, 1997), 86.

9   Alexander Moore, "Walt Disney World: Bounded Ritual Space and the Playful Pilgrimage Center," *Anthropological Quarterly*, 53(October 1980), 211–212; Christopher Finch, *Walt Disney's America* (New York: Abbeville Press, 1978), 133.

10 John Hench with Peggy Van Pelt, *Designing Disney: Imagineering and the Art of the Show* (New York: Disney Editions, 2008), 63; Kathy Merlock Jackson and Mark I. West, editors, *Disneyland and Culture: Essays on the Parks and Their Influence* (Jefferson, NC: McFarland and Company, 2011), 13.

11 Eric Avila, *Popular Culture in the Age of White Flight: Fear and Fantasy in*

Of course, this type of experience should be expected at Walt Disney World. It is a place where past, present, and future all meet and coexist alongside fantasy and myth. Visitors do not just see but "enter into time and experience past and experience future" there.[12] The company goes to great lengths to create that atmosphere. Music and even smells are pumped out into the street, to play on historic nostalgia (both what might be called academic as well as personal). All of this is designed to help pull guests into the Magic Kingdom and help them accept the Disney way. It is a glimpse, a vision, of what might have been a guest's own hometown made manifest before them at the very start of their visit to the park.[13]

By far the biggest Dis-Historic element in Main Street, however, is the use of architecture. Like the rest of the park, and regardless of which one a guest might prefer, each Main Street is themed perfectly. Starting with Walt (who was personally invested in the idea of Main Street), and continuing to the present, Disney has become expert (perhaps *the* experts) at understanding how to design, create, and re-create "place in its most historic sense."[14] Disneyland's Main Street, for example, has more Gothic elements to it, is easily bigger, and has the feel of an actually re-created town. In the case of the Magic Kingdom, its Main Street is grander and more "Eastern Seashore Resort Victorian" in its appearance, and more "demanding" of its visitors with storefronts that harken back to what towns offered railroad travelers.[15] Walt wanted historically accurate façades for storefronts of the types of businesses that could have been, would have been on

---

Suburban Los Angeles (Los Angeles: University of California Press, 2004), 135; Dolores Hayden, *The Power of Place: Urban Landscapes as Public History* (Cambridge: The MIT Press, 1995), 11; Paul Jerome Croce, "A Clean and Separate Space: Walt Disney in Person and Production," *The Journal of Popular Culture*, 25 (Winter 1991), 92; Real, *Mass-Mediated Culture*, 55; Paul Goldberger, *Why Architecture Matters* (New Haven: Yale University Press, 2009), ix–x.

12   Richard Schickel, *The Disney Version: The Life, Times, Art and Commerce of Walt Disney, Third Edition* (Chicago: Ivan R. Dee Publisher, 1997), 325.

13   Charles Carson, "Whole New Worlds: Music in the Disney Theme Park Experience, "*Ethnomusicology Forum*, 13(November 2004), 229–230.

14   Richard Francaviglia, "History after Disney: The Significance of 'Imagineered' Historical Places," *The Public Historian*, 17(Autumn 1995), 73.

15   Judith A. Adams, *The American Amusement Park Industry: A History of Technology and Thrills* (Boston: Twayne Publishers, 1991), 144–145; Leonard E. Zehnder, *Florida's Disney World: Promises and Problems* (Tallahassee: The Peninsular Publishing Company, 1975), 138; Andrew Kiste, *A Historical Tour of Walt Disney World* (Theme Park Press, 2015).

Main Street.[16] Because this was to be "everyone's hometown" according to Walt,[17] it needed to look like a town in the space available to it in the park. Therefore, all the Main Streets utilize forced perspective (a trick Walt's Imagineers had learned in doing movies) to make the buildings appear taller than they actually are.[18]

Because Main Street was to be the park's sole entry point, the street and its buildings are a constant reference for guests. As Imagineer Dick Irvine noted, Walt believed that "people who were reminiscing about their childhood would imagine a town square, Main Street as smaller than it actually was. [By using scale line] it would have a sort of storybook feeling to it."[19] However, it was a storybook steeped in cultural nostalgia. As Imagineer John Hench said, "You don't have to have been part of that period to recognize it or respond to it." What Walt was going after was "the spirit that built all those main streets."[20] By using forced perspective, Disney effectively "eliminated the contradictions" that the wide variety of main streets across America had produced.[21] Disney's version became the standard version.

Architecture's importance is even larger than just providing a theme for what is essentially a mall on either side of Main Street. The construction of the parks, with their façades, was part of a long tradition of American "imitative arts," which includes, from an architectural standpoint, borrowing from actual buildings.[22] Architecture invokes not just themes, but associations, and so is intrinsic to the

---

16 Marling, editor, *Designing Disney's Theme Parks*, 90; Marling, "Disneyland, 1955," 195; Warren Leon and Roy Rosenzweig, editors, *History Museums in the United States: A Critical Assessment* (Chicago: University of Illinois Press, 1989), 159; Richard Snow, "Disney: Coast to Coast," http://www.americanheritage.com/content/disney-coast-coast, 2 June 2014; M. Jeffrey Hardwick, *Mall Maker: Victor Gruen, Architect of an American Dream* (Philadelphia: The University of Pennsylvania Press, 2004), 29, 34, 40–41.

17 Dave Smith, *The Quotable Walt Disney* (New York: Disney Editions, 2001), 65.

18 Jason Surrell, *The Haunted Mansion: Imagineering a Disney Classic* (New York: Disney Editions, 2015), 11.

19 Irvine, Dick. "Disney Biography: Bob Thomas' Interview with Dick Irvine 1968", Lectures and Transcripts, Walt Disney Studio Archives, Burbank, California.

20 Hench, John (1). Cal-Arts Interview 1973, Lectures and Transcripts, Walt Disney Studio Archives, Burbank, California.

21 Hench, John and Dick Irvine. "Walt Disney Biography 1968" Lectures and Transcripts, Walt Disney Studio Archives, Burbank, California.

22 Marling, editor, *Designing Disney's Theme Parks*, 185.

idea of nostalgia that is at the heart of Dis-History.[23] The idea with the park architecture was to "build the very structure of myth, with themes from the depths of the American consciousness," according to Vincent Scully.[24] Myth can be a close relation of nostalgia—as both work upon our assumptions about how things were and are, and the further removed we are from the place where the mythic memory happened, the more we romanticize it. Disney's parks, starting with the Main Street entrances, give us a physical rendering of our myths and nostalgia, strengthening our sense of self. As Yi-Fu Tuan put it, "The past needs to be rescued and made accessible."[25] The parks do just that for guests who are willing to take the journey.[26]

Much of Main Street's allure is its obvious nostalgia. People like Main Street, even though it invokes a time period that most guests, even in the 1950s, had never lived through or had memories of.[27] As Gary Cross notes, "As progress advanced in the nineteenth century, so did nostalgia for lost communities."[28] Main Street is a reminder of what was left behind in the second half of twentieth-century America.[29] Not everyone grew up in a small town, but everyone who visits Disneyland or Walt Disney World collectively visits Walt's Main Street, and what they see influences how they remember not just their trip but also the history that Main Street represents. Here, Disney is democratizing the past, and giving guests a "universally" true first experience with it.[30] The streets offer a sense of "home"—which need not be a physical

---

23 Beth Dunlop, *Building a Dream: The Art of Disney Architecture* (New York: Harry N. Abrams, 1996), 53; Bob Thomas, *Walt Disney: An American Original* (New York: Disney Editions, 1994), 218–219; Neal Gabler, *Walt Disney: The Triumph of the American Imagination* (New York: Vintage Books, 2007), 498; Judith A. Adams, *The American Amusement Park Industry: A History of Technology and Thrills* (Boston: Twayne Publishers, 1991), 98, 144; Gary Cross, *Consumed Nostalgia: Memory in the Age of Fast Capitalism* (New York: Columbia University Press, 2015), 208–209.

24 Dunlop, *Building a Dream*, 8.

25 Yi-Fu Tuan, *Space and Place: The Perspective of Experience* (Minneapolis: University of Minnesota Press, 1977), 85, 122, 187, 194–197.

26 Nick Lantzer, as told to the author, during our July 2014 trip; Alexis de Tocqueville, *Democracy in America* (New York: Mentor, 1984), 172

27 Thomas Hine, *Populuxe* (New York: Alfred A. Knopf, 1986), 152.

28 Gary Cross, *Consumed Nostalgia: Memory in the Age of Fast Capitalism* (New York: Columbia University Press, 2015), 8–9.

29 Dunlop, *Building a Dream*, 117.

30 Richard Francaviglia, "History after Disney: The Significance of 'Imagineered' Historical Places," *The Public Historian*, 17(Autumn 1995), 71.

place we have lived, but one that allows us to be grounded and connect with the wider world.[31] Unlike where they grew up or where they live now, this Main Street is never going to change. Not only is it locked in time, but also it will never be redeveloped. As such, it gives off a sense of permanence that is lacking in modern life.[32]

None of this is to say that Main Street is not without its contradictions or problems. When Disneyland opened in 1955, for example, the newness of the asphalt and the July heat (perhaps anecdotally) caused the high heels of women's shoes to stick to its streets.[33] But, as was mentioned in the previous chapter, Disneyland was made possible, in part, because of the automobile and the mobility it provided—and yet Walt largely excluded it from the park and came to detest certain aspects of the automobile culture emerging in the 1950s. As such, he designed Main Street as a pedestrian zone, even though it was constructed at a time when the love of automobiles was perhaps at its peak in the United States. Additionally, Main Street is a nostalgic homage to small-town America, built at a time when the small towns that inspired it were vanishing if not already gone.[34] It is also full of "nostalgia for a supposedly uncomplicated, decent, hard-working, crime-free, rise-up-and-salute-the-flag way of life that is the stuff of Middle America's dreams." However, it is also a clashing example of what declining American urban centers in the 1950s and 1960s no longer were.[35] Walt saw Main Street as rejecting what urban areas had become. He disliked the notion that in order to live in the modern city, one had to sacrifice the values learned in less urban locations.[36] He knew these beliefs, this ideology, had obvious marketing potential to guests. As Karal Marling recounts a Disney park official describing Main Street: "Here is a period in America ... when progress was a good word and ... there was an intense optimism about what we were doing with our lives."[37]

At the same time, Main Street, U.S.A. must be understood, in part, as something that Hollywood was doing. It was a movie motif for

---

31   Janelle L. Wilson, *Nostalgia: Sanctuary of Meaning* (Lewisburg: Bucknell University Press, 2005), 33.

32   Jackson and West, editors, *Disneyland and Culture*, 217.

33   Marling, "Disneyland, 1955,"168.

34   Dunlop, *Building a Dream*, 35, 121.

35   Stephen F. Mills, "Disney and the Promotions of Synthetic Worlds," *American Studies International*, 28(October 1990), 73; Marling, "Disneyland, 1955," 193; Jackson and West, editors, *Disneyland and Culture*, 41.

36   Eric Avila, *Popular Culture in the Age of White Flight: Fear and Fantasy in Suburban Los Angeles* (Los Angeles: University of California Press, 2004), 113, 119.

37   Marling, "Disneyland, 1955," 197.

small-town America.[38] As much as Disney was a product of Hollywood, Walt's "Main Street" was influenced by his own past.[39] In 1938, Walt wrote a letter to the *Marceline News* about growing up in the town: "To tell the truth more things of importance happened to me in Marceline than have happened since—or are likely to in the future."[40]

Walt, according to critics, was always a "provincial Midwesterner"—patriotic, awed by technology, and largely unassuming toward the rest of the world.[41] He is, in their view, a work of historic construction, but not out-of-hand fabrication. Walt was more than a name. He was a symbol. He was the company in the minds of the public. Walt understood that he had created a mythos around himself and his company. As he put it, "Disney is something we've built up in the public mind over the years. It stands for something and you don't have to explain what it is to the public. They know what Disney is when they hear about our films or go to Disneyland. They know they're going to get a certain quality, a certain kind of entertainment."[42] Nowhere is this seen more clearly than in the case of C.V. Wood, Disneyland's first general manager, who was fired by and later involved in a legal battles with Walt and the company. Wood's name has been scrubbed from the company's official history involving the construction of the park, as Wood's conduct did not fit the Walt model.[43]

With Main Street, Walt was quite literally re-creating his past and in some ways improving his own childhood memories.[44] Marceline, a community created by the Atchison, Topeka, and the Santa Fe railroad as a "division point" so that passengers heading west could reach more than one destination, inspired Main Street. It was very much a

---

38 Avila, *Popular Culture in the Age of White Flight*, 104–105.

39 Jackson and West, editors, *Disneyland and Culture*, 45; Neal Gabler, *Walt Disney: The Triumph of the American Imagination* (New York: Vintage Books, 2007), 76.

40 "The Marceline I Knew by Walt Disney," http://www.waltdisneymuseum.org/the-marceline-i-knew-by-walt-disney/, 2 October 2015.

41 James Howard Kunstler, *The Geography of Nowhere: The Rise and Decline of America's Man-Made Landscape* (New York: Touchstone Book, 1993), 219.

42 Jeff Kurtti, *Walt Disney's Imagineering Legends and the Genesis of the Disney Theme Park* (New York: Disney Editions, 2008), xiii.

43 Todd James Pierce, *Three Years in Wonderland: The Disney Brothers, C.V. Wood, and the Making of the Great American Theme Park* (Jackson: University of Mississippi Press, 2016), 4–5, 247–251.

44 Cher Krause Knight, *Power and Paradise in Walt Disney's World* (Gainesville: University Press of Florida, 2014), 40, 62.

created community.[45] However, Walt did not remember the Marceline that was emerging when the family moved to Kansas City. The Main Street he knew in reality, rather than his "historical imagination," had "raw and rutted" dirt streets, with no trees but rather telegraph/telephone poles lining the way, and a simple train depot. It was not the town that had paved its streets, where there were twenty cars driving around, where there was "a new school, a new power plant and a new waterworks," and a new theater was on its way.[46] While small towns like Marceline were on the decline even as Walt was growing up there,[47] it (and for that matter, Fort Collins, Colorado, where Disney Imagineer Harper Goff was from) "looked" like a small town should.[48]

For the Imagineers, Main Street, U.S.A. was viewed as a means to not just funnel people into the park, but as a way to introduce them to the Disney experience. As such, it has been replicated in subsequent parks the world over. Disneyland Paris, like its American namesake, has a Main Street, U.S.A. That is where the overt similarities end, at least when it comes to the uses of American history. For American visitors, one of the chief differences between this Main Street, transplanted to France, and the ones they might have walked back home, comes in the veneration of the Statue of Liberty. Though they considered a Jazz Age rendition of the thoroughfare (which would have been a rather radical break with the past), Imagineers opted for the more traditional turn-of-the-century model because it was so different from the surrounding area (especially when considering the proximity of the park to Paris).[49] However, the concept does not work everywhere. Tokyo Disney has no Main Street, U.S.A. It has a "world bazaar" instead (though its Disney

---

45 Marling, "Disneyland, 1955," 193; Michael Barrier, *The Animated Man: A Life of Walt Disney* (Los Angeles: University of California Press, 2007), 9; Robin Allan, *Walt Disney and Europe: European Influences on the Animated Feature Films of Walt Disney* (Indianapolis: Indiana University Press, 1999), 3.

46 Richard Snow, "Disney: Coast to Coast, "http://www.americanheritage.com/content/disney-coast-coast, 2 June 2014; Neal Gabler, *Walt Disney: The Triumph of the American Imagination* (New York: Vintage Books, 2007), 10, 18; Marty Sklar, *Dream It! Do It!: My Half-Century Creating Disney's Magic Kingdoms* (New York: Disney Editions, 2013), 68; Dave Smith and Steven Clark, *Disney: The First 100 Years* (New York: Hyperion, 1999), 5.

47 Steven Watts, *The Magic Kingdom: Walt Disney and the America Way of Life* (New York: Houghton Mifflin Company, 1997), 6.

48 Gabler, *Walt Disney*, 12; Main Street, U.S.A. General (DL). Walt Disney Studio Archives, Burbank, California.

49 Andrew Lainsbury, *Once Upon an American Dream: The Story of Euro Disneyland* (Lawrence: University of Kansas Press, 2000), 53–56.

Sea area does have an "American Waterfront," covered to contend with weather, with some American touches, but it is mainly a shopping mall). Disneyland Hong Kong has a Main Street, U.S.A., but it is much smaller in scale than any of the others.[50] Shanghai Disney opted to introduce guests to Mickey and his friends rather than to American small-town nostalgia that had no basis in China.

Disney readily admits that what they are doing is essentially a "falsification" of the past, done both for "entertainment" purposes as well as to get at "deeper truths."[51] Such a statement implies that there might be things missing. As real as it all looks, we must remember that the entire park is artificial.[52] As such, what is and what is not there was done for real reasons. Walt sought to "improve" on the past. Or perhaps it is just a case of "selective amnesia."[53] By using the past, Walt was inviting people to escape the world they lived in. Not just with its 1950s Cold War fears (or later international or domestic concerns), but suburbia itself. He envisioned the park as a place where people were having fun, were happy, and were together with friends and family. To Walt, those were the things that made for real experiences, were indeed the stuff of reality, or at least the things that really mattered. While visitors bring their own realities with them, they walk on streets crafted by Walt. Walking through the park is like following in his footsteps.[54]

The Parks' Reality

Any notion that you are in a re-created downtown, however, is quickly dashed by several inescapable facts. First, despite the signage and the building façades, the moment you step inside you are no longer under the illusion of being in the late nineteenth century. You are, instead, very much in a twenty-first century shopping center. Except this one is full of only Disney merchandise, from clothing to food, to toys to jewelry, and of course, collectibles. Main Street has been called "an

---

50   Eric Smoodin, editor, *Disney Discourse: Producing the Magic Kingdom* (New York: Routledge, 1994), 192–193.

51   Warren Leon and Roy Rosenzweig, editors, *History Museums in the United States: A Critical Assessment* (Chicago: University of Illinois Press, 1989), 162.

52   Allan, *Walt Disney and Europe*, 230.

53   Leon and Rosenzweig, editors, *History Museums in the United States*, 161–162.

54   Marling, "Disneyland, 1955," 196; Michael Steiner, "Frontierland as Tommorowland: Walt Disney and the Architectural Packaging of the Mythic West," *Montana: The Magazine of Western History*, 48(Spring 1998), 12; Christopher Finch, *Walt Disney's America* (New York: Abbeville Press, 1978), 49; Gabler, *Walt Disney*, 499.

antique shop in reverse: the buildings are old-fashioned, the products modern."[55] It is a fully functional shopping mall, where guests are so taken in by the theming that buying things is both secondary and often happens with little thought to the eventual bill. This is the genius of Disney parks from a business standpoint.[56]

The second debunking event as you stroll down Main Street is that your eyes and your feet are drawn toward Cinderella Castle. Not only is it the actual focal point of the park, but it is also completely out of place for a re-created nineteenth-century American cityscape.[57] That contrast is stark and in turn makes Main Street, if you turn your gaze away from the castle, even more appealing. It is so very American. Not just in that nostalgic throwback to yesterday, but also as a democratic center for public life. A place for shopping, yes, but a place where people come together and that everyone can occupy and feel welcome. It is the true (if not geographic) center of the park, and unlike most modern cities, Main Street is designed with a sense of direction and purpose. Here everyone is equal.[58]

Other things make this street not only different from the past but also from our present. Main Street is devoid of cars, as are the parks themselves (save for amusements and rides). Guests tend to get around on foot. Though the streets have no vehicles on them, most guests (unless crossing or taking a picture) tend to still use the sidewalks along Main Street, rather than walk in the street itself. "By forcing his guests to walk along Main Street, by banishing the automobile from the domain, Walt was suggesting that something was amiss in the car-mad culture outside the park."[59] That people walk the park with little complaint shows that Walt may have been on to something.

For all that you see in and along Main Street as you walk, it does not take very long before guests begin to notice that a few things, a

---

55   Michael R. Real, *Mass-Mediated Culture* (Englewood Cliffs, New Jersey: Prentice-Hall, 1977), 54.

56   Jackson and West, editors, *Disneyland and Culture*, 150–154; Sharon Zukin, *Point of Purchase: How Shopping Changed American Culture* (New York: Routledge, 2005), 221.

57   Sharon Zukin, *Landscapes of Power: From Detroit to Disney World* (Los Angeles: University of California Press, 1993), 217–218.

58   Zukin, *Landscapes of Power*, 51, 241; Yi-Fu Tuan, *Space and Place: The Perspective of Experience* (Minneapolis: University of Minnesota Press, 1977), 42, 178.

59   Karal Ann Marling, editor, *Designing Disney's Theme Parks: The Architecture of Reassurance* (New York: Flammarion, 1997), 87; Marling, "Disneyland, 1955," 187; Jane Jacobs, *The Death and Life of Great American Cities* (New York: Vintage Books, 1992), 347.

few institutions, are missing from Main Street that were just as much a part of cityscapes as the city hall or barbershop once were. Any student of history, strolling down Walt's street, will quickly notice the absence of the saloon, for example. From a historian's perspective, this is quite odd, as saloons were a mainstay of American main streets (and side streets) during the late nineteenth and early twentieth centuries. Saloons served as small businesses (often linked to large breweries) and community centers (often for immigrant groups) and they could be found in rural and urban areas.[60] However, their absence serves to remind us that Dis-History is not about re-creating the past as it was, but rather as it might have been.

Indeed, the very nature of drinking alcohol in America during the period Main Street depicts prompted one of the largest reform movements in the nation's history. Temperance had begun as a reform during the Second Great Awakening in the early 1800s. It had picked up again in the 1870s, first as the Women's Crusade and then branching into powerful national organizations like the Woman's Christian Temperance Union, the Prohibition Party, and the Anti-Saloon League. By the time Mickey Mouse appeared, these groups had helped make America dry and were fighting to keep national Prohibition and their beloved Eighteenth Amendment intact and a part of the Constitution.[61]

Therefore, the great "cancerous tumor on the body politic," as reformers termed it, is missing, as are the reformers who made it so. Perhaps we can say that this Main Street town has gone dry, although not by reformers. Walt forbade, and the company for years after his death followed his edict, alcohol sales in the park (save for select occasions for special guests), though it was not because he was a "total abstainer." The ban on alcohol had more to do with a business decision to try to cut down on disorderly conduct and promote an image of family-centered fun, in line with the utopian nature of the Disney parks.[62]

In the minds of late nineteenth- and early twentieth-century reformers, on the other hand, the saloon was a one-stop shopping mart for sin

---

60 Perry R. Duis, *The Saloon: Public Drinking in Chicago and Boston, 1880–1920* (Chicago: University of Illinois Press, 1999).

61 Norman H. Clark, *Deliver Us from Evil: An Interpretation of American Prohibition* (New York: W.W. Norton and Company, 1976); K. Austin Kerr, *Organized for Prohibition: A New History of the Anti-Saloon League* (New Haven: Yale University Press, 1985); Catherin Gilbert Murdock, *Domesticating Drink: Women, Men, and Alcohol in America, 1870–1940* (Baltimore: The Johns Hopkins University Press, 1998).

62 Bob Thomas, *Walt Disney: An American Original* (New York: Disney Editions, 1994), 159; Mark Gottdiener, *The Theming of America: Dreams, Visions, and Commercial Spaces* (New York: Westview Press, 1997), 138.

and crime. However, since there are no saloons along Main Street, it seems to show that at Disney parks, there is no crime—in theory, it does not exist.[63] Perhaps we could have noticed that without thinking of the saloon. After all, while there is at least a building that says "fire department" as part of the town square, Main Street has no similar building for its town police department. In Disney's reimagined Main Street, there simply is no need for such a force. Before you reach Main Street, a largely unseen security force is protecting you without the need to make its presence known. The collective sense is that Disney's guests are law-abiding and orderly, without need of a reminder.

However, if a guest were thinking that crime had vanished thanks to divine intervention, they would soon notice that there is also no house of worship on Main Street either. Perhaps even more noticeably absent from Disney's Main Street than the missing saloons are the lack of churches. There are no church steeples as part of the Main Street skyline. Guests looking for religion have to visit the Norway pavilion in Epcot. Here they can find a stave church. One might argue that this is proof that to Disney, religion is somehow "foreign" as a concept, and not part of the American way of life.[64] Doing so, however, would miss the very complex relationship Disney has with religion, and what it means for Dis-History.

Unlike the saloon, which we can understand for the business reasons sketched out above, the absence of a church is more interesting because one was originally going to be included as part of Main Street as well as another as part of the proposed Haunted Mansion (which included a graveyard). Main Street's church even had a name, "the Little Church around the Corner," because it was set to occupy a small side street off Main Street. Neither proposed edifice was ever built.[65]

The lack of faith institutions (at a time when the promotion of civil religion was high in the United States) is even more problematic when we consider Walt's own history with organized religion. The Disneys were a "deeply religious" family when Walt was a child in Chicago. Their life "orbited" St. Paul Congregational Church, where Elias served as a deacon and Flora served as the congregation's treasurer. Walt even was named for the minister and baptized there. There was little doubt

---

63 William F. Van Wert, "Disney World and Posthistory," *Cultural Critique*, 32(Winter, 1995–1996), 192–193.

64 Clifford Geertz, *The Interpretation of Cultures* (New York: Basic Books, 2000), 126–127.

65 Jackson and West, editors, *Disneyland and Culture*, 47; Karal Ann Marling, editor, *Designing Disney's Theme Parks: The Architecture of Reassurance* (New York: Flammarion, 1997), 59.

that Elias was devout in matters of faith. He had a "stern Protestant morality," having grown up in a strict Wesleyan Methodist home. Yet, when the family moved to Marceline, they rarely attended church, though Elias continued to demand moral rectitude from his children.[66]

The easy answer is that Walt Disney rejected his religious roots, a rebellion against both his father and God, and left no place for either in his parks. Some might argue that Disney had embraced a secular/scientific view of the world, indeed that Walt was a "secular humanist" who "decided on the separation of Church and State in his magic kingdom." Some might allege that this is because Disney has long been associated with the dark arts, of witches, warlocks, and wiccans.[67] For further proof, one could note there is rarely a mention of God in any of the films Walt oversaw, or even of religion, save for the secular variety.[68] Indeed, some commentators have speculated that Disney was replacing established religion with one of his own. Anthropologist Alexander Moore argued that at Walt Disney World, Disney had created a "bounded ritual space" akin to pilgrimage centers, with its own rituals and even (to a degree) its own liturgical calendar and that Disney is a religion unto itself.[69]

Obviously, as a corporation, Disney cannot be in the business of encouraging people to go places, like to church, where they might spend their time and money as opposed to going to its parks.[70] Yet,

---

66 Gabler, *Walt Disney*, 8; Richard Schickel, *The Disney Version: The Life, Times, Art and Commerce of Walt Disney, Third Edition* (Chicago: Ivan R. Dee Publisher, 1997), 46-47; Michael Barrier, *The Animated Man: A Life of Walt Disney* (Los Angeles: University of California Press, 2007), 13; Mark I. Pinsky, *The Gospel According to Disney: Faith, Trust, and Pixie Dust* (Louisville: Westminster John Knox Press, 2004), 15-16; Steven Watts, *The Magic Kingdom: Walt Disney and the America Way of Life* (New York: Houghton Mifflin Company, 1997), 17; Bob Thomas, *Building a Company: Roy O. Disney and the Creation of an Entertainment Empire* (New York: Hyperion, 1998), 8-9.

67 Stephen F. Fjellman, *Vinyl Leaves: Walt Disney World and America* (Boulder: Westview Press, 1992), 350; Jackson and West, editors, *Disneyland and Culture: Essays on the Parks and Their Influence*, 47; Douglas Brode, *Multiculturalism and the Mouse: Race and Sex in Disney Entertainment* (Austin: University of Texas Press, 2005), 199.

68 Pinsky, *The Gospel According to Disney*, 3; Virginia A. Salamone and Frank A. Salamone, "Images of Main Street: Disney World and the American Adventure," electronic version, 87.

69 Alexander Moore, "Walt Disney World: Bounded Ritual Space and the Playful Pilgrimage Center," *Anthropological Quarterly*, 53(October 1980), 207-208, 211; William Arnal, "The Segregation of Social Desire: 'Religion' and Disney World," *Journal of the American Academy of Religion* 69(March 2001), 2.

70 Benjamin R. Barber, *Jihad vs. McWorld* (New York: Ballantine Books, 1996), 116.

from an historic (if not Dis-Historic) standpoint, not including religion is equally problematic.[71] If Main Street is about a re-created American past, how can God be so clearly written out of the story—considering the importance faith (both private and public) have played in American history? Perhaps the answer is found in digging a bit deeper into Walt's complex personal and corporate relationship with religion.

According to Bob Thomas, "Walt considered himself religious," even if "he rarely went to church." Perhaps he had had enough "religiosity" growing up and had little time for "sanctimonious preachers." He also "did not believe in mixing religion and entertainment," and never made a "religious film."[72] As for his children, Walt wanted his daughters to find a church of their own. They attended various religious, private schools and he made sure that they went to Sunday school at Hollywood Presbyterian Church. Diane, eventually, became an Episcopalian and Sharon a Presbyterian.[73] That being said, a Protestant clergyman gave a prayer of blessing at Disneyland's opening,[74] and one of Walt's favorite things to attend at the park was the Christmas Candlelight Processional, a tradition that started in 1955, and that includes hymns and the Gospel reading of Jesus' birth.[75] When Walt died, the Episcopal minister from Diane's church performed the service.[76]

Thus, despite what some critics allege, Walt was hardly opposed to religion. He believed that religious freedom was important, indeed that it "was central to the American way of life."[77] What he forged for the company and its movies and parks was, according to Mark Pinsky, "a consistent set of moral and human values ... largely based on Western, Judeo-Christian faith and principles, which together constitute a 'Disney gospel,'"[78] a reinterpretation of Christianity for "mass culture."[79] Walt was supportive of Norman Vincent Peale's

---

71 De Tocqueville, *Democracy in America*, 150–151.

72 Thomas, *Walt Disney*, 194–195; Didier Ghez, editor, *Walt's People: Volume 6: Talking Disney with the Artists Who Knew Him* (New York: Xlibris Corporation, 2008), 176.

73 Barrier, *The Animated Man*, 191; Pinsky, *The Gospel According to Disney*, 17–18.

74 Watts, *The Magic Kingdom*, 392.

75 "The Season of Giving: Walt and the Candlelight Processional," http://www.waltdisney.org/storyboard/season-giving-walt-and-candlelight-processional, 5 June 2014.

76 Gabler, *Walt Disney*, 633.

77 Watts, *The Magic Kingdom*, 348.

78 Pinsky, *The Gospel According to Disney*, xi.

79 Gabler, *Walt Disney*, xiv.

power of positive thinking.[80] He talked about the importance of prayer in his life as well as believed that studying the Scripture was an important pursuit. Indeed, he attributed his success in creating a business that brought "clean, informative entertainment to people of all ages" in large part to his "Congregational upbringing."[81] Disney saw Church and State as institutions that "are guarantors of the rights of the poor, the downtrodden, and the dispossessed"[82] and sought to uphold, not deter, those values. Walt believed his religious beliefs were expressed through what he did. He wanted to make sure "that in our movie work the highest moral and spiritual standards are upheld." He sought to "live a good Christian life" and believed "firmly in the efficacy of religion."[83]

So, why is there no church on Main Street? Not including one seemingly removes moral struggle from the idyllic world Disney created. There is another reason. Walt worried about anyone being offended or feeling excluded.[84] If this was true of his movies, it was even more so of his parks. Perhaps Walt steered Main Street away from displaying religion because he did not want to commodify it.[85] While he did not place a church in his park (unlike what Walter Knott did at the nearby Knotts Berry Farm),[86] he still wanted his stories to have some sort of moral lesson to them. He did not think that you did children any favors by discounting that there was evil in the world and wanted to show them that "good can always triumph over evil."[87]

---

80 Watts, *The Magic Kingdom*, 58–59.
81 Pinsky, *The Gospel According to Disney*, 21.
82 Tison Pugh and Susan Aronstein, editors, *The Disney Middle Ages: A Fairy-Tale and Fantasy Past* (New York: Palgrave Macmillan, 2012), 143.
83 Dave Smith, *The Quotable Walt Disney* (New York: Disney Editions, 2001), 256–257.
84 Pinsky, *The Gospel According to Disney*, xiii.
85 Barber, *Jihad vs. McWorld*, 83.
86 Walter Knott actually acquired a church building, placed it in Ghost Town, and had a minister conduct services there as a fully functioning house of worship from 1955 until 2004 (when the church building was relocated to better accommodate wedding requests and the new owners of the park who were not as devoted to the faith as the Knotts family had been). See, "Knott's Berry Park Church of Reflections," http://www.knottschapel.com/history/index.htm, 1 June 2016; *New York Times*, 28 June 2003.
87 Barrier, *The Animated Man*, 106; Pinsky, *The Gospel According to Disney*, 2; Michael R. Real, *Mass-Mediated Culture* (Englewood Cliffs, New Jersey: Prentice-Hall, 1977), 48, 76–77; Janet Wasko, *Understanding Disney: The Manufacture of Fantasy* (Cambridge: Polity Press, 2001), 118–119.

Religious leaders have not always known what to make of Disney, church or no church in the park. Historically, religion, in particular Christianity, has been a constant in American life, though in the form of religious pluralism. Even as secular and religious spheres coexisted alongside each other, faith remained an important means to promote community involvement.[88] Then came Disney, borrowing moral themes and talking of building culture. By the 1990s, some who had thought Disney was a friend in upholding American values, underpinned by Protestant (if not Judeo-Christian writ large) morality under Walt, came to believe that this heritage was being abandoned. In part this had to do with Michael Eisner who both broadened the company's markets and raised its profits, while also being viewed as both secular and either intensely private about or agnostic toward his Jewish heritage. In 1997, such arguments came to a head when the Southern Baptist Convention, the largest Protestant denomination in the country, called for its members to boycott Disney. While Eisner clearly got the better of the SBC's Richard Land when the two appeared on CBS's *60 Minutes*, Disney did see a decline in revenue (though there is little evidence that it was caused by the SBC's boycott), and both sides largely let the matter fade into history.[89]

The saloon and the church are not the only institutions missing from Main Street. There is no school either,[90] though that is perhaps more understandable from an historic main-street example. However, these omissions tell us a good deal. There is a cultural cleansing or purifying afoot with Dis-History. Its quest for standardization always carries with it the risk of losing the spirit of the work and history being adapted. Historians and critics have blasted Dis-History for this sanitization, and for good reason, though such omissions are hardly out of the norm, even for professional historians.[91] Indeed, to a degree,

---

88 Robert N. Bellah, Richard Madsen, William M. Sullivan, Ann Swidler, and Steven M. Tipton, *Habits of the Heart: Individualism and Commitment in American Life* (Los Angeles: University of California Press, 1996), 219–227; Pinsky, *The Gospel According to Disney*, 6-11.

89 Pinsky, *The Gospel According to Disney*, 123, 127–128, 240–241, 254–261; Wasko, *Understanding Disney*, 214. Perhaps ironically, one of the most overtly religious films (next to 1978's *Small One*) also dates from the same time as the SBC boycott, *The Hunchback of Notre Dame*. See, Pinsky, *The Gospel According to Disney*, 114-117, 167-172; Pugh and Aronstein, editors, *The Disney Middle Ages*, 229; Eleanor Byrne and Martin McQuillan, *Deconstructing Disney* (Sterling, Virginia: Pluto Press, 1999), 8–13.

90 Adams, *The American Amusement Park Industry*, 98.

91 Schickel, *The Disney Version*, 226–227.

such arguments are moot. Academic historians do not talk about everything (including the saloon and religion, or even schools) in their classrooms. They make choices, just like Disney.

Nor can Disney be faulted for not being a museum, even if Dis-History uses inspired history. Disney never bills itself as creating an "authentic replication of an era" the way Colonial Williamsburg does, nor a place where visitors can "re-experience a kind of personal identification with a national identity." It is not attempting to forge "official history" into "collective memory" as a museum might. Disney only vows to curate its own history. As Eric Gable and Richard Handler noted of their study of Colonial Williamsburg, "Visitors indeed remember their visits to Colonial Williamsburg, but their specific memories would seem to have little to contribute to any 'collective memory' of a 'national history.'" This is important because of the criticism that Disney receives for its use of Dis-History. As Gable and Handler note, people who come to Colonial Williamsburg bring their expectations and knowledge, as well as how Colonial Williamsburg itself "used to be" when they visit. Whether one is talking about a Disney park or a history park like Williamsburg, memories are perhaps the most important thing that people take away from such places.[92] It is with memory and nostalgia that Disney excels. Unlike Colonial Williamsburg, Disney's use of Dis-History allows guests to bring those things with them. Experiencing the past (even Disney's version and uses of it) *does* become part of a collective/personal memory.

A Standard American Story

Main Street, then, is the first place many guests experience Dis-History. As Richard Snow points out, author Sinclair Lewis found his fictional Main Street "foul with hypocrisy ... and blighted aspirations. He wasn't wrong. But neither was Walt Disney" when it came to describing the ethos of Main Street constructed by his Imagineers.[93] There was much good that came from the main streets across America, even if they all were not perfect or even similar to Walt's imagined one. If Main Street is supposed to be an idealized past, as critics have charged Disney of creating, then in reality Walt was crafting some sort of Golden Age myth (that we have fallen from and must seek to restore) steeped in our collective memory.[94]

---

92 Eric Gable and Richard Handler, "Public History, Private Memory: Notes from the Ethnography of Colonial Williamsburg, Virginia, USA," *Ethnos: Journal of Anthropology*, 65:2 (2000), 237–244.

93 Richard Snow, "Disney: Coast to Coast," http://www.americanheritage.com/content/disney-coast-coast, 2 June 2014.

94 Douglas Brode, *Multiculturalism and the Mouse: Race and Sex in Disney*

Such a formulation is hardly surprising. Walt's idea of culture was middle class, Midwestern American. With it came a heavy dose of nostalgia and a love affair with "classical" themed literature and architecture.[95] In addition, he saw nothing wrong with extolling and celebrating the values of the common American, like hard work, patriotism, and family. Walt believed that most people who viewed his films were like him, and that he reflected their values. In many ways, the parks were built on these American values and the assumption that guests already subscribe to them.[96] Walt was prepared to defend both those values and the company that he built around them.

Nowhere was Walt's beliefs in his Main Street values better seen than when the company was hit by a strike in 1941. The Disney studio had grown incredibly in the thirteen years since *Steamboat Willie* was released, and had just revolutionized animation with the success of *Snow White*, which had allowed Walt to build a large, modern studio complex. However, growth and the pace of production also destroyed the sense of camaraderie that had existed when Walt was one of the "boys," helping to make the cartoons that made the new studio possible. Walt's promises to individuals, the failure to always live up to those promises (both of which usually revolved around pay), and the fact that his name (and the credit that came with it) was part and parcel with any Disney release generated a good deal of resentment among his work force.[97]

While the strikers had many legitimate grievances, they also misunderstood Walt's position. Running the studio was more difficult and time consuming than many of the employees realized on a day-to-day basis. They might be working on one assignment for one picture. Walt

---

Entertainment (Austin: University of Texas Press, 2005), 255; Jackson and West, editors, *Disneyland and Culture*, 192.

95 Schickel, *The Disney Version*, 212–213; Watts, *The Magic Kingdom*, 190–191.

96 Watts, *The Magic Kingdom*, 347–348, 400–401; Jane Kuenz, Karen Klugman, Shelton Waldrep, and Susan Willis, editors, *Inside the Mouse: Work and Play at Disney World* (Durham: Duke University Press, 1995), 57; Robin Allan, *Walt Disney and Europe: European Influences on the Animated Feature Films of Walt Disney* (Indianapolis: Indiana University Press, 1999), 212.

97 Didier Ghez, editor, *Walt's People: Volume 2: Talking Disney with the Artists Who Knew Him* (Theme Park Press, 2015), 138; Didier Ghez, editor, *Walt's People: Volume 3: Talking Disney with the Artists Who Knew Him* (Theme Park Press, 2016), 24-25; Didier Ghez, editor, *Walt's People: Volume 4: Talking Disney with the Artists Who Knew Him* (Theme Park Press, 2016), 130; "My Review of the Walt Disney Documentary—Mr. Fun's Journal," http://floydnormancom.squarespace.com/blog/2015/9/17/my-review-of-the-walt-disney-documentary, 17 September 2015.

was overseeing multiple projects all at once. He was the company in very real ways. Walt's feelings of personal betrayal were exacerbated by how much he had invested in his animation staff.[98] Additionally, the strike was deadly serious for the company's economic bottom line (the financial peril of which Walt did not fully disclose to his employees).[99]

All these tensions boiled over during an attempt unionize the studio. Some 300 of the 1000 Disney employees joined the picket lines. Walt took a hardline and felt betrayed by the strikers. He disliked and clashed with the union leader, Herbert K. Sorrell, whom he thought was trying to destroy his studio. He also did not always receive the best advice from his lawyer, Gunther Lessing, who tended to reinforce Walt's instincts (sometimes without facts to back them up). Federal arbitration eventually ushered in a union, along with higher wages, better benefits, and more recognition for the animators, but it also led to a good number of firings (when future cutbacks needed to be made in staff, Disney always started with those who had stayed on the picket lines). The strike destroyed for Walt the idea that his studio was one big happy family, and he became much more serious about his business in the years to come.[100] Walt felt, and in some respects with good reason, that the strike was personal.[101]

Part of his political self, and thus the eventual parks, was forged in the strike.[102] While his father Elias was a populist and a socialist,

---

98   Didier Ghez, editor, *Walt's People: Volume 7: Talking Disney with the Artists Who Knew Him* (New York: Xlibris Corporation, 2008), 136–137; Don Hahn and Tracey Miller-Zarneke, *Before Ever After: The Lost Lectures of Walt Disney's Animation Studio* (New York: Disney Editions, 2015).

99   Schickel, *The Disney Version*, 256–257; Thomas, *Walt Disney*, 171; Eric Smoodin, *Animating Culture: Hollywood Cartoons from the Sound Era* (New Brunswick, NJ: Rutgers University Press, 1993), 127, 134–135; Watts, *The Magic Kingdom*, 98-99, 220, 226. Walt always felt that when employees left, especially to rivals, it was an act of betrayal. See, Leslie Iwerks and John Kenworthy, *The Hand Behind the Mouse: An Intimate Biography of the Man Walt Disney Classed "The Greatest Animator in the World,"* (New York: Disney Editions, 2001), 147.

100   Ghez, editor, *Walt's People: Volume 3*, 52, 74–77, 84–93, 160; "We Must Keep the Labor Unions Clean," http://historymatters.gmu.edu/d/6458/, 18 October 2015.

101   Davis, Marc. Interviewed by Bob Thomas, 1973, Lectures and Transcripts, Walt Disney Studio Archives, Burbank, California.

102   Wasko, *Understanding Disney*, 16–17, 98; Christopher Finch, *Walt Disney's America* (New York: Abbeville Press, 1978), 25-26, 31; Barrier, *The Animated Man*, 6–7, 170; Watts, *The Magic Kingdom*, 204–205; Gabler, *Walt Disney*, 358–359. Gabler seems to think (366-367) that right-wingers in the government overly influenced Walt when it came to communism and the strike.

who lionized both William Jennings Bryan and Eugene Debbs,[103] Walt became more conservative after the strike. He believed the people behind his labor issues were communists. As he told the House Un-American Activities Committee in 1947, he did not "believe it [communism] is a political party. I believe it is an un-American thing. I feel if the thing can be proven un-American that it ought to be outlawed. I think in some way it should be done without interfering with the rights of the people." The strike, Walt's anti-communism, and the Cold War in general helped propel him to build a park that would represent and enshrine the kinds of values found on any American Main Street.[104]

Before he could do that, the values of Main Street had to be literally defended from outside threats. No sooner had the strike ended than Walt and his company were enlisted in fighting World War II.[105] The war, which began in Europe in 1939, had already cut off Disney's access to European markets. Though America's entry into the conflict caused additional disruptions in his production schedule, there was also never any doubt that Walt would wed his company to the Allied cause.[106] Both he and Roy had served during World War I,[107] and as war clouds grew larger on the horizon, they looked for ways in which they might be of service again.[108]

Part of this was for financial reasons. It is easy to argue in retrospect, with Disney's success, that money was never an issue. During the war years, however, having just survived the strike and with foreign markets frozen, it was a dangerous time for the studio. Some 40 to 50 percent of Disney's revenues came from foreign markets. The war was

---

103 Barrier, *The Animated Man*, 13; Gabler, *Walt Disney*, 13.

104 Kathy Merlock Jackson, editor, *Walt Disney: Conversations* (Jackson: University of Mississippi Press, 2006), 16–17, 38–41; Gabler, *Walt Disney*, 450-453; Henry A. Giroux, *The Mouse that Roared: Disney and the End of Innocence* (New York: Rowman and Littlefield, 1999), 128–129; Barrier, *The Animated Man*, 201; Ted Morgan, *Reds: McCarthyism in Twentieth-Century America* (New York: Random House, 2003); Watts, *The Magic Kingdom*, 283–284; "We Must Keep the Labor Unions Clean," http://historymatters.gmu.edu/d/6458/, 18 October 2015.

105 J.B. Kaufman, *South of the Border with Disney: Walt Disney and the Good Neighbor Program, 1941-1948* (New York: Disney Editions, 2009), 8.

106 Richard Shale, *Donald Duck Joins Up: The Walt Disney Studio During World War II* (Ann Arbor: UMI Research Press, 1982), 20–21.

107 Thomas, *Walt Disney*, 46-47; Gabler, *Walt Disney*, 39; Watts, *The Magic Kingdom*, 10–11; "The American Flag," http://www.waltdisney.org/storyboard/american-flag, 5 June 2014.

108 Gabler, *Walt Disney*, 412; Watts, *The Magic Kingdom*, 228.

a direct assault on the studio's bottom line. Those lost revenue streams had to be made up somewhere. Government work was one way to do that. Walt was accused of making money, indeed of profiting, from his war movies. However, that was not the case. He could have made more money from his war contracts, but he was focused on helping the United States win the war. Disney was hardly alone, amongst corporations or Hollywood studios, in looking for government work. Few could match the unique and varied outputs of the House of Mouse.[109]

The federal government, as it turned out, needed Disney. While mutually beneficial, the government understood that Disney's films were an incredibly powerful tool. Walt turned the studio over to the armed forces during World War II, both as a facility (an anti-aircraft unit was deployed on the grounds in the wake of Pearl Harbor) as well as in terms of churning out a plethora of training (some of which were top secret, like the one on the Norden bombsight) and propaganda films.[110] The staff believed there was value in the films, and in the ideas and messages they were conveying. There was excitement in what they were doing, of being part of the war effort.[111]

For his part, Walt realized that his company had the training necessary to take complex subjects and make them easy to understand (at least on a basic level) because of their work in standardizing literature and fairy tales.[112] Despite the number and nature of the films, the relationship between Disney and the government was not always a happy one. Walt did not enjoy having to constantly travel to Washington to hammer out contract details, nor did he like having to deal with the demands of military and governmental officials, who did not understand the animation process, but always seemed to have critiques to offer. Additionally, Walt resented having to find proof as to why his

---

109   Ghez, editor, *Walt's People: Volume 4*, 105; Didier Ghez, editor, *Walt's People: Volume 6: Talking Disney with the Artists Who Knew Him* (Theme Park Press, 2015), 157; Ghez, editor, *Walt's People: Volume 7*, 109, 148; Thomas, *Building a Company*, 152; Eric Smoodin, *Animating Culture: Hollywood Cartoons from the Sound Era* (New Brunswick, NJ: Rutgers University Press, 1993), 136–150; Gabler, *Walt Disney*, 383, 389–390.

110   Smoodin, *Animating Culture*, 5; "In Defense of Walt Disney," http://www.waltdisney.org/storyboard/defense-walt-disney, 5 June 2014; Watts, *The Magic Kingdom*, 229; Shale, *Donald Duck Joins Up*, 12; Christopher Finch, *Walt Disney's America* (New York: Abbeville Press, 1978), 174; Didier Ghez, editor, *Walt's People: Volume 1: Talking Disney with the Artists Who Knew Him* (Theme Park Press, 2014), 183; Thomas, *Walt Disney*, 175.

111   Ghez, editor, *Walt's People: Volume 3*, 54-55, 187, 192-193; Ghez, editor, *Walt's People: Volume 4*, 178.

112   Thomas, *Walt Disney*, 176–177.

animators should not be drafted, and chafed under the lack of content control and distribution decisions for the films, as well as the increases in governmental security that often seemed burdensome.[113]

Some of the studio's work came after Nelson Rockefeller, head of the Office of the Coordinator of Inter-American Affairs, recruited Walt to conduct some "Disney Diplomacy" on behalf of the United States in Central and South America. Rockefeller did not want direct propaganda. The U.S. needed to be seen as a "good neighbor" in order to combat Nazi influence. Walt, members of his family, and dozens of employees visited Central and South America three times between 1941 and 1943, with the end result nearly two dozen different short or feature films (the best known of which teamed Donald Duck up with Panchito and Joe Carioca in *The Three Caballeros* and *Saludos Amigos*), which prompted better relations between the Americas and a public relations goldmine for Disney.[114]

More government contracts came after the South America trips and films. The Treasury Department asked Disney to help get Americans to pay their income taxes. Once again, Donald Duck was tasked with the job, and like his good-will films for South and Central America, the Duck was up to the task. The Disney film, entitled *The New Spirit*, employed Donald to convince his fellow citizens that it was their patriotic duty, especially in wartime, to help fund Uncle Sam. It was "the most widely seen, as well as the most controversial of all the Disney wartime films," largely because Donald dreams of being in Nazi Germany. It was also, according to Richard Shale, "an instant success," with evidence of its power shown by an increase in tax receipts going to the government following its debut.[115]

---

113 Shale, *Donald Duck Joins Up*, 36-38; Iwerks and Kenworthy, *The Hand Behind the Mouse*, 155, 167; Ghez, editor, *Walt's People: Volume 7*, 48–49, 55, 141; Barrier, *The Animated Man*, 184-185; Thomas, *Walt Disney*, 178–179.

114 Kaufman, *South of the Border with Disney*, 12–14, 17–18, 22, 25, 69, 102, 244–245; Gabler, *Walt Disney*, 371, 394–395; Smoodin, editor, *Disney Discourse*, 12, 132–133, 140–149,161; Andrew Parker, Mary Russo, Doris Sommer, and Patricia Yaeger, editors, *Nationalism and Sexualities* (New York: Routledge, 1992), 24–26; Iwerks and Kenworthy, *The Hand Behind the Mouse*, 160-161; Shale, *Donald Duck Joins Up*, 44–49, 54, 99, 108; Smoodin, *Animating Culture*, 101–102; Watts, *The Magic Kingdom*, 246–247; Douglas Brode, *Multiculturalism and the Mouse: Race and Sex in Disney Entertainment* (Austin: University of Texas Press, 2005), 92–93. The teaming of Donald Duck, Panchito and Joe Carioca was revived for a short film that is now part of the Mexico pavilion at Epcot.

115 Thomas, *Walt Disney*, 180-181; Shale, *Donald Duck Joins Up*, 27-29; Smoodin, *Animating Culture*, 168–183. Today, it is possible to read the over 300 pages of FBI files on Disney (or at least those that are not heavily redacted). See, "The

Walt knew that using Donald Duck in the tax film was essentially making a Donald Duck movie for free. And, as William L. O'Neill relates, the war did not stop Hollywood from "making comedies and musicals," with the vast majority of the 2500 films produced during the war years have nothing really to do with the war.[116] However, Walt had in mind making a feature film that could support U.S. war interests, make the studio money, and be as revolutionary as *Snow White*. For his source material, he turned to Alexander P. De Seversky's 1942 magnum opus, *Victory Through Air Power*, with thoughts of convincing the public and the government to win the war from the skies above.

De Seversky, a Russian ex-patriate and World War I flying ace, was, in the words of one critic, an "air extremist." The film, *Victory Through Air Power*, perhaps more so than the book it was based on, shaped public opinion about what could be accomplished by airplanes in modern warfare. De Seversky's book "slammed War Department orthodoxy" on how to fight a war, a theme that the movie explored. Released in 1943, the film arrived before audiences were well aware of German and Japanese airpower, and unsure if what they were watching was entertainment or propaganda. By utilizing live action, film footage, and animation, Disney made De Seversky's point that Allied air superiority could crush Nazi Germany. It also may have helped influence decision makers to give the D-Day landings more air support. Critics (including many within the military) blasted the film for holding out the idea that bombers could win a war. For all the public-policy success the movie helped to create, ultimately it was done at a financial loss for Disney as a studio. Walt later said that making the movie was a rash and somewhat "stupid thing to do," but he made the film anyway. According to Ward Kimball, *Victory Through Airpower* "served its purpose at the time."[117]

The end of World War II left Disney "in a precarious position," as its "strong momentum" from the pre-war years was gone, as were

---

FBI: The Vault, Walter Elias Disney," http://vault.fbi.gov/walter-elias-disney, 19 June 2014.

116   William L. O'Neill, *A Democracy at War: America's Fight at Home and Abroad in World War II* (New York: The Free Press, 1993), 258.

117   O'Neill, *A Democracy at War*, 141, 256, 315-316; Thomas, *Walt Disney*, 182–186; Watts, *The Magic Kingdom*, 234–237; Smoodin, editor, *Disney Discourse*, 44-45; Shale, *Donald Duck Joins Up*, 67–75; Gabler, *Walt Disney*, 390-394, 405; "Oldies and Oddities: The Disney War Plan," http://www.airspacemag.com/history-of-flight/oldies-and-oddities-the-disney-war-plan-137911052/?no-ist, 13 August 2014; Didier Ghez, editor, *Walt's People: Volume 5: Talking Disney with the Artists Who Knew Him* (Theme Park Press, 2016), 28, 65.

its government contracts (which the government was often slow in paying for anyway). The war films allowed the studio to stay open and in the public eye, if not turn a profit. While the company was in poor financial shape, it was also ready to get back in the swing of things.[118] If there was a benefit to the wartime experiences, it was that their work helped shield Walt and the company from some criticism and mute much of the internal strife left over from the strike.[119] It also gave Disney the chance to try different kinds of artistic endeavors (training, educational, even commercial work) with its films, which in turn helped open the company up to the idea of trying something equally new in the construction of a park.[120]

Additionally, the war years gave Disney a unique perspective on the American experience. The movies, the eventual parks, the merchandise, all made Walt Disney a very wealthy man and the embodiment of the American Dream.[121] Disney's values were Middle American, and yet he found a way to make them universal. In the process, he became a "symbol for American culture."[122] Walt himself asserted, "There's an American theme behind the whole park. I believe in emphasizing the story of what made America great and what will keep it great."[123] He also assumed that his success not only vindicated the American system but also could be replicated.[124] As the Second World War ended, he referred to the United States as "the mightiest nation in history."[125]

Critics see such statements and their translation into park attractions as "grandiose" and proof of American exceptionalism.[126] Walt did not care. Nor do the millions who have walked along Main Street

---

118 Kaufman, South of the Border with Disney, 263; Shale, Donald Duck Joins Up, 80, 112; Thomas, Walt Disney, 201; Watts, The Magic Kingdom, 237–238.

119 Smoodin, Animating Culture, 103–104.

120 Shale, Donald Duck Joins Up, 109; Barrier, The Animated Man, 188–189.

121 Joe Flower, Prince of the Magic Kingdom: Michael Eisner and the Re-Making of Disney (New York: John Wiley and Sons, Inc., 1991; Theme Park Press, 2017), 10.

122 Finch, Walt Disney's America, 32; Watts, The Magic Kingdom, 37; Smoodin, Animating Culture, 16.

123 Henry A. Giroux, The Mouse that Roared: Disney and the End of Innocence (New York: Rowman and Littlefield, 1999), 36.

124 Richard Schickel, The Disney Version: The Life, Times, Art and Commerce of Walt Disney, Third Edition (Chicago: Ivan R. Dee Publisher, 1997), 158.

125 Walt Disney, "Mickey as Professor," The Public Opinion Quarterly, 9(Summer 1945), 125.

126 William F. Van Wert, "Disney World and Posthistory," Cultural Critique, 32(Winter, 1995–1996), 200.

and into the Magic Kingdom. Perhaps we should see Main Street as a "festival marketplace," a gathering place of people who bring their own assumptions to what Disney has prepared for them. A place that is both a public space while also being one that is safe, secure, and private, all at the same time.[127] It is a place that is a gateway to a world of fantasy, including a whole Fantasyland.

---

127 Don Mitchell, *Cultural Geography: A Critical Introduction* (Malden, Massachusetts: Blackwell Publishing, 2000), 135–137.

CHAPTER FOUR

A Small World of Fantasy(land)

Experience Cinderella Castle

Looking down Main Street, guests' eyes are eventually transfixed by a castle. In Disneyland (and several of the other parks as well), it is Sleeping Beauty Castle. However, in the Magic Kingdom guests encounter Cinderella Castle. A massive structure, guests can be excused if, at first glance, they believe for a moment that the only way such a large castle (one that is much larger than its California cousin) could have come to reside in the midst of Florida was with a little faith, trust, and pixie dust. The castle is not just a focal point or a passageway to other lands; it is an attraction in its own right, complete with a restaurant where guests can dine with Cinderella and other Disney princesses, as well as view one of the best pieces of artwork in the Magic Kingdom—a mosaic tile display that shows Cinderella's story. The whole experience of seeing, entering, and being a part of the castle's routine can be an "amazing" one for younger guests.[1]

Cinderella Castle presides over the largest area of the Magic Kingdom, Fantasyland. In many ways, Fantasyland is nearly a kingdom unto itself. Few guests probably realize it (due to walking the pathways and their focus being on getting to the next attraction), but if they approach Cinderella Castle from Main Street, they will come to a plaza (with the famed Walt and Mickey statue at its center) that is actually an island. One of Disney's own intercoastal waterways stretches from Adventureland to Tomorrowland, and helps create a frontal moat for the castle itself. Sidewalls, landscaping, and pathways use their own version of forced perspective to shield Fantasyland from the rest of the park, making a guest's arrival in the area that much more special. However, though an artificial kingdom to be sure,

---

1 Nick Lantzer, as told to the author, during our July 2014 trip.

the experiences that guests have in Fantasyland are quite real and are shaped by the forces of Dis-History.[2]

Castles are central to both the parks and to our understanding of Dis-History. They do not imply historic themed entertainment, but rather fantasy.[3] They are places where guests can be transformed and new experiences can be had.[4] The Disney castles are not concerned with "realism" in the sense that they are meant to be re-created European castles. The Imagineers of Disneyland Paris created their version of Sleeping Beauty Castle complete with a dragon beneath it.[5] The Shanghai park's castle has an underground boat ride.[6] Though very American, Disney has no problems with kings, queens, or royalty.[7] They are fixtures of the past, and in some ways very Dis-Historic. In Fantasyland, Walt was bringing European stories to his American audience, forging a common culture in the process.[8]

Walt called objects that pull a guest along a certain avenue a "wienie"—something visual that lures people forward, all the while setting the scene of what is to come.[9] The castle is the chief wienie for the Magic Kingdom. In the case of Disneyland, it is literally at the center of the park. However, the castle is ultimately more than just a lure. It is symbolic of Dis-History's attempt to create a culture. All cultures need history (which guests have walked through and along via Main Street), but they also need myths. As Joseph Campbell argued, myths reveal, "truths disguised for us under the figures of religion and mythology."[10]

---

2   Robin Allan, *Walt Disney and Europe: European Influences on the Animated Feature Films of Walt Disney* (Indianapolis: Indiana University Press, 1999), 230.

3   Tison Pugh and Susan Aronstein, editors, *The Disney Middle Ages: A Fairy-Tale and Fantasy Past* (New York: Palgrave Macmillan, 2012), 39; Beth Dunlop, *Building a Dream: The Art of Disney Architecture* (New York: Harry N. Abrams, 1996), 99.

4   Pugh and Aronstein, editors, *The Disney Middle Ages*, 50–51.

5   Andrew Lainsbury, *Once Upon an American Dream: The Story of Euro Disneyland* (Lawrence: University of Kansas Press, 2000), 69–72.

6   "Disney CEO Iger's Empire of Tech," http://fortune.com/2014/12/29/disney-ceo-bob-iger-empire-of-tech/, 12 January 2015.

7   Pugh and Aronstein, editors, *The Disney Middle Ages*, 126.

8   Kathy Merlock Jackson and Mark I. West, editors, *Disneyland and Culture: Essays on the Parks and Their Influence* (Jefferson, NC: McFarland and Company, 2011), 32; Richard Schickel, *The Disney Version: The Life, Times, Art and Commerce of Walt Disney, Third Edition* (Chicago: Ivan R. Dee Publisher, 1997), 356.

9   John Hench with Peggy Van Pelt, *Designing Disney: Imagineering and the Art of the Show* (New York: Disney Editions, 2008), 50.

10   Joseph Campbell, *The Hero with a Thousand Faces* (Princeton: Princeton University Press, 1949), vii.

Like Campbell, Walt understood the power of myth when it came to cultural formation,[11] thanks to famed architect Frank Lloyd Wright, who talked to the company's artists in February 1939 and told them what the nation needed was culture.[12] Walt and his team believed that they were on the verge of doing some truly unique and innovative things, things that could only be done in America.[13] The Fantasyland they constructed is now where we turn to see Dis-History attempt this goal.

The Fantasy of Standardization

The attractions in Fantasyland are perhaps best understood as adaptations of Disney's version of children's literature. The rides, especially, are like their own version of Disney's movies and "amplify" what the films depict.[14] In Fantasyland, guests can fly over London (and go "off to Neverland") with Peter Pan. They can ride on Prince Charming's carrousel (the only prince to get a ride—though you can also attempt to pull the Sword from the Stone if the possibility of ruling England one day is attractive to you). They can whirl around on the Mad Hatter's tea cups, journey under the sea with the Little Mermaid, visit Belle's cottage, the Beast's castle, and Gaston's tavern. They can ride in the mines with the Seven Dwarfs or spend time adventuring with Winnie the Pooh. Indeed, guests can hardly turn around without bumping into a Disney character, or being lured to dine in a themed restaurant. If there is a place for synergy between Disney's characters, rides, and movies, Fantasyland is the easiest place to find it.[15]

It is hardly surprising that in his quest to create American culture, Walt turned to fairy tales such as the ones that inspired his movies and rides, to visually create "a mythical literature."[16] As science fiction writer John C. Wright notes, "The best way to find reality is through fairyland."[17] Indeed, as far back as the 1700s, Europeans were placing

---

11 Didier Ghez, editor, *Walt's People: Volume 4: Talking Disney with the Artists Who Knew Him* (New York: Xlibris Corporation, 2007), 154–155.

12 Don Hahn and Tracey Miller-Zarneke, *Before Ever After: The Lost Lectures of Walt Disney's Animation Studio* (New York: Disney Editions, 2015), 360.

13 Hahn and Miller-Zarneke, *Before Ever After*, 281.

14 Jackson and West, editors, *Disneyland and Culture*, 87–88, 96.

15 Douglas Brode, *Multiculturalism and the Mouse: Race and Sex in Disney Entertainment* (Austin: University of Texas Press, 2005), 219.

16 Alexander Moore, "Walt Disney World: Bounded Ritual Space and the Playful Pilgrimage Center," *Anthropological Quarterly*, 53(October 1980), 212.

17 John C. Wright, "The Superversive Literary Movement Stakes Its First Claim," http://www.scifiwright.com/, 16 September 2014.

stories in far-off places (like the Orient), not because they were retelling tales from foreign lands, but because by locating them amongst such locales, they could talk about contemporary issues without seeming to do so.[18] In a Dis-Historic sense, while often based on older fairy tales, Fantasyland is the area of the park where Disney brought Americanized medieval Europe for both its guests and the common culture it was creating. Even though some of the princesses, in their Disney version, are products of a later time (the seventeenth or eighteenth centuries), the tone of the stories remains medieval—a past more open to fantasy than the present. Guests see it represented in various ways, from the abundance of castles to the aforementioned Sword in the Stone. Here are legends crafted to fit a Disney audience.[19]

Fantasyland clearly shows Disney's quest for story standardization. It is not because of children—though children more easily accept fantasy and have a better sense of familiarity with the characters that guests meet in Fantasyland.[20] Disney, after all, is doing more than just having a theme park for kids. It is actually tapping into something much larger, for fairy tales were never meant solely for children. Fairy tales hold universal appeal, partially based on nostalgia, but also because there are elements and themes that both children and adults can appreciate.[21] These are "wonder tales," as Jack Zipes notes, and are timeless" in their morals, if not their settings. It makes perfect sense that Disney gravitated to them.[22]

Nor is it surprising that he was criticized for doing so. As Douglas Street argued, such stories are part of a genre of literature that has "been long maligned." Indeed, in the nineteenth century, many "authors, critics, and parents felt that if children were exposed to fairy tales and other forms of nonrealistic literature, they would become

---

18 Jack Zipes, *When Dreams Came True: Classical Fairy Tales and Their Tradition* (New York: Routledge, 1999), 14–15, 18.

19 *The Imagineering Field Guide to the Magic Kingdom at Walt Disney World: An Imagineer's Eye Tour* (New York: Disney Editions, 2005), 78; Pugh and Aronstein, editors, *The Disney Middle Ages*, 3, 14, 88-89, 116–117; Jackson and West, editors, *Disneyland and Culture*, 97; Robin Allan, *Walt Disney and Europe: European Influences on the Animated Feature Films of Walt Disney* (Indianapolis: Indiana University Press, 1999), 16; Eric Smoodin, *Animating Culture: Hollywood Cartoons from the Sound Era* (New Brunswick, NJ: Rutgers University Press, 1993), 14.

20 Jackson and West, editors, *Disneyland and Culture*, 208; Richard Schickel, *The Disney Version: The Life, Times, Art and Commerce of Walt Disney, Third Edition* (Chicago: Ivan R. Dee Publisher, 1997), 324.

21 Zipes, *When Dreams Came True*, 1; Schickel, *The Disney Version*, 207-209.

22 Zipes, *When Dreams Came True*, 4, 26.

incapable of accepting or even of perceiving reality." Zipes argues that as the oral tradition of fairy tales gave way to a literary tradition (which became the official version), with the stories written down in "high" versions of the language, they were (on some level) taken from the common people and given only to the well educated. The transition to written instead of spoken also meant that the stories were less likely to be shared communally but rather read by the individual in isolation.[23] While Disney is perhaps the best known for their adaptations, they are hardly the only company seeking to rework children's stories, either at the present or historically.[24] The Grimms had done it themselves.[25] Disney's "utopian, idealized form" is similar, according to Michael Real, to what Dante did to the medieval Europe in *The Divine Comedy*.[26] What Walt achieved, on some level, was taking the stories back for popular, common culture, first by creating an animated version,[27] and then by giving them life in the parks.

Disney's versions of the stories are powerful, in large part because they are supported by multiple genres for consumers. The park attractions are based on movies (which often come with songs), which are in turn based on books (both original and Disney versions). Thus, it is hardly surprising that the Disney versions become the standard version of classic fairy tales for most Americans.[28] In many ways, Walt's goal to create a common American canon of literature was widely successful. If nothing else, since people know the Disney version of the story, they at least know the story. Fantasyland became a place where Disney got to show that their version of European fairy tales could overcome cultural

---

23 Elizabeth Bell, Lynda Haas, and Laura Sells, editors, *From Mouse to Mermaid: The Politics of Film, Gender, and Culture* (Indianapolis: Indiana University Press, 1995), 21–25.

24 Douglas Street, editor, *Children's Novels and the Movies* (New York: Frederick Ungar Publishing Company, 1983), xv, xix, 197.

25 Zipes, *When Dreams Came True*, 72–73.

26 Michael R. Real, *Mass-Mediated Culture* (Englewood Cliffs, New Jersey: Prentice-Hall, 1977), 47.

27 Janet Wasko, *Understanding Disney: The Manufacture of Fantasy* (Cambridge: Polity Press, 2001), 127–128.

28 Wasko, *Understanding Disney*, 113, 125–126, 129–130; Benjamin R. Barber, *Jihad vs. McWorld* (New York: Ballantine Books, 1996), 97; John Schultz, "The Fabulous Presumption of Disney World: Magic Kingdom in the Wilderness," *The Georgia Review*, 42(Summer 1988), 285; Terri Martin Wright (1997) Romancing the Tale: Walt Disney's Adaptation of the Grimms' "Snow White", *Journal of Popular Film and Television*, 25:3, 98–108, DOI: 10.1080/01956059709602756.

and linguistic barriers.[29] In addition, what critics fail to appreciate is that sometimes the Disney adaptation is superior to the original.[30]

The baseline for Disney standardization is to keep the moral element of good versus evil, even if you have to alter and condense the rest of the story. Walt believed that without that element, the classic fairy tales he was presenting "long since would have died because they would have no meaning." Children, he argued, understood this much better than adults did.[31] As Walt put it: "To captivate our varied and worldwide audience of all ages, the nature and treatment of the fairy tale, the legend, the myth have to be elementary, simple. Good and evil, the antagonists of all great drama in some guise must be believably personalized. The moral ideals common to all humanity must be upheld. The victories must not be too easy. Strife to test valor is still and always will be the basic ingredient of the animated tale, as of all screen entertainments."[32]

As such, Disney did not shy away from introducing children to the idea that there was good and evil in the world (even if some parents worried those representations of "witches, ogres, giants, and dragons" might be "overexciting for their children). As Walt himself put it, "I don't believe in playing down to children. I didn't treat my youngsters like fragile flowers, and I think no parent should. ... Most things are good and they are the strongest things, but there are evil things, too, and you do a child no favor by trying to shield it from reality. The important thing is to teach a child that Good always triumphs over Evil, and that is what our pictures do."[33]

Beyond that, Walt's vision for the parks and thus for Dis-History rested on two principles. As he put it, the first was that "virtue triumphs over wickedness in our fables," and the second was that "laughter is America's most important export."[34] Walt tasked the Imagineers who created Disneyland with turning those ideas into reality for the guests. You can see it in the attractions, such as Mr. Toad's Wild Ride, Pinocchio's Daring Journey, and Snow White's Scary Adventure, which all still exist at Disneyland and have a darker, scarier feel to them. They also follow their respective movies closely. In Disneyland's

---

29 Andrew Lainsbury, *Once Upon an American Dream: The Story of Euro Disneyland* (Lawrence: University of Kansas Press, 2000), 66–68.

30 Street, editor, *Children's Novels and the Movies*, 39.

31 Kathy Merlock Jackson, editor, *Walt Disney: Conversations* (Jackson: University of Mississippi Press, 2006), 68–69.

32 Dave Smith, *The Quotable Walt Disney* (New York: Disney Editions, 2001), 6.

33 Jackson, editor, *Walt Disney: Conversations*, 54.

34 Christopher Finch, *Walt Disney's America* (New York: Abbeville Press, 1978), 292.

Fantasyland, we might add into the mix the Alice in Wonderland attraction as well, to get the intensity of the park and its devotion to these ideals. Starting with Snow White, many Disney movies and their eventual, subsequent rides had moments parents objected to as "scary" for their children.[35] However, by sticking to Walt's formula, Disney has tended to go for thrills, not fear, in its park attractions.

Disney's quest for standardization in a cultural canon is seen clearly in the various princess stories the studio has released. Though Sleeping Beauty and Cinderella might boast of park castles, the reason there is such a place called Fantasyland at all is because of Disney's first princess, Snow White. "The fairest one of all," after all, really launched the Disney animation empire and made the eventual parks possible. Her story was chosen, in part, because as a boy, Walt had seen a film (though he remembered it as a play) of the Snow White story. In creating their version for the silver screen, Disney animators not only had to contend with crafting a full-length movie (a feature, not a short, which was a gamble for the studio), but also synthesize and standardize a variety of versions of Snow White's story, creating in the process a "definitive American form to an international folk classic."[36]

Snow White "is a simple story faultlessly told." Not only did it launch an entirely new medium, it gave the company the financial resources to build a larger studio, and it successfully captured the tale for audiences across the country and that world. Those were no small accomplishments. The United States was full of immigrants, most from Europe, at the time *Snow White* debuted. Many people were familiar with the story, but Disney defined it for them in a singular way, and for generations to come. The movie also established the Disney brand's "social contract" with the American public: if they saw Walt's movies, they could expect good, family-friendly films.[37]

---

35 Richard Schickel, *The Disney Version: The Life, Times, Art and Commerce of Walt Disney, Third Edition* (Chicago: Ivan R. Dee Publisher, 1997), 220–221.

36 Janet Wasko, *Understanding Disney: The Manufacture of Fantasy* (Cambridge: Polity Press, 2001), 131; David Whitley, *The Idea of Nature in Disney Animation* (Burlington, VT: Ashgate, 2008), 32–33; Bob Thomas, *Building a Company: Roy O. Disney and the Creation of an Entertainment Empire* (New York: Hyperion, 1998), 108–109; Neal Gabler, *Walt Disney: The Triumph of the American Imagination* (New York: Vintage Books, 2007), 217–218; Robin Allan, *Walt Disney and Europe: European Influences on the Animated Feature Films of Walt Disney* (Indianapolis: Indiana University Press, 1999), 37; Finch, *Walt Disney's America*, 233; Michael Barrier, *The Animated Man: A Life of Walt Disney* (Los Angeles: University of California Press, 2007), 2–3; Didier Ghez, editor, *Walt's People: Volume 2: Talking Disney with the Artists Who Knew Him* (Theme Park Press, 2015), 81.

37 Finch, *Walt Disney's America*, 232, 237; Mark I. Pinsky, *The Gospel According*

However, *Snow White*'s success set an almost impossible bar and burden on future Disney animation.[38] Audience expectations grew with each new film announced and few films, at least in the mind of Walt, were ever as perfectly done as *Snow White*. In the years to come, critics would attack the company for animating people rather than animals (they blasted Disney's desire for "monolithic realism" in its animation—in short, that the people and animals actually looked like people and animals), and for delving into children's literature and folk tales rather than creating more "folk art" with Mickey, Donald, and the rest of the Fab Five.[39]

Publicly at least, Walt had little patience for such criticism.[40] He argued that "literary versions of old fairy tales are usually thin and briefly told. They must be expanded and embellished to meet the requirements of theater playing time, and the common enjoyment of all members of movie-going families."[41] As he put it: "To translate the world's great fairy tales, thrilling legends, stirring folk tales into visual theatrical presentations and to get back warm response of audiences in many lands have been for me an experience and a lifetime satisfaction beyond all value."[42] With Dis-History, Walt believed the common American culture he was creating incorporated both folk tales and folk art. Furthermore, the best way to educate children and their parents (and subsequent generations) in the stories of that culture was through animating (what some believed to be) children's literature. Walt said, "We are not trying to entertain the critics. I'll take my chances with the public."[43] Moreover, he had supporters, beyond just his audience. As Beverly Lyon Clark said, "We value childhood. But we also dismiss

---

to Disney: Faith, Trust, and Pixie Dust (Louisville: John Knox Press, 2004), 27.

38   Wasko, *Understanding Disney*, 129–130; Terri Martin Wright (1997) "Romancing the Tale: Walt Disney's Adaptation of the Grimms' "Snow White", *Journal of Popular Film and Television*, 25:3, 98–108, DOI: 10.1080/01956059709602756; Barrier, *The Animated Man*, 296.

39   Beverly Lyon Clark, *Kiddie Lit: The Cultural Construction of Children's Literature in America* (Baltimore: The Johns Hopkins University Press, 2003), 169-178; Richard Schickel, *The Disney Version: The Life, Times, Art and Commerce of Walt Disney, Third Edition* (Chicago: Ivan R. Dee Publisher, 1997), 222–225; Karal Ann Marling, editor, *Designing Disney's Theme Parks: The Architecture of Reassurance* (New York: Flammarion, 1997), 125.

40   Clark, *Kiddie Lit*, 183.

41   Dave Smith, *The Quotable Walt Disney* (New York: Disney Editions, 2001), 19.

42   Smith, *The Quotable Walt Disney*, 8.

43   Smith, *The Quotable Walt Disney*, 12.

it." Historically, Clark noted, Americans have a "love/hate relationship with fantasy." Thus, some of the disdain projected on Disney by critics was because of how children and juveniles were perceived, as well as how literature aimed for them as an audience is understood.[44]

The criticism did not stop Walt, nor did the perceived inability to match *Snow White* when it came to the princess-themed movies. In 1950, Walt Disney Studios released *Cinderella*. With the loss of revenue because of World War II, the company was hoping for another *Snow White*-level hit at the box office. The story that Disney told (and retold) and became the official version is not exactly the version that was told in the eighteenth and nineteenth centuries. The Brothers Grimm version, for example, has the stepsisters literally disfiguring themselves in the vain attempt to get their feet to fit in the glass slipper. While it is another example of Walt's quest for standardization, it was not the hit Disney had hoped for. Thus, as Disneyland was taking shape, the decision was made for Sleeping Beauty's castle to be constructed as the centerpiece of the park, not Cinderella's. On his television show, Walt promoted not only his park but also the soon-to-be released movie with previews and even a feature on Pyotr Ilyich Tchaikovsky, who composed the famed ballet based on the Sleeping Beauty story. While the movie had stronger revenues than *Cinderella* when it debuted in 1959, even combined the two films could not surpass *Snow White*'s box office totals.[45]

Regardless, Walt had achieved a Dis-Historic victory. He had shown that not only could you be faithful (though not rigidly so) to the source material (even if it varied), but you could also get at "the mind of the reader."[46] The result could be monetarily satisfying, but it could also produce a common cultural story and point of reference. All three of the princess stories had been drawn from stories collected by the Brothers Grimm, who had compiled them from a variety of European sources. Nevertheless, Disney had accomplished his goal of Americanizing them and creating a canon for citizens of the United

---

44 Clark, *Kiddie Lit*, 1, 130, 179–181.

45 Ghez, editor, *Walt's People: Volume 2*, 208; Didier Ghez, editor, *Walt's People: Volume 3: Talking Disney with the Artists Who Knew Him* (Theme Park Press, 2015), 160–161; John Schultz, "The Fabulous Presumption of Disney World: Magic Kingdom in the Wilderness," *The Georgia Review*, 42(Summer 1988), 283–285; William F. Van Wert, "Disney World and Posthistory," *Cultural Critique*, 32(Winter, 1995–1996), 193.

46 Wendell Aycock and Michael Schoenecke, editors, *Film and Literature A Comparative Approach to Adaptations* (Lubbock: Texas Tech University Press, 1988), 32.

States to draw from. Dis-History, in other words, was a success, one that was only reinforced with the creation of the parks. To top it off, Walt argued that Disney had "made the fairy tale fashionable again."[47]

Walt only partially relished that victory, at least when it came to Fantasyland. At its opening, he said Fantasyland "is the world of imagination, hopes, and dreams."[48] However, despite all it meant for Dis-History, his company, and the parks, Fantasyland was his least favorite area of Disneyland.[49] Working on animation was grueling and taxing, and the longer Disney was at it, the less Walt enjoyed it.[50] He grew tired "of animating familiar fairy tales because audiences were difficult to satisfy, even their expectations based on what they read in books."[51] Walt believed that delving into children's literature—because of peoples' attachments and interest in the characters—was the most difficult thing to do well, and that was always Disney's goal.[52]

The studio invested heavily in the films that helped bring about the creation of the park and Dis-History, nearly all of which correspond to the twenty-some-odd year period between *Snow White* and *Sleeping Beauty*. Walt believed that to "do the fantastic things, based on the real" his animators needed to "first know the real." He brought in teachers, lecturers, and had his animators take classes in drawing live (both people and animals) models so the renderings and sketches could be accurate. Artists were encouraged to travel as well. The point was to "maintain the illusion of life" and advance the story they were telling.[53]

However, the creation of a Dis-Historic cultural canon did not rest only on stories about princesses. In 1935, Walt, Lillian, Roy, and Edna Disney had all gone on a "grand tour" of Europe. The Disneys returned with hundreds of books on fairy tales and folk stories.[54] One of the stories they brought back with them was *Pinocchio*. Here was

---

47 Smith, *The Quotable Walt Disney*, 139.

48 Smith, *The Quotable Walt Disney*, 64.

49 Kathy Merlock Jackson and Mark I. West, editors, *Disneyland and Culture: Essays on the Parks and Their Influence* (Jefferson, NC: McFarland and Company, 2011), 30.

50 Thomas, *Walt Disney*, 220–221.

51 Jackson and West, editors, *Disneyland and Culture*, 24.

52 Kathy Merlock Jackson, editor, *Walt Disney: Conversations* (Jackson: University of Mississippi Press, 2006), 135

53 Don Hahn and Tracey Miller-Zarneke, *Before Ever After: The Lost Lectures of Walt Disney's Animation Studio* (New York: Disney Editions, 2015), 18, 30–32, 72–73, 175, 190–191, 294; Didier Ghez, editor, *Walt's People: Volume 4: Talking Disney with the Artists Who Knew Him* (Theme Park Press, 2016), 56–57.

54 Hahn and Miller-Zarneke, *Before Ever After*, 339, 343.

a protagonist who is a "flawed and imperfect" character, just about the opposite of *Snow White*. In some ways, it was a story that brought balance to the emerging cannon in terms of protagonists and tone, while still remaining magical and fantastic. Like many fairy tales, the *Pinocchio* that Disney first encountered was a story full of violence. While Walt did not shy away from portraying violent actions, he was also willing to use the standardization process to hint at, rather than show all, the violent nature of some of the stories he was adapting. Walt made the decision to alter the *Pinocchio* story so that audiences would actually care that the character transforms from a puppet into a real boy. To be literally true to the text would mean displaying Pinocchio's "nasty" behavior—which was sure to turn off viewers. Walt always believed *Pinocchio* was a better film than *Snow White*. If critics had a problem with the adaptation upon the film's release in 1940, Walt could point out that in some ways he had saved the work from obscurity. Carlo Collodi's story was originally released in 1882. While it found an audience in places like Bavaria, it was not hailed at the time in Italy the way Alessandro Manzoni's *The Betrothed* was.[55] Thus, Dis-History not only created a common canon, but it was saving (by adding) works that might be lost from that canon altogether.

The company took an even bigger risk and bigger step toward forging this Dis-Historic cultural collection that same year with the release of *Fantasia*. Walt hoped to bridge the gap between classical music and the common person with the movie, further establishing the broad common culture he hoped to forge for Americans. It was a gap he believed existed, at least in part, because most people liked to have visuals as reference points of memory. He worked closely with Leopold Stokowski of the Philadelphia Orchestra to wed music to animation pieces that were inspired by the composition (both literally and figuratively). Walt believed he was doing something new, and that doing so carried with it certain financial risks but great cultural rewards. He believed that he was going to bring "a little culture to the American people" with *Fantasia*. It drew heavily from Greek mythology

---

55   Michael R. Real, *Mass-Mediated Culture* (Englewood Cliffs, New Jersey: Prentice-Hall, 1977), 58; Janet Wasko, *Understanding Disney: The Manufacture of Fantasy* (Cambridge: Polity Press, 2001), 138; Zipes, *When Dreams Came True*, 141; Thomas, *Walt Disney*, 161; Barrier, *The Animated Man*, 139; Street, editor, *Children's Novels and the Movies*, 40.; Pinsky, *The Gospel According to Disney*, 32; Elizabeth Bell, Lynda Haas, and Laura Sells, editors, *From Mouse to Mermaid: The Politics of Film, Gender, and Culture* (Indianapolis: Indiana University Press, 1995), 63; Joseph Luzzi, "The Great Unread: What Makes a Classic Endure?—The Paris Review," http://www.theparisreview.org/blog/2014/08/26/the-great-unread/, 28 August 2014.

for several segments, brought the world the Sorcerer's Apprentice version of Mickey Mouse, and the finale (Moussourksy's "Night on Bald Mountain" teamed with Schubert's "Ave Maria") is perhaps the most overtly religious cartoon Walt ever authorized. *Fantasia* was the end of the critical love for Disney. Critics lamented being with audiences that responded to the animation more than to the music. They also blasted Disney's interpretation of the music, what they considered a lack of seriousness in the "middle-brow culture" he sought to create, and the very notion that Walt was trying to make the fantastic—the stuff of imagination—visual and even concrete. It proved to intellectuals how obtuse he was, and what poor taste he actually had.[56]

If there were limits to what Walt could do with constructing a Dis-History version of literature into animated film, he found it with 1951's *Alice in Wonderland*. Walt loved Alice, and had used some of the themes from Lewis Carroll's books as far back as the early 1920s, when he first blended live action with animation. As a result, he felt like he had to make Alice into an animated feature. Capturing her story on film, however, tested both Walt and his staff and few were happy with the end result.[57] As some of the animators later recalled, "Alice ... wasn't a real character you could identify with." The story is hard to get through. Although the individual sections are good,[58] Alice lacks a certain narrative heart, in Marc Davis' opinion, because all she can do is react to the madness around her.[59] Considering that Carroll's books' popularity in the United States is up for debate, whatever cultural knowledge exists today in the United States tends to be from Disney's version. Even when Walt felt disappointed, Dis-History still prevailed.

All of these classic Disney films found a home in the park system that the company developed, and all of their attractions are firmly

---

56 Neal Gabler, *Walt Disney: The Triumph of the American Imagination* (New York: Vintage Books, 2007), 301–314, 340–341, 427; Eric Smoodin, editor, *Disney Discourse: Producing the Magic Kingdom* (New York: Routledge, 1994), 220–224; Pinsky, *The Gospel According to Disney*, 37-38; Pugh and Aronstein, editors, *The Disney Middle Ages*, 98-99; Ghez, editor, *Walt's People: Volume 2*, 86; Ghez, editor, *Walt's People: Volume 4*, 68–69; Siegfried Kracauer, *Theory of Film: The Redemption of Physical Reality* (Princeton, New Jersey: Princeton University Press, 1997), 88–89; Steve Wasserman, "In Defense of Difficulty," http://www.theamericanconservative.com/articles/in-defense-of-difficulty/, 18 March 2015.

57 Ghez, editor, *Walt's People: Volume 2*, 208–209; Ghez, *Walt's People: Volume 4*, 81; Clark, *Kiddie Lit*, 153-155, 168–169; Pinsky, *The Gospel According to Disney*, 57.

58 Hench, John (1). "Interview with Bob Thomas", Lectures and Transcripts, Walt Disney Studio Archives, Burbank, California.

59 Davis, Marc. Interviewed by Bob Thomas, 1973, Lectures and Transcripts, Walt Disney Studio Archives, Burbank, California.

situated in Fantasyland. Snow White has her "scary adventure" in Disneyland (and her friends the dwarfs, on their new mine train ride in Florida). Sleeping Beauty and Cinderella (in California and Florida, respectively) have their castles. Pinocchio has a ride in Disneyland and a restaurant in the Magic Kingdom. Elements from *Fantasia* are found in Hollywood Studios and Disneyland's Fantasmic show, Disneyland's Mickey and the Magical Map show, and the Magic Kingdom's Fantasyland attraction, Mickey's PhilharMagic. Alice has her own attraction in Disneyland and her friends the Mad Hatter and Cheshire Cat have a teacup ride and restaurant in the Magic Kingdom. Indeed, nearly all the Disney animated classics, including *Dumbo* (1941) and *Peter Pan* (1953), are represented in the parks. The sole exception is 1942's *Bambi*. Many of them, as well as other classics (new and old—some of which have not been made into Disney films) also have miniature representations in Disneyland's Storybook Land boat ride.[60] The release and re-release of these films (on VHS, DVD, and Blu-ray), fueled by nostalgia and the search for more profits, only helps the company keep the stories before an ever-changing public.[61]

After Walt's death, there was something of a pause in the development of the Dis-Historic canon. Even though films like the *Black Cauldron* (1985), *Great Mouse Detective* (1986), and *Oliver and Company* (1988) drew from literature, they failed to find much traction either with the public or within the parks.[62] After Michael Eisner became the head of the company, he was urged to keep in place the production pipeline overseen by Walt's nephew Roy (who had a passion for animation), and Jeffery Katzenberg, who also came to the studio in the early 1980s. Together they created a second golden age for Disney animation starting with 1989's *The Little Mermaid* and 1991's *Beauty and the Beast*. Both films hold true to the old Disney template of true love conquering all, princess/prince dynamics, powerful songs, and over-the-top villains, all pulled from classic literature. New animation since then has attempted to resurrect both the Dis-Historic reliance on classic literature and the translation of many of those stories into attractions at the parks.[63]

---

60 Didier Ghez, editor, *Walt's People: Volume 6: Talking Disney with the Artists Who Knew Him* (New York: Xlibris Corporation, 2008), 250–251.

61 Michael D. Eisner, *Work in Progress* (New York: Random House, 1998), 190–191.

62 Of course, not even every film that Walt had greenlighted—even those that fit into the Dis-Historic canon concept, found a true home in the parks. Take, for example, *101 Dalmatians* (1961) and the *Jungle Book* (1967).

63 Peter Schweizer and Rochelle Schweizer, *Disney, The Mouse Betrayed: Greed,*

The second golden age brought newer kinds of critiques and criticisms. With now fifty-plus years of Dis-Historic cannon to analyze, academics emboldened by new currents within their various disciplines began to take aim at Disney and its films. One of the criticisms levied as the second wave of princess films began to take shape was that these movies were misogynistic and detrimental to how young girls could and should see themselves. None of this was surprising, these critics said, because Walt himself had been against women's rights, pointing to a lack of female animators at the studio during its first golden age. However, academic theory does not exactly fit with the historic facts, casting a much more complicated picture than either detractors or supporters might first argue. While, in the 1940s, opportunities for women were limited at the studio, Walt also made it clear that "if a woman can do the work as well, she is worth as much as a man." As he put it at the time, "We are not interested in low-price help. We are interested in efficient help." "I honestly believe," Walt went on, "that they [women] may eventually contribute something to this business that men never would or could."[64]

None of that is to say that Disney started hiring females as animators. Walt's comments were made in the midst of strike controversy (perhaps as both warning and challenge to male animators thinking of joining the unionization effort) and with war clouds on the horizon (and with them, the threat of very real labor shortages). There were women who worked at Disney during this period, including for a time Walt's wife Lillian (who had worked in the ink department before they were married), who actively contributed to both the movies and eventually the parks. Perhaps none of them compared to Mary Blair, who not only worked on such films as *Cinderella*, *Peter Pan*, and *Alice in Wonderland*, but also was one of the lead designers of the Small World Attraction and the stunning mural in Disney's Contemporary Hotel. However, sex discrimination in hiring is not really what the critics are getting at. Rather, it has more to do with how women are

---

Corruption, and Children at Risk (Washington, D.C.: Regnery Publishing, 1998), 140-145; James B. Stewart, *Disney War* (New York: Simon and Schuster, 2005), 102–103, 106–107, 233; Clark, *Kiddie Lit*, 130; David A. Bossert, *Remembering Roy E. Disney: Memories and Photos of a Storied Life* (New York: Disney Editions, 2013), 11, 64–65, 69; Eisner, *Work in Progress*, 170–173; Elizabeth Bell, Lynda Haas, and Laura Sells, editors, *From Mouse to Mermaid: The Politics of Film, Gender, and Culture* (Indianapolis: Indiana University Press, 1995), 134; Wasko, *Understanding Disney*, 134–135.

64 "In Defense of Walt Disney," http://www.waltdisney.org/storyboard/defense-walt-disney, 5 June 2014; Kathy Merlock Jackson, editor, *Walt Disney: Conversations* (Jackson: University of Mississippi Press, 2006), 17.

represented in Disney films and then the parks. Moreover, it has a name, the princess myth.⁶⁵

According to the critics, little girls who watch Disney movies see the princess only as women waiting for men to save them while wearing beautiful dresses. Little girls idolize the princesses, so the myth goes, and thus opt to be passive and let boys do things for and to them. For some critics, children being able to actually interact with princesses (and the occasional prince) in Fantasyland only exacerbates the princess myth even more. Not everyone is so sure, however, that Disney's version of the stories actually does what the critics claim. Douglas Brode, for example, argues that the standardization undertaken by Disney actually improves the stories in significant ways and "transformed patriarchal old fairy tales into contemporary feminist fables,"⁶⁶ culminating with films such as *Brave* and *Frozen* having no heroic prince at all, only powerful princesses. If Brode is correct, Dis-History's standardization and Americanization allows the stories to grow beyond their original forms.

Debates over the princesses and feminism, though interesting, do not really engage Dis-History as Walt constructed it. For him, the whole point of creating Dis-History was to form a common cultural canon and experiences. Critics of Disney's literary process have been present almost since the moment Dis-History came into being. Frances Clarke Sayers launched her attack on Disney in 1965. She was no passing critic, but rather a member of UCLA's faculty and an expert in children's literature. Her critique was prompted by remarks made by California's superintendent of public instruction, Max Rafferty, who called Walt Disney "the greatest educator of this century." Sayers would have none of it, blasting both the comment and Disney in a letter to the *Los Angeles Times*, in which she said it was time to "call him [Disney] to account for his debasement of the traditional literature of childhood, in films and in the books he publishes."⁶⁷

Sayers was far from finished. In a follow-up interview, done in the wake of her public letter, she continued to criticize Disney. She argued, "The number of books published by Mr. Disney has nothing to do with whether or not he is bringing literature to children. That judgment has got to be based on quality rather than quantity." Furthermore, Disney was a destroyer of folk lore, a man (and company—Sayers personalized

---

65   Jackson, editor, *Walt Disney*, 17; *Washington Post*, 25 January 2016.

66   Douglas Brode, *Multiculturalism and the Mouse: Race and Sex in Disney Entertainment* (Austin: University of Texas Press, 2005), 180–191, 266–268; Pinsky, *The Gospel According to Disney*, 142–143.

67   "Walt Disney Accused," http://archive.hbook.com/magazine/articles/1960s/dec65_sayers.asp, 29 May 2014.

her criticisms, perhaps because in 1965 Walt was still alive and still very much the face of the company) who "eliminates" some aspects of the old stories while going on to "accentuate" other aspects, causing a distorted story to emerge that is so obvious in its presentation (say, of good versus evil) as to leave nothing to the imagination. As she put it, "Disney takes a great masterpiece and telescopes it."[68] The problems with Dis-History's quest for standardization had, and have, far-ranging implications. Sayers worried, to a degree, about the mass-market nature of Disney's multimedia versions, but even more so how by taking a work and making it his own, Walt showed no "regard for the original author or to the original book."[69]

However, Sayers, writing and speaking about Disney in 1965, was also troubled by something else: "As a teacher at the university level, I see that one of the great lacks in the modern college student is a knowledge of the past. He lives in a kind of vacuum between birth and death with very little relationship to anything that has gone on before." Her worry was that Disney was filling that void to some degree: "I think Disney falsifies life by pretending that everything is so sweet, so saccharine, so without any conflict except the obvious conflict of violence."[70]

Much has been made of the Sayers critique, and rightfully so. However, as we have seen, Dis-History need not be negative if one grasps the main idea that Walt was attempting to forge a usable, collective mythology. Because of the animated nature of many of the films she criticized, Sayers may have missed the nuances or failed to grasp that in an hour and a half, you simply cannot do it all. Indeed, by saying the book is better than the movie, Sayers (and other critics) show a literary bias that gives neither animation nor movies their due as an art form, nor as a means to convey deeper cultural truths.

Walt, of course, had counter arguments for his critics. He believed that "films stimulate children to read books on many subjects."[71] In

---

68 "Walt Disney Accused," http://archive.hbook.com/magazine/articles/1960s/dec65_sayers.asp, 29 May 2014.
69 "Walt Disney Accused," http://archive.hbook.com/magazine/articles/1960s/dec65_sayers.asp, 29 May 2014. It is interesting to note that Walt did not always pursue authors for their works, sometimes they came to him hoping for the Disney treatment. Such was the case with Upton Sinclair, who pursued Walt for nearly thirty years until Walt agreed to do a movie based off his book *The Gnomobile*. See, Disney to Sinclair correspondence in the Upton Sinclair papers, Lilly Library, Indiana University, Bloomington, Indiana.
70 "Walt Disney Accused," http://archive.hbook.com/magazine/articles/1960s/dec65_sayers.asp, 29 May 2014.
71 Dave Smith, *The Quotable Walt Disney* (New York: Disney Editions, 2001), 14.

addition, he pointed out that "humans learned life's lessons by seeing real things or pictures with their eyes for ages before they began learning through written or spoken words."[72] He was confident that what Disney was doing with the Dis-Historic canon could help teachers and expand knowledge to students, for he was sure that there was a role for Disney (its films, books, and parks) to play in American "mass education."[73]

Critics and the arguments they enter into with Dis-History are to be expected. However, Dis-History's most pressing issue is not the need to receive the blessing of academics. Rather, it is how to handle being utilized in the parks, places that create memories and that trade in nostalgia, while also needing to be able to change and adapt attractions as the years go on and new guest expectations and interests develop. Guests can become attached to a ride, not because it is the best attraction in the park, but because of memories associated with it.[74] Disney faced backlash, for example, when its *20,000 Leagues Under the Sea* ride was rebranded around *Finding Nemo* in Disneyland and eliminated altogether in the Magic Kingdom. More Dis-Historic contention was felt when Mr. Toad's Wild Ride was rethemed in Florida (though it survives in California) around the Many Adventures of Winnie the Pooh. While both attractions are based off classic children's literature, Toad was not only one of the original park rides brought to Walt Disney World, but it also had cinematic roots in the golden age of Disney animation. All that is left to remind guests of what once was is an Imagineered painting of Toad passing the deed of property over to Owl within the Pooh ride itself.

Perhaps the largest undertaking was the early 2010s expansion of Fantasyland in the Magic Kingdom. In order to find the space, Disney opted to eliminate Mickey's Toontown Fair (which itself had replaced two earlier Mickey-centric attractions, and was similar to Disneyland's Mickey's Toontown), meaning that while the little mouse who started it all could still be found for photo ops in the park, his home was literally bulldozed to make way for more princess-themed attractions. Perhaps no one in Florida and Fantasyland benefited more than did Belle. The heroine of *Beauty and the Beast* was already well represented in Epcot (where she can be found in her native France, of course, but also, strangely enough, as the hostess at the Akershus restaurant in the Norway pavilion), but now guests can visit her enchanted cottage (which actually is her father's home) that whisks you to the Beast's castle (where guests get to re-enact the famous first dance with Belle

---

72 Smith, *The Quotable Walt Disney*, 163.
73 Smith, *The Quotable Walt Disney*, 164–167.
74 Jackson and West, editors, *Disneyland and Culture*, 6.

herself), before exiting to what could be a very enchanted meal at the Be Our Guest food service area (expertly crafted by the Imagineers to replicate the interior of the Beast's castle). In addition to that, there is a quick service possibility at Gaston's tavern. Not to be forgotten, guests can also venture to Prince Eric's castle (from the *Little Mermaid*) for an adventure under the sea. All this casts a shadow over the other new spire in Fantasyland, Rapunzel's tower (from the movie *Tangled*) which forms not only part of the entryway to the land, but also serves as a large rest/bathroom area. The expansion also changed Snow White's role in Fantasyland a bit. Her original ride is now gone. However, in the new Fantasyland, her friends, the Seven Dwarfs, have a mine ride adventure planned for guests. The immersive nature of the newer rides is not lost on guests and the memories they generate, even if older guests still remember the former attractions fondly.

It is understandable that Disney would want to update the parks. Those changes are also carefully balanced against the Dis-Historic process. The company is well aware that expansion and change carry with it the cost of collective memory. Disney knows that younger guests may not be able to have the same experiences as their parents or grandparents did. Making sure that they do come back, though, that the bonds that remain are stronger than the ones lost, is a constant balancing act. Dis-History forces the company to be mindful of the past even as it presses toward the future.[75]

Small World: Imperialist Statement or Utopian Vision?

As we have seen, Dis-History in Fantasyland is not just about creating a standardized canon. It is about expanding that canon. The rides are meant to convey the meaning of cultural myths, standardized by Disney, to guests.[76] Since the end of World War II, American power has been such that American culture became dominate globally. Disney is a part of that domination. Because Disney seemed to embody American values, it came to be viewed as pushing an American ideology because it is an American company. Its true strength is that it has staying power, from generation to generation.[77] What this means for Dis-History is that whatever Walt might have intended it to do for Americans, its reach is now global in scope in ways that he could hardly have imagined.

---

75 Judith A. Adams, *The American Amusement Park Industry: A History of Technology and Thrills* (Boston: Twayne Publishers, 1991), 71.
76 Pugh and Aronstein, editors, *The Disney Middle Ages*, 63.
77 Bell, Haas, and Sells, editors, *From Mouse to Mermaid*, 44, 136.

A SMALL WORLD OF FANTASY(LAND)

Walt could imagine quite a bit—including the children of the world singing about peace and harmony. Nestled near the castle in the Magic Kingdom sits Small World. In this boat ride, guests are whisked away on a global journey, the ubiquitous song lyrics ("it's a small world after all, it's a small world after all...") being the chief constant, as doll-like animatronic children sing it throughout the journey. However, guests note as well that the song is sung in their native languages, until the conclusion. The children are all dressed in culturally correct clothing. It remains one of the most popular attractions in every Disney park it is a part of and it is "the happiest cruise that ever sailed around the world."[78]

It is hardly a surprise. Small World was one of, if not the most, popular attraction that Disney built for New York's 1964 World's Fair. Like the other World's Fair attractions, Small World was a rush to the finish, but it was "beloved" by all who visited it.[79]

In the parks, worlds and races coexist in ways that often do not happen in Disney films or in the world outside.[80] However, that does not stop critics from lambasting the attraction and what it stands for. While some focus on the theme song, most of its detractors focus instead on the utopian stylings of Small World's global vision. According to its critics, Disney forces nations into categories, which defines and teaches foreigners that American ways and things are better than what they have.[81] Critics also claim that what Disney actually did was put forward racial, ethnic, and national stereotypes that foster a "distorted self-image,"[82] while also acting as an agent of "cultural appropriation" and American imperialism.[83]

---

78 Stephen F. Fjellman, *Vinyl Leaves: Walt Disney World and America* (Boulder: Westview Press, 1992), 274–275; Douglas Brode, *Multiculturalism and the Mouse: Race and Sex in Disney Entertainment* (Austin: University of Texas Press, 2005), 2; William A. Covino, "Walt Disney Meets Mary Daly: Invention, Imagination, and the Construction of Community," *JAC* 20(Winter 2000), 153; Wasko, *Understanding Disney*, 63.

79 Neal Gabler, *Walt Disney: The Triumph of the American Imagination* (New York: Vintage Books, 2007), 593; Brode, *Multiculturalism and the Mouse*, 1, 3; Steven Watts, *The Magic Kingdom: Walt Disney and the America Way of Life* (New York: Houghton Mifflin Company, 1997), 416.

80 Pugh and Aronstein, editors, *The Disney Middle Ages*, 212.

81 Ingolf Bogeler and Anthony R. De Souza, editors, *Dialectics of Third World Development* (Montclair, NJ: Allanheld, Osmun & Company, 1980), 122, 126–129.

82 Bogeler and De Souza, editors, *Dialectics of Third World Development*, 130.

83 Brenda Ayres, editor, *The Emperor's Old Groove: Decolonizing Disney's Magic Kingdom* (New York: Peter Lang, 2013), 5.

Such charges are hardly unique to Small World, of course. Critics have held up Donald Duck as proof positive that Disney is an agent of American imperialism. While this is not readily seen in his movie appearances (save, perhaps, in *Saludos Amigos*), it *is* when one looks at Disney comics.[84] Part of the problem is that Donald Duck could be construed as a stereotype himself, of the United States—loud and abrasive with his opinions, hard to understand, and overly patriotic in his sailor suit of red, white, and blue.

If Small World is imperialistic, then critics should note its location. It is in Fantasyland, not Tomorrowland. Douglas Brode argues that Small World, in fact, was a harbinger of diversity or multiculturalism in American life. Indeed, according to Brode, in this respect Walt Disney and his company were very much ahead of not just the rest of America but also the rest of the world in the 1950s and 1960s.[85] The interesting thing is that cultural/national pride is showcased as part of this spirit of unity. Perhaps even more telling is the lack of any governmental institutions. Small World is hardly calling out for a single world government. Rather, this feeling of unity is grassroots, a recognition that everyone shares the planet. And that is a fantastic, powerful statement.

Questions of Fantasy

Fantasyland raises other fundamental questions. If we accept that the parks, with their hub-and-spoke pattern, were Walt's "mental map" of the world, what does it mean that Fantasyland is at the center? What else should be implied by its neighbors, Liberty Square and Tomorrowland? What exactly are we to make of a place in the United States of America, a place that champions, at least on some level, not only American ideals but American ingenuity and business, whose parent company is often the face of American culture and cultural imperialism, that has "Cinderella Castle [as] symbolically and functionally central" to its hope to create American myths? All of these are fair questions to ponder. John Schultz, who articulated the previous statement, laments "democracy's perverse fascination with royalty," something that was noted at least as far back in the American experience as Alexis de Tocqueville in the 1830s.[86]

Perhaps we would do better to try to understand Fantasyland and

---

84 John Taylor, *Storming the Magic Kingdom: Wall Street, the Raiders, and the Battle for Disney* (New York: Alfred A. Knopf, 1987), 25.

85 Brode, *Multiculturalism and the Mouse*, 1–2.

86 John Schultz, "The Fabulous Presumption of Disney World: Magic Kingdom in the Wilderness," *The Georgia Review*, 42(Summer 1988), 277.

Dis-History's employment of a castle there in another way, and for that we should ponder de Tocqueville some more. The famed French visitor to the United States in the nineteenth century wrote in his *Democracy in America* that "nothing struck me more forcibly than the general equality of condition among the people. I readily discovered the prodigious influence which this primary fact exercises on the whole course of society; it gives a peculiar direction to public opinion, and peculiar tenor to the laws; it imparts new maxims to the governing authorities, and peculiar habits to the governed."[87]

If it seems odd or out of place to quote de Tocqueville, go back and reread the first part of the quote: "Nothing struck me more forcibly than the general equality of condition among the people." A man who grew up within a society where a noble class (castles) still clung to existence despite the French Revolution ("liberty, equality, fraternity") and the rise and fall of Napoleon, de Tocqueville's France had seen war, societal upheaval, and change on a scale Americans both during his tour and to the present could scarcely comprehend. In America, de Tocqueville found a new kind of society, one where equality was a bedrock principle. A place where, until Walt, perhaps, castles only existed in the imagination, and after Walt, in the realm of fantasy.

Everywhere you go within Walt Disney World (and perhaps even more so in Disneyland), you stand in line. However, there is something very democratic about that experience. There is a sense of fairness—everyone waits (even if you got into the park early, even if you use Fast Pass)—at some point in the day. You will stand in line, displaying a good deal of order and good behavior, not because you are in a kingdom (with a monarch looking over you from their castle), but because that is the right thing to do. People keep moving and eventually you get to the attraction you are aiming for. The lines are so well laid out (and much of them under shade if not inside and air conditioned) that you do not even notice the Florida weather.[88] Just as important, you are all (friends, family, fellow guests) sharing this experience together.

In Walt Disney World, guests inhabit that virtue de Tocqueville noticed. Here, equality of condition flourishes. In Fantasyland, everyone can visit the castle. Everyone can take part in delving into mythic stories. Everyone is equal in encountering Dis-History. And equality, Americans believe, is what their nation is all about.

---

87 Alexis de Tocqueville, *Democracy in America* (New York: Mentor, 1984), 26.
88 Fjellman, *Vinyl Leaves*, 205–209.

CHAPTER FIVE

Give Me Liberty (Square)!

Experience the Hall of Presidents

Just outside Fantasyland's castle walls, guests to the Magic Kingdom find the Hall of Presidents, a "shrine" of sorts to American democracy and history.[1] Disney bills it as an opportunity to "behold all 43 U.S. Presidents on stage together in a patriotic celebration tracing the history of the United States." Modeled after Independence Hall in Philadelphia, the attraction has included historic items such as George Washington's dental appliances and Abraham Lincoln's leather portfolio in its exhibit cases. Inside the 700-seat theater, guests not only get to witness all the nation's chief executives, via audio-animatronic representation, but also are provided with a sweeping presentation of American history.[2]

The idea of the hall started with Walt Disney himself, who originally conceived it in the late 1950s. Disney's program idea was for a show called "One Nation Under God." Conceptualized for Disneyland in 1958, the program would have had a short film, followed by a reveal of all the presidents, and then Lincoln would give a speech. The project was initially shelved because the technology did not exist to make it a reality.[3] By the 1964 World's Fair, however, Disney was able to create the "Visit with Mr. Lincoln" show for the state of Illinois, and the hall idea was quickly brought back to life. Walt saw the fair as a means to showcase not only what his Imagineers could do, but also as a means to test the popularity of Disney attractions for a possible second park. In addition to Illinois, Disney worked with Ford Motor Company, General Electric,

---

1 Alexander Moore, "Walt Disney World: Bounded Ritual Space and the Playful Pilgrimage Center," *Anthropological Quarterly*, 53(October 1980), 215.

2 "Hall of Presidents," https://disneyworld.disney.go.com/attractions/magic-kingdom/hall-of-presidents/, 19 February 2014. Following the 2016 presidential election, the hall was closed so that Imagineers could prepare to add Donald J. Trump to the show.

3 "Hall of Presidents Original Show," http://waltdatedworld.bravepages.com/id223.htm, 3 June 2014.

and Pepsi-Cola to design attractions. Walt "played hardball" with the State of Illinois for the funding needed to build Lincoln.[4] In the end, he and his Imagineers needed every penny. Though Walt had pitched the idea to Robert Moses, which helped get Disney into the World's Fair, under his original timetable, Lincoln should have been ready in five to ten years. Now, Walt had just over a year.[5]

Walt put a good deal of his own time and energy into the Lincoln project, perhaps working harder than he had since launching Mickey Mouse, and seemed to thrive under the challenge and the deadline of the fair. He wanted Lincoln (and eventually the other presidents) to be an automation—not just because he believed it showcased American technology, but because it was an innovative means to show America's progress as a nation. The Lincoln automation required the creation of all sorts of new technology, becoming a new field of entertainment, which the Imagineers labeled audio-animatronics. Lincoln was "the most sophisticated expression" of audio-animatronics yet developed. It, and the other presidents that followed, was the future's technology made more real than nearly anything in Tomorrowland, but drawing from and representing the past by bringing Lincoln to life in the present.[6] While there really was not enough time, or technology, to fulfill Walt's ambition for showing all the presidents at the fair, he was confident that if Lincoln proved successful, his idea for a hall would eventually be realized.[7]

The goal with the Lincoln auto-animatronic was to "give the illusion of life." And not just any life, but the life of one of America's most

---

4 Warren Leon and Roy Rosenzweig, editors, *History Museums in the United States: A Critical Assessment* (Chicago: University of Illinois Press, 1989), 163; "Hall of Presidents Original Show," http://waltdatedworld.bravepages.com/id223.htm, 3 June 2014; "Look Closer: Great Moments with Mr. Lincoln," http://www.waltdisney.org/storyboard/look-closer-great-moments-mr-lincoln, 5 June 2014; "Great Moments with Mr. Lincoln, "http://www.imagineeringmyway.com/greatmoments%27swi.html, 3 June 2014; Neal Gabler, *Walt Disney: The Triumph of the American Imagination* (New York: Vintage Books, 2007), 581.

5 Dave Smith, *The Quotable Walt Disney* (New York: Disney Editions, 2001), 206.

6 Christopher Finch, *Walt Disney's America* (New York: Abbeville Press, 1978), 74.

7 Leslie Iwerks and John Kenworthy, *The Hand Behind the Mouse: An Intimate Biography of the Man Walt Disney Classed "The Greatest Animator in the World,"* (New York: Disney Editions, 2001), 213–214; Richard Schickel, *The Disney Version: The Life, Times, Art and Commerce of Walt Disney, Third Edition* (Chicago: Ivan R. Dee Publisher, 1997), 335; Gabler, *Walt Disney*, 582; Steven Watts, *The Magic Kingdom: Walt Disney and the America Way of Life* (New York: Houghton Mifflin Company, 1997), 412–413, 417.

important presidents. As Marc Davis, one of Disney's Imagineers, noted "We weren't creating a mechanical man. We were creating the illusion of a man, an illusion of Abraham Lincoln." Achieving that goal was very difficult for the Imagineers. The entire undertaking was both new and incredibly sophisticated, and everyone involved was "nervous" about completing it on time. The Imagineers could craft a good deal of Lincoln, but there were just as many obstacles to its completion, and problems with the animatronic seemed to grow as the fair got closer. Lincoln didn't work at first. It seemed vastly too complicated. Others might have walked away from it. Walt did not.[8] The Imagineers turned to Lockheed Martin's hydraulic division for input on parts. The end result, though, was a crowd pleaser. "Lincoln is man-size—and so realistic it seems made of flesh and blood." And guests were wowed by getting to see a representation of the president deliver the real Lincoln's actual words.[9]

Critics, on the other hand, were horrified by what the Imagineers had created. Some blasted the concept, arguing that God had plagued the construction of the audio-animatronic Lincoln because Walt was trying to re-create the dead president.[10] As one reviewer put it, the Lincoln "electronic robot" was carrying Disney's "concept of cartoon realism to what may be its ultimate point." Critics labeled it as a "grotesquery," dehumanizing to actual humans, and worried that people, because it was Lincoln, would come to worship the machine as if it were the actual president returned to life—literally a Biblical "graven image."[11]

Nothing critics said could diminish Walt's love of the attraction. As a boy, Walt had dressed up as Lincoln before his school classmates and recited the Gettysburg Address. His principal was so taken by the performance, he had Walt go to all the classrooms to recite it. Lincoln and

---

8   Hench, John (1). December 1974 Interview, Lectures and Transcripts, Walt Disney Studio Archives, Burbank, California.

9   Bob Thomas, *Walt Disney: An American Original* (New York: Disney Editions, 1994), 311–312; Eric Smoodin, editor, *Disney Discourse: Producing the Magic Kingdom* (New York: Routledge, 1994), 66; Gabler, *Walt Disney*, 580, 594-595; Didier Ghez, editor, *Walt's People: Volume 5: Talking Disney with the Artists Who Knew Him* (Theme Park Press, 2016), 223; Didier Ghez, editor, *Walt's People: Volume 6: Talking Disney with the Artists Who Knew Him* (New York: Xlibris Corporation, 2008), 219.

10 Thomas, *Walt Disney*, 311–312; Gabler, *Walt Disney*, 580, 594–595.

11 Michael Barrier, *The Animated Man: A Life of Walt Disney* (Los Angeles: University of California Press, 2007), 293; Kathy Merlock Jackson, editor, *Walt Disney: Conversations* (Jackson: University of Mississippi Press, 2006), 82; Richard Schickel, *The Disney Version: The Life, Times, Art and Commerce of Walt Disney, Third Edition* (Chicago: Ivan R. Dee Publisher, 1997), 332, 335, 337.

American history held a special place in Walt's heart ever after.[12] As he later put it, "I have always felt that too few people realize that Lincoln's concepts and philosophies are as useful, as necessary, as applicable today as they were when he pronounced them a century ago. His analysis of freedom and its true meaning, his approach to justice and equality, his own courage and strength –all are as vital in the 1960s as they were during the mid-1800s."[13] Walt loved the show, often tearing up as the performance built to a close.[14] Nor was he alone. Despite the worries of some of the initial critics, the show is also quite powerful. Unlike the Lincoln memorial in Washington, Disney's Lincoln actually speaks to those who come to visit.[15]

Today, the Mr. Lincoln show is part of a shrine both to him and to Walt Disney at the Disneyland Opera House. Located on Main Street, the theater both captures Disney history (a Dis-Historic museum to Walt and his company, akin to One Man's Dream in Florida's Hollywood Studios) as well as the stirring words of America's sixteenth president. Disneyland's Great Moments with Mr. Lincoln has elements of what guests who have visited Epcot and the Magic Kingdom's related attractions have come to expect, including similar images and repeated songs. But Lincoln's words (given voice by actor Royal Dano) are as powerful as when he first uttered them. And Great Moments includes a multicultural Hall of Distinction and showcases various historical displays. The waiting area also includes striking Imagineer paintings, perhaps especially the one of Lincoln alone in the midst of the Civil War, that help strike the appropriate tone before guests enter to see and hear the version of the sixteenth president that Walt helped create.

Lincoln was always a first step. Walt's original plan for Disneyland was for Main Street to connect with Liberty Street (where there would be Edison Square, to talk about American technology and innovation,

---

12 Stephen F. Fjellman, *Vinyl Leaves: Walt Disney World and America* (Boulder: Westview Press, 1992), 69–70.

13 Great Moments with Mr. Lincoln Attraction File, Walt Disney Studio Archives, Burbank, California.

14 "Look Closer: Great Moments with Mr. Lincoln," http://www.waltdisney.org/storyboard/look-closer-great-moments-mr-lincoln, 5 June 2014; "The Disneyland Story presenting Great Moments with Mr. Lincoln," https://disneyland.disney.go.com/attractions/disneyland/disneyland-story/, 19 February 2014; "Great Moments with Mr. Lincoln, " http://www.imagineeringmyway.com/greatmoments%27swi.html, 3 June 2014; Thomas, *Walt Disney*, 38; Gabler, *Walt Disney*, 27.

15 Schickel, *The Disney Version*, 336.

and a New Orleans Square to depict the South).[16] The Magic Kingdom revived the idea, giving rise to Liberty Square, home to the Hall of Presidents. Here, the Imagineers returned to Walt's original vision of "One Nation Under God," and brought to life not just another Lincoln, but all the nation's presidents via audio-animatronics. Key events like the Constitutional Convention, the Whiskey Rebellion, the Nullification Crisis, Sectionalism, and the Civil War, along with scenes showcasing Thomas Edison, the Wright brothers, automobiles, movies, and World War II were a part of the original show put in place for the park's opening. The narrator then noted, "It was a time of transition, a time of progress. But the fundamental philosophy of freedom, the belief in the rights of the individual and the dignity of man remained unaltered. The Constitution was still the rock." Then, before the reveal of all the presidents, a film clip was shown of a Saturn V rocket taking astronauts to the moon, once again merging Walt's love of history with his belief in technology and progress.[17]

Visitors today are greeted by signage that proclaims "Welcome to the Hall of Presidents, A Celebration of Liberty's Leaders." There are portraits of Thomas Jefferson, Woodrow Wilson, Ronald Reagan, George Washington, Andrew Jackson, James Monroe, Franklin Roosevelt, Jimmy Carter, and of course, Abraham Lincoln in the gallery. There is also some presidential memorabilia, gowns worn by First Ladies, two paintings of George Washington, and the carpet seal straight from the White House. Starting with Bill Clinton, all the modern presidents have offered their own voices to the Disney script.[18] Actor Morgan Freeman now narrates the show, and while including all the presidents can cause some people historical discomfort, it is interesting to see who guests do (and do not) applaud, reflecting both the political preferences and memories of the particular audience, as well as the power of a Dis-Historic representation to solicit such reactions to begin with. Yet, the Hall of Presidents truly is a unifying, nationalistic show. And Lincoln remains at the center of it all.[19]

---

16   Gabler, *Walt Disney*, 564.
17   "Hall of Presidents Original Show," http://waltdatedworld.bravepages.com/id223.htm, 3 June 2014.
18   Peter Schweizer and Rochelle Schweizer, *Disney, The Mouse Betrayed: Greed, Corruption, and Children at Risk* (Washington, D.C.: Regnery Publishing, 1998), 265; *The Nation*, 22 November 1993.
19   Leon and Rosenzweig, editors, *History Museums in the United States*, 164; Jane Kuenz, Karen Klugman, Shelton Waldrep, and Susan Willis, editors, *Inside the Mouse: Work and Play at Disney World* (Durham: Duke University Press, 1995), 67; Stephen F. Fjellman, *Vinyl Leaves: Walt Disney World and America*

The hall is a patriotic attraction, not a partisan one. Walt said that when he closed his eyes "the American flag is waving in both of them and up my spine is growing this red, white, and blue stripe."[20] By the time Disneyland was built, both Walt and Roy had moved from the populism and socialism of their father to embrace the Republican Party. And while that transformation was real[21] and was reflected from time to time by the company (Disney's animation division crafted a commercial for Dwight Eisenhower's campaign in 1952, with Roy writing a member of the campaign staff after the election that "we are all very happy at the outcome of the election"),[22] more often than not, they publicly blurred the lines between their personal, public, and corporate politics in significant ways, just as they blurred the lines between education and entertainment.[23] But like Eisenhower, Disney was investing in his parks the idea of a civil religion that upheld the American values Dis-History was helping to articulate via its cultural canon in the midst of the Cold War.[24]

(Boulder: Westview Press, 1992), 69–70.

20 Dave Smith, *The Quotable Walt Disney* (New York: Disney Editions, 2001), 176.

21 Jim Korkis, *Who's Afraid of the Song of the South?* (Orlando: Theme Park Press, 2012), 198–202; Ingolf Bogeler and Anthony R. De Souza, editors, *Dialectics of Third World Development* (Montclair, NJ: Allanheld, Osmun & Company, 1980), 132; Thomas, *Walt Disney*, 227; Gabler, *Walt Disney*, 448.

22 Roy O. Disney to Jacqueline Cochran, 14 November 1952; Bill Anderson to Jacqueline Cochran, 19 November 1952; Jacqueline Cochran Papers, Eisenhower Campaign Series, Box 2, Dwight D. Eisenhower Presidential Library.

23 Gabler, *Walt Disney*, xiii; Douglas Brode, *Multiculturalism and the Mouse: Race and Sex in Disney Entertainment* (Austin: University of Texas Press, 2005), 262; Kathy Merlock Jackson and Mark I. West, editors, *Disneyland and Culture: Essays on the Parks and Their Influence* (Jefferson, NC: McFarland and Company, 2011), 188; Steven Watts, *The Magic Kingdom: Walt Disney and the America Way of Life* (New York: Houghton Mifflin Company, 1997), 70, 71, 76. Walt could also be covertly overt in his politics. In September 1964, he was in Washington, D.C. to receive the Medal of Freedom from President Johnson. Before the ceremony, he had his driver swing by the Lincoln Memorial so that he could stand with his childhood hero. He then went to the ceremony, where he wore a visible Goldwater pin. See Thomas, *Walt Disney*, 327–328; Schickel, *The Disney Version*, 355-356.

24 Gabler, *Walt Disney*, 480–481; Eric Smoodin, *Animating Culture: Hollywood Cartoons from the Sound Era* (New Brunswick, NJ: Rutgers University Press, 1993), 151–168; Watts, *The Magic Kingdom*, 349; Rick Perlstein, *Before the Storm: Barry Goldwater and the Unmaking of the American Consensus* (New York: Hill and Wang, 2001), 327; Eric Avila, *Popular Culture in the Age of White Flight: Fear and Fantasy in Suburban Los Angeles* (Los Angeles: University of California Press, 2004), 116–117.

Walt was working to affirm the American way of life, a place where liberty and freedom were given, and opportunity and progress were expected. Stephen Mills has argued that Disney capitalized on the post-war period, and the rise of American hegemony, to "create not just a profitable enterprise but a heroic agency to promote U.S. values far beyond the limitations inherent in the movies. He saw a window of opportunity to create not a sterile monument to American values but a dynamic agency by which he could promote them, helping to resolve what he saw as a crisis in U.S. society." By raising awareness among Americans of their principles and leaders from the past, Walt was striving to protect the American society of the future by reminding it of its past.[25] As he put said, "It seems to me, that the first duty of culture is to defend freedom and resist all tyranny."[26] Walt's fellow citizens in the 1950s understood his message and gravitated toward it.

Like other aspects of Dis-History, the hall has its critics. It has been condemned for placing the presidents into a show that deprives them of their historic context and complexities, while promoting a "great man" theory of history that has no room for dissent or controversy.[27] And while social historians (who tend to argue for a "bottom-up" version of history, rather than a "top-down" model) were just starting to gain academic traction during Walt's later years, starting with some of the studio's post-war films, critics had latched onto and attacked Disney for using American history and culture as a means to make money (while also standardizing folklore and myth).[28] Thus, they see Liberty Square and Frontierland (the topic of the next chapter) as promoting "history as it should have been," cleaned up and reworked by Disney, not as it actually was.[29] Furthermore, the attraction's "unquestioning

---

25 Stephen F. Mills, "Disney and the Promotions of Synthetic Worlds," *American Studies International*, 28(October 1990), 71; Avila, *Popular Culture in the Age of White Flight*, 38–39; Watts, *The Magic Kingdom*, 348.

26 Dave Smith, *The Quotable Walt Disney* (New York: Disney Editions, 2001), 230.

27 Jane Kuenz, Karen Klugman, Shelton Waldrep, and Susan Willis, editors, *Inside the Mouse: Work and Play at Disney World* (Durham: Duke University Press, 1995), 67; Stephen F. Fjellman, *Vinyl Leaves: Walt Disney World and America* (Boulder: Westview Press, 1992), 71; John Schultz, "The Fabulous Presumption of Disney World: Magic Kingdom in the Wilderness," *The Georgia Review*, 42(Summer 1988), 287, 290; Jackson and West, editors, *Disneyland and Culture*, 117; Kuenz, Klugman, Waldrep, and Willis, editors, *Inside the Mouse*, 168–169.

28 Watts, *The Magic Kingdom*, 250–251.

29 Fjellman, *Vinyl Leaves*, 79; John Schultz, "The Fabulous Presumption of Disney World: Magic Kingdom in the Wilderness," *The Georgia Review*, 42(Summer 1988), 286; Jason Sperb, *Disney's Most Notorious Film: Race,*

patriotism"[30] strikes many critics as anathema, while others are perplexed by Disney's ability to work with the National Archives to create exhibits in its parks as well as to showcase items from within the Presidential Library System.[31] There are even those who complain of the content of the show (arguing it needs more humor or satire) and the hall's layout, arguing that guests are so far away from the presidential audio-animatronics that they cannot truly appreciate the detail and craftsmanship.[32]

Even with such a wide variety of criticisms, the hall remains a popular attraction and one of the most overtly educational ones in the Magic Kingdom. It makes people realize "you get a sum total of something that's much bigger than any one of these individual guys."[33] Guests still come to it, just as they will go and watch Great Moments with Mr. Lincoln at Disneyland, not because it is the only way to interpret the past, but because it is a good way to view the Dis-Historic version of American History—one that is uplifting and like the parks themselves, if not exceptional than at least somewhat magical.

Beyond the Hall and into the Square

At the Magic Kingdom, the Hall of Presidents is housed in Liberty Square. According to Christopher Finch, "It is not surprising to find that at the heart of Walt Disney World is Liberty Square, and at the heart of Liberty Square is the Hall of Presidents."[34] After all, it is the attraction that serves as the best example of Walt's formulation of Dis-History to be not just about forging a culture via fairy tales and myths, but forging an *American* culture that is steeped in history. It is an area of the park whose architecture harkens back to eighteenth-century Philadelphia and Boston. The attention to detail is akin to what one might find either on a Hollywood set or at a living history museum, the latter being the kind of place where "American

---

Convergence, and the Hidden Histories of Song of the South (Austin: University of Texas Press, 2012), 28.

30 Henry A. Giroux, *The Mouse that Roared: Disney and the End of Innocence* (New York: Rowman and Littlefield, 1999), 44; Gabler, *Walt Disney*, 612.

31 *The Nation*, 10 July 2012.

32 Ghez, editor, *Walt's People: Volume 5*, 37; Judith A. Adams, *The American Amusement Park Industry: A History of Technology and Thrills* (Boston: Twayne Publishers, 1991), 146.

33 Hench, John (1). "Interviewed by Gabe Essoe 1972," Lectures and Transcripts

34 Christopher Finch, *Walt Disney's America* (New York: Abbeville Press, 1978), 133-136.

history [is] consumed by eager tourists" in search of a simulated past that is found alive, not in the dead words of books.[35] There is, in other words, an authentic feel to Liberty Square, as if here is where the "true spirit of America" can be found.[36]

But it is the spirt of "a new nation," as a plaque tells visitors, which is "is waiting to be born." Guests are surrounded by representations that invoke the Revolutionary era and the theming of "liberty" goes beyond just the name of the square. There is a Liberty tree (which historically was an elm, though in the Magic Kingdom it is a Southern live oak), with its historic tie to the Stamp Act Crisis, where colonists assembled to protest. There is an exact copy of Philadelphia's Liberty Bell, cast from the same mold as the original. The riverboat that plies the waters nearby is named the *Liberty Belle*. And there is the Liberty Tree Tavern, a favorite of many guests for an all-American-inspired meal. There are public stocks, now used for fun family pictures, not for punishment or denying people of their liberty.[37]

As Walt and his Imagineers first conceived it, Liberty Square was originally going to be Liberty Street, and flow out from Main Street. It was an effort to "dramatize the story of America's historical heritage and its relation to the concept of freedom of enterprise." Initially, Disney hoped it would open in the fall of 1957, and would cover the Revolutionary War period (1770–1780) with halls dedicated to the Declaration of Independence and to the nation's presidents.[38] Outside of the halls, where the street would have shops themed around colonial merchants, there would be an "absence of liberty."[39] Walt wanted Liberty Street's attractions to be free, and he also wanted a series of 24-minute films made for television and schools on American history, with topics to be covered including the Revolution, the Constitution, and the Bill of Rights.[40]

---

35 Leon and Rosenzweig, editors, *History Museums in the United States*, 163–164; Mark Gottdiener, *The Theming of America: Dreams, Visions, and Commercial Spaces* (New York: Westview Press, 1997), 147.

36 *The Imagineering Field Guide to the Magic Kingdom at Walt Disney World: An Imagineer's Eye Tour* (New York: Disney Editions, 2005),65.

37 Virginia A. Salamone and Frank A. Salamone, "Images of Main Street: Disney World and the American Adventure," electronic version, 87.

38 Liberty Street (Misc. DL) file, *News from Disneyland*, Walt Disney Studio Archives, Burbank, California.

39 Liberty Street (Misc. DL) file, Outline for Liberty Street, Walt Disney Studio Archives, Burbank, California.

40 Liberty Street (Misc. DL) file, Interoffice Memo, 2/11/59, Walt Disney Studio Archives, Burbank, California.

But the ultimate denial of liberty in American history, slavery, finds no mention here. Much of the history Disney opts to use in its Liberty Square theming is New England or northeast in its origins, while Frontierland is the west throughout American History. The company tends to avoid probing very deeply into the history of the south.[41] The reason, of course, is that to do so would require making at least tacit mention of the Civil War and slavery, a "hard fact," as numerous historians have pointed out. The closest Liberty Square comes to nearly having to do so is with the inclusion of the Haunted Mansion, and then only because of where the attraction is located in Disneyland. In the California park, the mansion is located in New Orleans Square, a decision that made some sense (bringing a different cultural theming to southern California) and meant that the exterior of the mansion was going to be heavily influenced by southern mansions.[42] By placing the Magic Kingdom's mansion in Liberty Square, the decision was made to theme it as a nineteenth-century Dutch Gothic from the Hudson River, keeping the theme of confronting 999 ghosts (and to a degree, death itself—something that modern guests are much more removed from than their ancestors were), but no longer needing to engage the nation's history of slavery while being physically located in a former Confederate state.[43] As Disney's network of parks has expanded internationally, the location and stories associated with the mansion have changed accordingly, as these American issues fade before Imagineering innovation.[44]

Liberty Square, then, is a place where represented history mixes with historic-inspired fantasy. Indeed, it is in Liberty Square that visitors first experience an attempt by Disney to craft a "heroic mythohistorical American past," according to anthropologist Alexander Moore.[45] Walt had soaked up history while growing up, when the subject "treated the settling of the North American continent and the

---

41 Fjellman, *Vinyl Leaves*, 65.

42 "Haunted Mansion," http://www.disneyparkhistory.com/haunted-mansion.html, 13 March 2015; Jason Surrell, *The Haunted Mansion: Imagineering a Disney Classic* (New York: Disney Editions, 2015), 12-13.

43 *The Imagineering Field Guide to the Magic Kingdom at Walt Disney World: An Imagineer's Eye Tour* (New York: Disney Editions, 2005), 70

44 In Tokyo, the Mansion is in Fantasyland. In Paris, it is in Frontierland. And in Hong Kong, it is in an area known as Mystic Cove. See, Jason Surrell, *The Haunted Mansion: Imagineering a Disney Classic* (New York: Disney Editions, 2015), 41-43, 50-53, 117.

45 Alexander Moore, "Walt Disney World: Bounded Ritual Space and the Playful Pilgrimage Center," *Anthropological Quarterly*, 53(October 1980), 212.

early history of the United States as very serious subjects,"[46] and he was "fascinated" by historic myths—the stories that grew up around actual events.[47] In crafting Dis-History, Walt had to decide what he wanted to represent and what he hoped guests would remember.[48] He opted to stress the concept of liberty and gave guests the chance to encounter some of the leaders of the United States. Here, Dis-History is giving the American past a theme asking guests to preserve it and to carry it forward. And sometimes this Dis-Historic challenge has caused the company to think about doing even more.

The Failure of the Vision: Disney's Great America Park

The Disney name, or brand, has real value. People know what to expect from it. Much of that value has to do with the legacy that Walt, and the animation division of the ever-growing company, created in the minds of Americans. From the company's perspective, that image has to be protected. At the same time, by the early 1980s, a decision was made to grow, expand, and diversify in ways that Walt Disney, and even his brother Roy, had never imagined possible.[49] The company that the Disney brothers founded and led worked well so long as they were both alive, but it was unprepared when they both passed from the scene and Dis-History was faced with a new corporate leadership that was not a part of its creation.[50]

When Walt died, Roy stepped in and took over running the company. However, the elder Disney brother also realized that while he could maintain the company (and make sure Walt Disney World got built), he would not, due to his own age, be able to push it forward. His immediate job was to assure employees, stockholders, and the public that the Disney they knew would continue. To do that, Roy realized that it could not continue to be run strictly as a family business any longer. So he created a much more corporate structure, bringing Donn Tatum

---

46   Christopher Finch, *Walt Disney's America* (New York: Abbeville Press, 1978), 133.

47   Finch, *Walt Disney's America*, 136.

48   Benedict Anderson, *Imagined Communities: Reflections on the Origin and Spread of Nationalism* (New York: Verso Press, 1998), 197–198; Benjamin R. Barber, *Jihad vs. McWorld* (New York: Ballantine Books, 1996), 135–136.

49   Schweizer and Schweizer, *Disney, The Mouse Betrayed*, 135-139; Michael Wallace, "Serious Fun," *The Public Historian*, 17(Autumn 1995), 83.

50   Didier Ghez, editor, *Walt's People: Volume 1: Talking Disney with the Artists Who Knew Him* (Theme Park Press, 2014), 68, 80.

(vice president of administration, known as a "Roy man"), E. Cardon Walker (from the marketing department, known as a "Walt man"), Ron Miller (Walt's son-in-law and a film producer), Roy's son Roy E. (who was in the animation department), and two of the company's long-time producers, Bill Walsh and Bill Anderson, into an executive committee.[51] Roy died in 1971, shortly after the Magic Kingdom opened, and over the next few years, Tatum, Walker, and Miller all succeeded him in running the company. While committed to the company's success and Dis-History's role in it, none of them were a match for the Disney brothers when it came to actually leading the company.[52]

The committee system Roy created to run the company produced lots of ideas, but after he died, it had no real head to make sure things actually got done. The creative people needed a unified vision. They were largely working off of Walt's vision, but he was no longer there to act as an "umpire" or guide for their various ideas.[53] In many ways, the committee was not ready for the changes in the motion picture market during the 1970s. The Disney executives were largely insular and stayed out of the Hollywood scene and network to a large extent. Under both Tatum and Walker, the company seemed cautious, if not tentative. Both men understood the Disney image, did not want to harm the company's reputation, and they wanted things done correctly. They also were averse to embracing some new technology. Walker, for example, refused to approve various expenses, including the then new technology of car phones.[54]

By the early 1980s, the company was in the hands of Walt's son-in-law, Ron Miller. Miller was well liked personally within the company. He had played football at both the collegiate and professional levels, and had served in the Army before coming to work as a producer for the Disney studio. Like Walker, Miller wanted to imitate Walt's formula for success, but (perhaps because he was younger) was also

---

51 Joe Flower, *Prince of the Magic Kingdom: Michael Eisner and the Re-Making of Disney* (New York: John Wiley and Sons, Inc., 1991), 59; Janet Wasko, *Understanding Disney: The Manufacture of Fantasy* (Cambridge: Polity Press, 2001), 30.

52 Eric Smoodin, editor, *Disney Discourse: Producing the Magic Kingdom* (New York: Routledge, 1994), 97–99; Bob Thomas, *Building a Company: Roy O. Disney and the Creation of an Entertainment Empire* (New York: Hyperion, 1998), 304, 311-314, 339-341; Flower, *Prince of the Magic Kingdom*, 50, 52, 57; Marty Sklar, *Dream It! Do It!: My Half-Century Creating Disney's Magic Kingdoms* (New York: Disney Editions, 2013), 6–7.

53 Flower, *Prince of the Magic Kingdom*, 5, 51–54.

54 Wasko, *Understanding Disney*, 31; Flower, *Prince of the Magic Kingdom*, 83–87.

willing to push the company in new directions.⁵⁵ Miller, in many ways, laid the groundwork for much of the success Disney had in the late 1980s and early 1990s, and beyond. As Jim Korkis points out, Miller's initiatives or things that opened on his watch included expanding into cable television (the Disney Channel), expanding the parks (Epcot, Tokyo Disney), expansion into more adult-themed movies (*Splash* starring Tom Hanks, for example) with a new studio label (Touchstone Pictures), giving young animators (like Tim Burton) their first opportunities, the release of the first Walt Disney Home Entertainment videotapes, forays into new kinds of computer animation (like *Who Framed Roger Rabbit* and *Tron*) that mixed with live action. All these things happened on Miller's watch.⁵⁶

The problem was that it took years for some of these changes and innovations to bear fruit, and time was not on Miller's side. The Tatum/Walker years paralyzed the studio. Revenues were, generally speaking, down in the parks and with both live-action and animated films (some of which were box office bombs, shortages were developing in the production pipeline, and the new initiatives were not yet generating much money (and costing money in the process).⁵⁷

The listlessness and internal dissension only fed speculation that the company was ripe for a hostile takeover. As corporate raiders began to make runs on Disney stock, Miller and his advisors became frantic in heading them off. Try as they might to solve the various challenges, those leading the Disney company found that the mid-1980s were a perilous time for a company that had publicly traded shares on Wall Street, due to the perception that its assets were worth much more than its stock. In 1984 Disney became the target of a hostile takeover bid, led by Saul Steinberg, who planned to divvy it up and sell off the pieces. Miller essentially bought him off, paying some $60 million to buy back stock, while also recruiting "white knights" in the form of the Bass family to purchase additional Disney stock, to keep it out

---

55 Flower, *Prince of the Magic Kingdom*, 57, 140.

56 "In Praise of Ron Miller," http://www.mouseplanet.com/11189/In_Praise_of_Ron_Miller, 15 October 2015.

57 Andi Stein, *Why We Love Disney: The Power of the Disney Brand* (New York: Peter Lang, 2011), 36; Michael D. Eisner, *Work in Progress* (New York: Random House, 1998), 116, 156–157, 168–169; Flower, *Prince of the Magic Kingdom*, 138–139; John Taylor, *Storming the Magic Kingdom: Wall Street, the Raiders, and the Battle for Disney* (New York: Alfred A. Knopf, 1987), viii-ix, 3–7, 14, 20–21, 24, 27, 95; Alan Bryman, *Disney and His Worlds* (New York: Routledge, 1995—ebook version), 39; Eric Smoodin, editor, *Disney Discourse: Producing the Magic Kingdom* (New York: Routledge, 1994), 78-79.

of the hands of the corporate raiders. Beyond saving itself immediately, Disney leadership seemed to have no plans to make sure such a raid on the company never happened again.[58]

Miller had other issues to deal with as well. His cousin-in-law, Roy E. Disney, was disgruntled with the direction the company was headed. Roy felt that his ideas were ignored, his voice unheard, and had even suffered the ultimate indignity of losing his company parking spot. In protest, he resigned from the board and went into real-estate investment, making new partnerships outside of the Disney orbit. In the wake of the Steinberg takeover attempt, Roy was brought back onto the board. There he began working with one of his real-estate contacts, Stanley Gold, to begin unseating Miller.[59]

Roy felt he had to make the move to preserve both the family company and his own financial success. He was dedicated to the company. Roy found it a burden, at times, to have the last name of Disney, because it came with responsibilities. His decision to unseat Miller caused a rift within the family, but the eventual change in management also helped kickstart the company's second golden age. He loved the studio that his father and uncle had built, and believed it needed to be dedicated to the art of animation (and to the artists that produced it), not just be run like a regular company. Roy believed strongly in the animation division and had pushed to standardize the voices of characters, meaning that for the first time Disney was locking in their voice talent.[60]

Energized, Roy began advancing Michael Eisner to head the company his uncle and father had started. Eisner had a proven Hollywood track record, but little corporate experience and no proof he could do any better at the job than Ron Miller. Eisner was brought in to lead the company on September 22, 1984. He had always wanted to work at Disney and was ready for new challenges after working at Paramount and ABC. To many, Disney was a "dusty" company. It seemed to be passing on movies that became hits, was only slowly embracing home-video sales, was hardly advertising its parks, and in many ways was coasting on its past. Eisner's job was to reverse those perceptions as quickly as possible. But changing the corporate culture also meant changing many of the people in the corporation and, some felt, the corporate values Walt had instilled in the company that bore

---

58 Flower, *Prince of the Magic Kingdom*, 100–101, 110–111, 116–117; David A. Bossert, *Remembering Roy E. Disney: Memories and Photos of a Storied Life* (New York: Disney Editions, 2013), 130–134.

59 Flower, *Prince of the Magic Kingdom*, 62–63; Stein, *Why We Love Disney*, 35.

60 Bossert, *Remembering Roy E. Disney*, 37, 41, 46–47, 77, 126–127, 129, 136, 144–145; Flower, *Prince of the Magic Kingdom*, 148.

his name.⁶¹ Of course, Eisner had much to learn about how Disney operated. But he had the support of Roy E. Disney who had gotten to know him a few years before, while both served on the board of the California Institute of the Arts. He was poised to bring fresh thinking to the company, including how it used Dis-History.⁶²

Corporations are not ruined or saved by one man, and in those first few years, Eisner had a team in place that made Disney's turnaround happen.⁶³ Frank Wells was a key part of this transformation. Wells was a Rhodes Scholar and former vice-chairman of Warner Brothers; he was also "more conservative than Eisner in many ways," according to Joe Flower, and "a stronger voice for tradition." He was, in other words, Eisner's Roy. Eisner relied on Wells a great deal, and the two men started to craft new ways to maximize and diversify products, including making more money from the park system.⁶⁴ For help with reinvigorating the movie arm of the studio, Eisner turned to Jeffrey Katzenberg, who was wonderful at building relationships with talent and picking scripts.⁶⁵ Those who had worked with Walt were traumatized by the changes that came to the studio. It was not how it had once been.⁶⁶

---

61   John Taylor, *Storming the Magic Kingdom: Wall Street, the Raiders, and the Battle for Disney* (New York: Alfred A. Knopf, 1987), 206–209, 220; Michael Wallace, *Mickey Mouse History and Other Essays on American Memory* (Philadelphia: Temple University Press, 1996), 160–161; Schweizer and Schweizer, *Disney, The Mouse Betrayed*, 4-11; Flower, *Prince of the Magic Kingdom*, 40–41, 68-69, 134–135, 152.

62   Marty Sklar, *Dream It! Do It!: My Half-Century Creating Disney's Magic Kingdoms* (New York: Disney Editions, 2013), 232; Taylor, *Storming the Magic Kingdom*, 54–55, 78–79, 154, 198, 210–211; James B. Stewart, *Disney War* (New York: Simon and Schuster, 2005), 44, 62; Michael D. Eisner, *Work in Progress* (New York: Random House, 1998), 117; Bossert, *Remembering Roy E. Disney*, 11.

63   Eric Smoodin, editor, *Disney Discourse: Producing the Magic Kingdom* (New York: Routledge, 1994), 86; Flower, *Prince of the Magic Kingdom*, 163.

64   Smoodin, editor, *Disney Discourse*, 80–81, 86, 93; Eisner, *Work in Progress*, 4, 147–148, 208–209, 213–221; Janet Wasko, *Understanding Disney: The Manufacture of Fantasy* (Cambridge: Polity Press, 2001), 32; Flower, *Prince of the Magic Kingdom*, 162, 170–173, 191; Bossert, *Remembering Roy E. Disney*, 137; Stewart, *Disney War*, 32; Stein, *Why We Love Disney*, 37; Schweizer and Schweizer, *Disney, The Mouse Betrayed*, 29–30, 39.

65   Eisner, *Work in Progress*, 147; Taylor, *Storming the Magic Kingdom*, 240–243. As Taylor points out, Eisner's revolution would not have been possible had corporate raiders not been circling Disney and forced the company to shake things up in order to survive intact (246).

66   Didier Ghez, editor, *Walt's People: Volume 5: Talking Disney with the Artists Who Knew Him* (Theme Park Press, 2016), 385–386.

Part of Eisner's quest to truly corporatize Disney was his belief in taking "quality shots" (and lots of them) to win people's hard-earned money. His team had lots of ideas in those first few years. Some were great, some were not, but virtually all of them were tested out by Disney in one form or another.[67] Eisner understood in ways that Miller did not (but Walt had) that it was not enough for Disney to put out a product that appealed to parents and children, nor was it enough to even diversify to the point where the company turned out films that appealed to a wider audience. The leadership of the company also had to promote the corporation, both to the general public as well as to the investors on Wall Street.[68]

The new management team knew that if they could combine all their "profit centers" they could make more money. The easiest way to do that while also strengthening the Disney brand was focusing on the parks, which continued to be a money-maker for Disney. Wells believed the parks were "underutilized" and along with others began pushing to better advertise them. Eisner wanted the parks to revamp, grow, and expand. The problem, of course, was that parks undergoing massive construction projects might deter people from coming at all in the short term (or, worse yet, going to a competitor's park). The solution was to expand the number of parks Disney owned, giving guests more choices and diverting them to new parks (once built) while the older ones underwent construction. Eisner envisioned a "third generation theme park," themed around different concepts, potentially located in areas other than Florida or California.[69]

Disney's America was going to be the company's first step in this new direction.[70] Turing to Dis-History, Eisner's team took a fresh look at Walt's ideas and concepts for what became Liberty Square. The new park they soon envisioned would be smaller than its American cousins, and themed around American history. Eisner and his team selected the greater Washington, D.C. area for the park and found 2,300 acres (owned by Exxon) a mere twenty miles from the nation's capital. Eisner was sure they could find additional land just as easily. Virginia was especially attractive because of existing theme parks, historic sites, and cultural attractions within the state, as well as its

---

67 Flower, *Prince of the Magic Kingdom*, 184, 194–195.
68 Taylor, *Storming the Magic Kingdom*, 247
69 Eisner, *Work in Progress*, 234–235; Flower, *Prince of the Magic Kingdom*, 153, 158, 185-186, 238; Cary Carson, "Mirror, Mirror, on the Wall, Whose History is the Fairest of Them All?" *The Public Historian*, 17(Autumn 1995), 63; James B. Stewart, *Disney War* (New York: Simon and Schuster, 2005), 60.
70 Michael Wallace, "Serious Fun," *The Public Historian*, 17(Autumn 1995), 84.

GIVE ME LIBERTY (SQUARE)!

proximity to airports and population centers. It was hoped that, once completed, the American-made revenues would help fund further development of Disneyland and Walt Disney World, as well as make up for the financial crisis that seemed to be enveloping the recently opened park in France.[71]

In some ways, the park idea was Eisner's attempt to utilize Dis-History in a new way. The company had done a good deal of planning, and believed they were being both historically accurate as well as providing edutainment (entertainment that also educated) based attractions. Unlike Walt's purchase of land in Florida some three decades before, Disney's acquisition and plans for a new park leaked to the press well ahead of the company's schedule.[72] And so, in November 1993, the company was forced to announce that the new park "would be a 'serious fun celebration' of U.S. history," and stated it would be "a source of pride and unity for all Americans." The park was to cover American history from 1600 to 1945—with additional land set aside for future development as needed. Crossroads USA would be a typical nineteenth-century town setting, complete with retail space. President's Square would host a setting for animatronic American statesmen of the past to interact with park guests. Native America would re-create a Powhatan Indian village and have a water ride inspired by Lewis and Clark's travels west. The Civil War Fort would include areas to discuss both the Union and Confederate soldiers' experiences, a Circle-Vision movie, and a nighttime reenactment of the *Monitor* and *Merrimac* ironclad battle. Enterprise would showcase a factory town of the late nineteenth and early twentieth centuries, and have a roller coaster called the Industrial Revolution. We The People would discuss immigration in an Ellis Island-type setting, and why people (from Native Americans to the present) came to America, as well as conflict between groups. Victory Field was to be based around a World War II airfield, complete with computer-simulated parachute drops and tank and weapons displays. State Fair would include a Ferris wheel, a small roller coaster, and baseball-themed entertainment. And the Family Farm would showcase crops, dairy cattle, ice-cream making, a country wedding, barn dancing, and a buffet, all in the most ideal way possible. Of course, like its counterparts in California and Florida, the park was to be encircled by antique steam trains as well.[73]

---

71 Eisner, *Work in Progress*, 319-323; Michael Wallace, *Mickey Mouse History and Other Essays on American Memory* (Philadelphia: Temple University Press, 1996), 162–163.

72 Eisner, *Work in Progress*, 323–325.

73 Wallace, "Serious Fun," 84; Marcia G. Synnott, "Disney's America: Whose

The proposed park relied on the "Disney way" of construction, design, and requisite appeals to nostalgia. Crossroads USA was based off of Main Street. President's Square was a revamped Hall of Presidents. The CircleVision movie about the Civil War, was similar to what Disney has done at Epcot, while the re-created ironclad battle is akin to Fantasmic at Hollywood Studios, with a dose of Rivers of America from Disneyland thrown in for good measure. The World War II battle simulations sound quite familiar to anyone who has ever gone on Star Tours (the Star Wars ride) at Hollywood Studios. And the trains would have likely been the only non-pedestrian conveyance in the park.[74]

Disney officials believed they could construct a park that truly engaged guests about the nation's history. They believed they could do so without hiding portions of that history (at least including the blemishes, if not always the warts), while still retaining the sense of pride, patriotism, and progress that Walt had first instilled at Disneyland. They were not proposing a "Pollyanna" view of history in the least and acknowledged that there were areas within American history that could be contentious. However, they believed that they could inspire guests to go learn more about the topics they presented. Indeed, Disney offered Colonial Williamsburg, Mount Vernon, and the Smithsonian the opportunity to have kiosks at the park, to let guests know about other area attractions.[75]

What Disney had not planned for was how quickly opposition formed. The first wave came from the Piedmont Environmental Council (aided by landowners with last names like DuPont and Mellon—the state's "new" first families) who questioned the water and air pollution (not to mention the traffic) the estimated 30,000 daily visitors would generate. They feared an influx of Disney guests into their community, which would also bring "gaudy hotels and restaurants, and the Disneyland-ization of their corner of Virginia."[76] More

---

Patrimony, Whose Profits, Whose Past?" *The Public Historian*, 17 (Autumn 1995), 49, 54-55; "Disney's America and the Historian's Dilemma," http://www.themeparkinsider.com/flume/201311/3753/, 19 February 2014.

74 Wasko, *Understanding Disney*, 173.

75 Michael Wallace, *Mickey Mouse History and Other Essays on American Memory* (Philadelphia: Temple University Press, 1996), 164; Synnott, "Disney's America: Whose Patrimony, Whose Profits, Whose Past?," 56–57; Wallace, "Serious Fun," 85; Cary Carson, "Mirror, Mirror, on the Wall, Whose History is the Fairest of Them All?" *The Public Historian*, 17(Autumn 1995), 62; Flower, *Prince of the Magic Kingdom*, 190.

76 Otis L. Graham, Jr., "Editor's Corner: Learning Together: Disney and the Historians," *The Public Historian*, 16(Autumn, 1994), 6; "Disney's

damning, and surprising to Disney, was the opposition from historians. Forming the Protect Historic America group, C. Vann Woodward, John Hope Franklin, James McPherson, Arthur M. Schlesinger, Jr., David McCullough, Shelby Foote, and Ken Burns all came out as opposed to the park, as much for its proposed size as for its mix of history and education. Woodward, in particular, believed that Disney was attempting to create "synthetic history" in an area rich with "real history" already, including the nearby Manassas National Battlefield Park.[77] Both sides viewed Virginia as the nexus of the national nativity narrative and had concerns about what a park based on Dis-Historic broad culture might do to their "old" Virginia.

The questions historians laid at the feet of Disney's proposal had as much to do with presentation at they did with content. The group believed Disney was proposing little more than a historical veneer on consumerism. Could Dis-History do anything but "dumb down" America's story? Could Disney really capture the horrors of war or slavery? What would it make of labor unrest? Would the Native American area deal with the conquest of the west (and at least the broken treaties, if not what some historians argued was genocidal warfare)? Would just an American-centric park really attract enough visitors to justify its existence? They also raised concerns about what this Dis-Historic park was going to omit: problems that industry/corporations cause, as well as issues centering on race, class, and gender, and conflict. The "selective reconstruction of the past" is always problematic they pointed out. How much more so in a theme park?[78]

Dis-History's mythic past has long frustrated historians, as we have seen. But with Disney's America, the company was proposing to build an entire park around the concept in close proximity to where some of that history actually took place. Academic critics unloaded a good deal of scholarly rage at the proposed park.[79] Eisner did not help matters by making statements about how boring he found history

---

America and the Historian's Dilemma," http://www.themeparkinsider.com/flume/201311/3753/, 19 February 2014

77 Graham, Jr., "Editor's Corner: Learning Together: Disney and the Historians," 6.

78 Synnott, "Disney's America: Whose Patrimony, Whose Profits, Whose Past?,", 45–47; "Disney's America and the Historian's Dilemma," http://www.themeparkinsider.com/flume/201311/3753/, 19 February 2014; Wasko, *Understanding Disney*, 173–174.

79 Patricia Mooney-Melvin, "Beyond the Book: Historians and the Interpretive Challenge," *The Public Historian*, 17(Autumn 1995), 76; William F. Van Wert, "Disney World and Posthistory," *Cultural Critique*, 32(Winter, 1995–1996), 213.

as a child, and other company officials only made matters worse by arguing that they could, through set pieces and cast members, make guests to the proposed park "feel," for example, as though they were really in the Civil War. Scholars openly worried that Disney might "cheapen" serious subjects by not going into enough detail or simply by having them in a park where fun was on the minds of its guests much more than learning.[80] George Sanchez of the University of Michigan said Disney "ignored" too much. Critics pointed out that the current parks were void of social conflict and that it was difficult to even imagine a theme park based on such a premise. Indeed, they argued, Disney did not even have the right to try and interpret such events for the general public.[81]

Many of the loudest professional critics challenged the park not because they were worried about mixing history with entertainment, but because a Disney version of that mixture would undoubtedly be more popular than what they themselves were doing. By the early 1990s, museums saw themselves in a battle with Disney for guests and consumer spending. As Cary Carson noted of the reaction at Colonial Williamsburg, Disney's proposed park "challenged our monopoly, it rattled our complacency, and it mocked our claims to entertain and educate the general public."[82] Disney "is both feared and admired by museums like Colonial Williamsburg." As such, many professional public historians believe Disney and its fellow theme-park "ilk" must be disparaged at every turn,[83] even as museums and historic centers admired and tried to emulate Disney's narrative theming and "technical wizardry that so entrances children and grown-ups."[84]

---

80 Synnott, "Disney's America: Whose Patrimony, Whose Profits, Whose Past,?" 52-53; Carson, "Mirror, Mirror, on the Wall, Whose History is the Fairest of Them All?", 66; Wallace, "Serious Fun," 87.

81 Eisner, *Work in Progress*, 328-330; Michael R. Real, *Mass-Mediated Culture* (Englewood Cliffs, New Jersey: Prentice-Hall, 1977), 82; William F. Van Wert, "Disney World and Posthistory," *Cultural Critique*, 32(Winter, 1995–1996), 189; Synnott, "Disney's America: Whose Patrimony, Whose Profits, Whose Past?" 53.

82 John Terrell, "Disneyland and the Future of Museum Anthropology," *American Anthropologist*, 93(March 1991), 152; Carson, "Mirror, Mirror, on the Wall, Whose History is the Fairest of Them All?" 61.

83 Eric Gable and Richard Handler, "Public History, Private Memory: Notes from the Ethnography of Colonial Williamsburg, Virginia, USA," *Ethnos: Journal of Anthropology*, 65:2 (2000), 242.

84 *New York Times*, 29 September 1994; Michael Wallace, *Mickey Mouse History and Other Essays on American Memory* (Philadelphia: Temple University Press, 1996), 21.

Opposition to the park left hidden the degree to which academic and public historians were united in their defense of history only by a common (Disney) opponent. People like to visit historic sites and academic historians often have a difficult time accepting the fact that once a place is preserved and an interpretation for what went on there is offered, the end result is a mixture of education and entertainment.[85] And yet, public historians understood all too well what Disney was trying to do and the pitfalls associated with trying to be informative as well as entertaining. Indeed, public historians knew that virtually all the questions that critics of the park were asking of Disney, as well as their more probing questions about presenting the past to popular audiences, could just as easily be leveled at them, and they, like Disney, would have just as hard of a time answering the critics' attacks with articulate answers that might settle the debate in their favor.[86]

Disney was surprised at the opposition of historians. After all, one of the company's arguments was that visitors would flow out of their encounter with Dis-History, inspired to visit national parks and battlefields nearby. Not to mention that the historians were objecting to a concept that had not been fully realized yet, let alone built—-the park was still in the planning phases.[87] Eisner had taken "a deep personal interest" in the proposed park both as a part of his larger agenda and because he was confident that Disney could "educate through entertainment" in ways that academics did not appreciate. He was shocked that so many in both the community and academia stood against the proposal. Eisner pointed to surveys that showed that few American high-school graduates really grasped their nation's history. But in trying to talk about it, and what Disney might be able to do about it, he came off as "smug and arrogant." He knew, in retrospect, how much this hurt their chances—almost as much as failing to realize the sheer number of wealthy landowners did.[88]

---

[85] Patricia Mooney-Melvin, "Beyond the Book: Historians and the Interpretive Challenge," *The Public Historian*, 17(Autumn 1995), 75–77; Wallace, *Mickey Mouse History*, 122–123; Gable and Handler, "Public History, Private Memory," 242–243.

[86] Douglas Greenberg, "History is a Luxury": Mrs. Thatcher, Mr. Disney, and (Public) History," *Reviews in American History*, 26(March 1998), 303; Carson, "Mirror, Mirror, on the Wall, Whose History is the Fairest of Them All?" 64.

[87] Graham, Jr., "Editor's Corner: Learning Together: Disney and the Historians," 6–7.

[88] Eisner, *Work in Progress*, 330-335; Synnott, "Disney's America: Whose Patrimony, Whose Profits, Whose Past?" 44; Wallace, "Serious Fun," 86; Wallace, *Mickey Mouse History and Other Essays on American Memory*, 166.

Ironically, part of the problem Disney faced with academics was that the version of Dis-History they were proposing for the new park was itself utilizing academic theory in formulating its lands, but doing so outside academia. The thematic grouping of, say, industrial heritage or immigration is an interesting way to study or showcase a topic, and something that is often found in scholarship and on college campuses. And, according to Richard Francaviglia, that may have hurt Disney's chances with professional historians, who viewed such ideas in a very proprietary sense.[89] Disney attempted in other ways to show historians that they could do history, indeed, that Dis-History had its place. One of their advisors was historian Eric Foner, who counseled Disney that no matter what they did, there was going to be criticism and that pressing ahead might be the only way to deal with it.[90]

However, the twin forces of opposition were devastating to the company's hopes for the park. The public relations onslaught from the landowners and the historians (which many on the Disney side of the dispute believed was fueled by misinformation) hurt the company's image. Indeed, Eisner was accused of being "the man who would destroy American history."[91] Additionally, the Euro-Disney park was in financial chaos, needing loans and outside investment to stay open.[92] And then, Frank Wells died in a helicopter crash, triggering a nasty succession crisis that eventually led to Jeffery Katzenberger leaving Disney. And to make matters worse, in the midst of all this, Eisner was forced to undergo emergency heart bypass surgery.[93]

Though initially inclined to fight and build the park, Disney, with little notice to its allies, eventually gave up. As the *New York Times* reported in September 1994, the project "was reviled by historians and environmentalists and hotly debated at local planning boards as well as the United States Senate." Despite the support of Virginia's governor and other political leaders, Disney lost the public-relations battle both locally and to a degree nationally, bordering on a debacle.

---

89 Richard Francaviglia, "History after Disney: The Significance of 'Imagineered' Historical Places," *The Public Historian*, 17(Autumn 1995), 74; Wallace, *Mickey Mouse History and Other Essays on American Memory*, 92.

90 Eisner, *Work in Progress*, 329–331.

91 Wallace, *Mickey Mouse History and Other Essays on American Memory*, 154–165; *New York Times*, 29 September 1994; Eisner, *Work in Progress*, 335; Stewart, *Disney War*, 190.

92 Synnott, "Disney's America: Whose Patrimony, Whose Profits, Whose Past?" 48.

93 Alan Bryman, *Disney and His Worlds* (New York: Routledge, 1995; ebook version), 60; Eisner, *Work in Progress*, 336–337.

After the announcement was made that Disney was shelving plans for the new park, some of the historians who had vocally opposed it did publicly concede that it might have some value, but needed to be located someplace other than Virginia.[94]

Ultimately, the demise of Disney's America did little to Dis-History or the company's use of the past. Eisner later called the failure of the history park as both "painful" and "enlightening." He also recognized that the name alone was a mistake. While they had wanted to associate "Disney with America and America with Disney," to critics the name implied Disney was trying to "own" American history.[95] But the demise of the park did not stop Eisner from pursuing new and interesting ideas within either Dis-History or the parks. And, in perhaps the ultimate irony, while the professional historians who had opposed the park might have achieved a sense of triumph, those who opposed it as a development have watched as much of the land Disney wanted to build on has been turned into the suburban sprawl they feared the House of Mouse would bring to their portion of Virginia.[96]

(Re)Vision: Dis-History After Disney's America

In some respects, it was the failure of Disney's America that led to the company reaching out to historians in a more systematic way and to a new era for Dis-History.[97] The company's ally, historian Eric Foner, helped rewrite the script for Abraham Lincoln in the parks. One of the nation's leading experts on slavery, anti-slavery, and Reconstruction, Foner told Disney that the Great Emancipator had to make mention of slavery for his importance to the nation to be appreciated. While contentious at the time, the changes he proposed are not nearly as controversial as some once imagined. Disney's Lincoln, after all, was still speaking words first uttered by the actual Abraham Lincoln.[98] The

---

94   Synnott, "Disney's America: Whose Patrimony, Whose Profits, Whose Past?" 43; *New York Times*, 29 September 1994; Schweizer and Schweizer, *Disney, The Mouse Betrayed*, 269-270; Stewart, *Disney War*, 191; Eisner, *Work in Progress*, 167, 327–328; Wallace, *Mickey Mouse History and Other Essays on American Memory*, 167.

95   Eisner, *Work in Progress*, 318–320.

96   "Disney's America and the Historian's Dilemma," http://www.themeparkinsider.com/flume/201311/3753/, 19 February 2014

97   Synnott, "Disney's America: Whose Patrimony, Whose Profits, Whose Past?" 51.

98   Eisner, *Work in Progress*, 326; Real, *Mass-Mediated Culture*, 69; Wallace,

focus of the Hall of Presidents became less about democracy and the presidents, and more about freedom as an "unfinished agenda." John Wiener saw the changes as "progressive."[99] Disney also started working with historian James Oliver Horton as well, who noted that if Disney was going to use history, then historians should help them do it well.[100]

One of the chief criticisms of Dis-History (historically) has been that it avoids dealing with "messy" aspects of the past. While that is true, to a degree, in the parks, it is not always accurate when it comes to Dis-History's cinematic application.[101] Perhaps nowhere are both of these Dis-Historic trends seen more clearly than in the animated film *Pocahontas*. First pitched at roughly the same time that Disney's America was being put on the drawing boards, the film was released the year after Disney pulled out of the Virginia park idea. Mark Pinsky speculates that this chain of events explains not only why the movie was made, but the version of the Pocahontas story that ultimately became part of the Disney canon.[102] Today, Pocahontas can be found as part of the Fantasmic show—a Disney water and fireworks display, utilizing characters, at both Disneyland and at Hollywood Studios. Why, exactly, is harder to pinpoint. Perhaps Pocahonas is there to serve as a reminder, both of Dis-History's importance and what might have been with Disney's America.

At the time, a Pocahontas animated film made perfect sense for Disney. The story was one, at least in its basic outline, that many Americans knew. A Native American princess saved English settlers (both in the form of John Smith and by aiding the colonists with relations with her people), thus averting disaster at Jamestown, the first permanent English settlement in the New World. Furthermore, it is enshrined as part of America's founding myth. In the United States Capitol, Pocahontas is represented twice. She is depicted saving John

---

"Serious Fun," 84; Richard Snow, "Disney: Coast to Coast," http://www.americanheritage.com/content/disney-coast-coast, 2 June 2014; Didier Ghez, editor, *Walt's People: Volume 1: Talking Disney with the Artists Who Knew Him* (Theme Park Press, 2015), 198.

99   Schweizer and Schweizer, *Disney, The Mouse Betrayed*, 266–269; Wallace, "Serious Fun," 84.

100   Graham, Jr., "Editor's Corner: Learning Together: Disney and the Historians," 7; Synnott, "Disney's America: Whose Patrimony, Whose Profits, Whose Past?" 57.

101   Eleanor Byrne and Martin McQuillan, *Deconstructing Disney* (Sterling, Virginia: Pluto Press, 1999), 111–113.

102   Mark I. Pinsky, *The Gospel According to Disney: Faith, Trust, and Pixie Dust* (Louisville: Westminster John Knox Press, 2004), 166.

Smith as part of the frieze along the rotunda dome, and a giant portrait also hangs in the Capitol, showing her baptism. With *Pocahontas*, Disney did not just want to make money. The company wanted to use the movie as a means to deal with criticism that it was racially and historically insensitive.[103] It was to be animated Dis-History.

Ultimately, though, *Pocahontas* is Disney-imagineered history, and in its own way, a very different type of Dis-History than what is found in the parks.[104] From a Dis-History perspective, *Pocahontas* is interesting for several reasons. The studio initially told their historic consultants that they wanted the film to be "historically accurate." However, what they meant, much to the dismay of many of the consultants involved, was that they wanted the details to be true, but the story itself was to serve more as an inspiration than a cinematic portrayal of what actually happened. So, while Disney studied Native American culture and spirituality, and grappled with race relations, they also decided to make nature itself a character, and ended up depicting what was soon to be named Virginia as an earthly paradise, where natives lived in pristine fellowship (with all the "colors of the wind") until the arrival of greedy English colonists, who disrupted this balance.[105]

And if that was all Disney opted to do with the story, it would be perhaps expected. But this was no fairy tale, this was Disney telling a historic event via animation. The changes and alterations just kept coming. Every Disney movie needs a villain, for example, and in *Pocahontas*, that villain is Sir John Ratcliffe, the "mercenary prospective governor" of the Jamestown colony. Ratcliffe's selection for the role is hardly surprising, as John Smith (the hero in both history and in Dis-History) did not like him. But historically, Ratcliffe was a more complicated figure, who met his death after being "betrayed" by Native Americans and nailed to a tree until dead. Disney's version of Ratcliffe seems more in tune with Spanish conquistadors than it does an agent of the British Crown and the Virginia Company. Alterations to the

---

103   Gary Edgerton and Kathy Merlock, "Redesigning Pocahontas: Disney, the "White Man's Indian," and the Marketing of Dreams," *Journal of Popular Film & Television*, 01956051, Summer96, Vol. 24, Issue 2. Accessed on 25 September 2014.

104   Henry A. Giroux, *The Mouse that Roared: Disney and the End of Innocence* (New York: Rowman and Littlefield, 1999), 101.

105   Edgerton and Merlock, "Redesigning Pocahontas: Disney, the "White Man's Indian," and the Marketing of Dreams." *Journal of Popular Film & Television*, 01956051, Summer96, Vol. 24, Issue 2. Accessed on 25 September 2014; Schweizer and Schweizer, *Disney, The Mouse Betrayed*, 151-157; David Whitley, *The Idea of Nature in Disney Animation* (Burlington, VT: Ashgate, 2008), 83.

story went on from there. Eisner objected that Pocahontas did not have a mother in the movie, as he wanted to avoid the appearance of "dysfunctional" native families. The problem was not the typical Disney one (that one or both parents was dead). The problem was that her father, Powhatan, was a polygamist. Furthermore, Powhatan is depicted in the film as ruling over a peaceful tribe threatened by the arrival of the English. In fact, the tribe was a confederacy of Powhatan's tribe and those tribes he had conquered and married into, who spent several years attempting to do the same to the newly arrived English.[106] And far from an idyllic setting with natives living in harmony with nature, natives in Powhatan-era Virginia used stone-age agricultural techniques, including the slashing and burning (which required moving every few years) of forests and fields that contributed to lessening crop yields. They also hunted widely (though only, as David Whitely points out, whites are depicted as trying to kill nature).[107]

And then there is the depiction of Pocahontas herself. The film shows her as a buxom teenager (or perhaps a woman in her twenties), when in fact at the time she first met John Smith she was perhaps ten or twelve years old. Disney's version has her fall in love with Smith, which is also ahistorical. Smith enjoyed spending time with her. Pocahontas was carefree in a way that the English settlers were not. And she was fascinated with him, and liked the fact that he treated her people with respect.[108] But she did not fall in love with him (despite saving his life from a possible ritual capture and near sacrifice). She married another settler, John Rolfe, with no evidence that she was enamored with Smith. Nor is there any discussion of Pocahontas' conversion to Christianity, and the historical issues surrounding it. While Eisner argued that the event took place after the movie, it is not a part of the sequel either, though her trip to England is, where she received a celebrity's welcome. Her death from small pox is also glossed over in the sequel.[109]

---

106   Frederic W. Gleach, *Powhatan's World and Colonial Virginia: A Conflict of Cultures*; electronic version (Lincoln: University of Nebraska Press, 1997), 23–24, 31.

107   Whitley, *The Idea of Nature in Disney Animation*, 82–86.

108   Philip L. Barbour, *Pocahontas and Her World* (Boston: Houghton Mifflin Company, 1969), 32–33; Alden T. Vaughan, *American Genesis: Captain John Smith and the Founding of Virginia* (Boston: Little, Brown, and Company, 1975), 48–49.

109   Schweizer and Schweizer, *Disney, The Mouse Betrayed*, 157-161; Byrne and McQuillan, *Deconstructing Disney*, 108; Gleach, *Powhatan's World and Colonial Virginia: A Conflict of Cultures*; electronic version, 3, 11, 74–75, 108, 111–121, 135; James Horn, editor, *Captain John Smith Writings With other Narratives of Roanoke, Jamestown, and the First English Settlement of America* (New York: The

Pocahontas the film does a disservice to Dis-History as constructed by Walt. By vowing to dispel stereotypes and claiming it is authentic, in some ways makes the historic story depicted more problematic for Dis-History as a concept. Pocahontas was a real person with a real story that historians largely know. Disney took the "essence" of her story, as if it were a myth, and made her story "better." The producers were "not impressed" with how the historic Pocahontas looked in pictures, so they "enhanced her," aged her, and made her "beautiful" by Hollywood's standards. And as critics point out, that is not all they did. The movie is in English, which Native Americans could not actually speak, but can in the movie, despite the fact they then cannot understand the English! Some critics even say that the movie makes the natives co-agents of their own genocide. Pocahontas' wedding, a mixture of both love and political maneuvering, gave the English a cash crop (tobacco) that put Jamestown on a firm financial footing. Despite its importance to both native culture and the success of the colony, tobacco garners little mention in the film.[110]

All that being said, what Disney was attempting to do with *Pocahontas*, while in a way different for its animated division, was consistent with live-action movies the company had been involved with since Walt's time. The studio was attempting to take the Native American side of the story seriously. As Douglas Brode notes, they did so in films like *Tonka* and *Squanto* much better than they did in *Pocahontas*. The film *Brother Bear*, in particular, deals with Native American myth and the fantastic in far better ways than the two films Disney has devoted to their native princess. While deserving some praise for trying to do better, the animated foray into Dis-History called *Pocahontas* ended up in only slightly better shape than the proposed Disney's America park.[111]

The problem for Disney and its cinematic use of Dis-History is that merely by attaching itself to a project, even if historical accuracy is

---

Library of America, 2007), 124, 188; Pinsky, *The Gospel According to Disney*, 164; Jacquelyn Kilpatrick, "Disney's Politically Correct Pocahontas," *Cineaste*, 21(Winter, 1995), 36; Vaughan, *American Genesis*, 36–37, 86–89, 93–94; Barbour, *Pocahontas and Her World*, 24–25, 154–159.

110 Wasko, *Understanding Disney*, 141–142; Kilpatrick, "Disney's Politically Correct Pocahontas," 36–37; Byrne and McQuillan, *Deconstructing Disney*, 109–110; Douglas Brode, *Multiculturalism and the Mouse: Race and Sex in Disney Entertainment* (Austin: University of Texas Press, 2005), 265; Whitley, *The Idea of Nature in Disney Animation*, 88.

111 Brode, *Multiculturalism and the Mouse*, 12-13; Whitley, *The Idea of Nature in Disney Animation*, 66, 81; Pinsky, *The Gospel According to Disney:*, 68, 220.

a goal, opens up questions about the uses of history for profit, as well as the lengths to which history can be used to advance a fictional storyline. Perhaps the best example of a success in this area is Pearl Harbor. In preparing for the film, Disney had the help of the U.S. Navy and several historians. Its blockbuster status meant that the film would be informing a generation that knew very little about the attack and U.S. entry into World War II. Thus, the film also required that Disney connect with veterans and show due reverence to what actually happened, even while employing artistic license as needed to push the "love story" angle of the plot, and how some characters (based on real people) were portrayed. It spawned other work, by *National Geographic* (to go beyond the Hollywood film) and the *Honolulu Advertiser* (to collect oral histories of those who lived through the attack). The film could be viewed, as it was by Daniel Martinez, the historian at the USS *Arizona* Memorial, as "a wonderful opportunity. The synergy of the film has created an audience anxious to learn."[112] That, of course, is not always the case. Ultimately, Dis-History cannot predict for Disney how its films and attractions will be interpreted by either guests or experts.[113]

Basing Dis-History in notions of popular history means that Disney is operating in the realm of a "public trust" or common knowledge, and while it might not be nuanced, such popular conceptions are also not always wrong either, and, as some observers have noted, is how Americans adopt all sorts of ideas, theories, and opinions.[114] Disney asks for expert advice. But in the end, it does what it wants to do. For the company and its guests, Dis-History does not end with any one film or even in Liberty Square. If anything, Liberty Square is a gateway to the largest representation of the concept at the parks: Frontierland and Adventureland.

---

112   Geoffrey M. White, "Disney's Pearl Harbor: National Memory at the Movies," *The Public Historian*, 24(Fall 2002), 98-108, 114; Kilpatrick, "Disney's Politically Correct Pocahontas," 37.

113   Schweizer and Schweizer, *Disney, The Mouse Betrayed*, 270–274; Robert Brent Toplin, editor, *Oliver Stone's USA: Film, History, and Controversy* (Lawrence: University Press of Kansas); Byrne and McQuillan, *Deconstructing Disney*, 152–159, 164–165; Giroux, *The Mouse that Roared*, 113.

114   Alexis de Tocqueville, *Democracy in America* (New York: Mentor, 1984), 148.

CHAPTER SIX

Dis-History's Mythic Frontier Adventure

Experience the Power of the Rails

As guests arrive at Walt Disney's Magic Kingdom, the first thing they actually encounter related to the park (whether they arrive on foot, by monorail, boat, bus, car, or ferry) is the railroad. Even before they walk down Main Street or catch a glimpse of the castle, their entryway into this world of fun and fantasy is designed to look like a train station, with a fully functional railroad system running atop the entrance and around the park.

Visually, the Walt Disney World railroad transports guests back to the age of steam power. Its track physically encircles the park, allowing guests to hop aboard and traverse the lands with ease if they opt not to walk. Departing from the Main Street station, with stops in Frontierland and Fantasyland, riders are offered a glimpse of the past as they travel, getting a feeling of being in a wilderness or untamed frontier (complete with Native American encampments) and perhaps of the future as they pass through Tomorrowland. Disneyland's version, even in its pared down, modern form, is even more explicit in its invocation of the past. The train ride in California transports guests through the Grand Canyon (inspired by one of the company's True-Life Adventure films), as well as back to the time of the dinosaurs.

The motivation behind the train was Walt's own love affair with railroads. His wife, Lillian, believed that the parks had much to do with her husband's near lifetime fascination with the Atchison, Topeka, and Santa Fe railroad that ran through his hometown of Marceline, Missouri. As we have seen with Main Street, Marceline cast a wide influence on Walt's imagination, and the town itself owed a great deal to the railroad that helped connect it to the rest of the nation.[1] His uncle Mike

---

1 Karal Ann Marling, "Disneyland, 1955: Just Take the Santa Ana Freeway

was an engineer for the Santa Fe, and Walt harbored a boyhood dream of following in his footsteps—even working for a time selling soft drinks and candy to railroad customers. Walt's passion for trains never left him. As an adult, not only did he love to talk about them, he also built one in his own backyard. Named the Carolwood-Pacific, Walt's private railroad was a one-eighth scale train system that ran on his property, complete with a tunnel that went under a portion of Lillian's flower garden.[2]

Thus, it was hardly surprising that when he was invited to attend the 1948 Chicago Railroad Fair, Walt enthusiastically agreed to go. The fair had life-size models and real artifacts (alongside reproductions), as well as exhibits. It was a prototype of sorts for the parks and perhaps even the outright birthplace of Dis-History.[3] It was no surprise when Walt approved the *Great Train Robbery* movie, since it combined a story set during the Civil War with trains (requiring Disney to purchase actual locomotives for use in filming).[4] When the decision was made to include a train as part of Disneyland, Walt insisted that all the details be correct with both the train and the station. His Imagineers were to produce an historically accurate depiction, not one of fantasy. The authentic, functional railroad was the first attraction finished at the park.[5] A Dis-Historic attempt at historic re-creation if not exactly presentation.

Walt's love of trains eventually translated itself into another attraction, long after his death: Big Thunder Mountain Railroad. The ride is a roller coaster themed on a railroad that goes through a western mining town. Known as an "E-ticket" ride (from a time when guests had to purchase ticket books at the entrance—with the best and most expensive rides taking an "E-ticket") Big Thunder is the anchor attraction of the Frontierland section of both Disneyland and the Magic Kingdom,[6] themed to capture, at least for some children, what

---

to the American Dream," *American Art*, 5(Winter-Spring, 1991), 177; Michael Barrier, *The Animated Man: A Life of Walt Disney* (Los Angeles: University of California Press, 2007), 9; John F. Stover, *The Life and Decline of the American Railroad* (New York: Oxford University Press, 1970), 54–55.

2 Richard Schickel, *The Disney Version: The Life, Times, Art and Commerce of Walt Disney, Third Edition* (Chicago: Ivan R. Dee Publisher, 1997), 35; Marling, "Disneyland, 1955: Just Take the Santa Ana Freeway to the American Dream," 177–179; Bob Thomas, *Walt Disney: An American Original* (New York: Disney Editions, 1994), 41.

3 Karal Ann Marling, editor, *Designing Disney's Theme Parks: The Architecture of Reassurance* (New York: Flammarion, 1997), 43.

4 Thomas, *Walt Disney*, 235.

5 Thomas, *Walt Disney*, 12; Barrier, *The Animated Man*, 20–21, 253.

6 Michael Eisner, *Work in Progress* (New York: Random House, 1998), 210-211.

the mythic "Wild West" was like. Its backstory is pulled from the western "gold rushes" that prompted boom towns to pop up overnight, whenever gold, silver, copper, or some other precious mineral was discovered. And at night it becomes clearer to see that the "mining town" you pass through while riding Big Thunder contains a saloon, complete with an upstairs area for "entertainment," as well as numerous other buildings needed to sustain a mining community. But in its twists and turns, guests glimpse not just the frontier as it is being settled and its resources extracted, but also experience a sense of adventure in the midst of their ride as they plunge into a wild wilderness.[7]

Big Thunder, like Walt's trains that helped inspire it, tap into something very American. The excitement of the frontier, the thrill of adventure, the power of steel, and the possibilities of manifest destiny are all infused in the attraction. Big Thunder invokes both the frontier as well as the spirt of adventure in ways that Fantasyland's Prince Charming Regal Carrousel simply never could. But Disney's use of railroads also showcases Dis-History's ability to tap directly into the past and to use history as an organizing principle. Like the gold rush that inspired it, Big Thunder (and all of Disney's railroads) are ridden by people from all over the world.[8] But when they sit down, they are in for a very American experience.

Capturing the Great American Myth

The trains that so captivated Walt's attention contributed to another historical fact that affected the course of his life. A few years before Walt was born, in 1893, historian Frederick Jackson Turner first presented his "frontier thesis" at the meeting of the American Historical Association held in conjunction with the World's Columbian Exposition. In it, Jackson noted that according to the superintendent of the census "the unsettled area [of the United States] has been so broken into by isolated bodies of settlement [in large part due to the railroads] that there can hardly be said to be a frontier line." For Turner, this meant American history was at a turning point, because "the existence of an area of free land, its continuous recession, and the advance of American settlement westward explain American development."

---

7 Didier Ghez, editor, *Walt's People: Volume 6: Talking Disney with the Artists Who Knew Him* (New York: Xlibris Corporation, 2008), 238; Susan Lee Johnson, *Roaring Camp: The Social World of the California Gold Rush* (New York: W.W. Norton & Company, 2000), 25-27, 186, 274, 339; Judith A. Adams, *The American Amusement Park Industry: A History of Technology and Thrills* (Boston: Twayne Publishers, 1991), 18.

8 Adams, *The American Amusement Park Industry*, 18.

Having unsettled land had allowed "American social development" to be "continually beginning over again on the frontier," which, according to Turner, meant that "the frontier promoted the formation of a composite nationality" as well as strengthened American "democracy."[9]

Few things better capture how Walt saw the possibilities of his parks than Turner's thesis, even with its flaws.[10] And the best physical embodiment of it for Dis-History is found in Frontierland. Not only do you literally have the concept of the frontier displayed prominently, as Richard Francaviglia points out—"so powerful is the name 'Frontierland' that its mere mention evokes images of 'the West' to most people,"[11] but another important facet of the thesis is found there as well, the "privileged locus of motion."[12] It was a new means of transportation, in particular the railroads, which so enamored Walt, that not only made the rapid settlement of the West possible but also ended the very notion of a frontier in American life. The railroads "vigorously played up the theme of a frontier-less New West," due to providing virtually unprecedented historic mobility of people and goods. The West became yet another American region as a result.[13] But the concept or idea of the West simply did not go away. Instead, it passed into the realm of myth where Disney found it.

Frontierland is not about the vanishing frontier, nor the surpassed frontier, but rather about its importance. The area taps into a reminder of the historical significance of the divide between civilizations and a symbolic reminder of that which defined Americans as a people—all through a mythic frontier space. Perhaps that is too much to wonder about in an area of a theme park, but not for Disney. If Main Street is how Walt remembered his hometown, then Frontierland is where he remembered his childhood dreams. Not that his family were pioneers, but the mythic frontier of farm and homestead alongside pretend play about an untamed country where the conflicts (both between people

---

9 "Frederick Jackson Turner: The Significance of the Frontier in American History 1893," http://nationalhumanitiescenter.org/pds/gilded/empire/text1/turner.pdf, 11 June 2014.

10 Donald Worster, *Under Western Skies: Nature and History in the American West* (New York: Oxford University Press, 1992), 7.

11 Richard Francaviglia, "Walt Disney's Frontierland as an Allegorical Map of the American West, "The *Western Historical Quarterly*, 30(Summer 1999), 157.

12 Andrea Carosso, "America's Disneylands and the end-of-century American Cityscape," *Revue francaise d'etudes americaines* 83(January 2000), 65.

13 Worster, *Under Western Skies*, 1, 12–13, 23, 33; Benedict Anderson, *Imagined Communities: Reflections on the Origin and Spread of Nationalism* (New York: Verso Press, 1998), 115.

and nature as well as between peoples) occurred. Walt was tapping into the mythic West in real ways, meant to appeal to Americans. And he did so beautifully.

For the frontier did not really vanish. Instead, it resided still "in the American imagination." Here, "history and legend mingle" freely, with many of the tales that become attributed to the hero being "clearly generic or traditional rather than historical." The western myth, on some level, is about "an ordinary people moving into an extraordinary land." And that is a concept that historians never really could control. Walt understood that people wanted heroes and that the "ruthless quest after truth" that historians crave does not always fit with such desires.[14] Frontierland, then, "fits" into a long American tradition of trying to understand the frontier and the "West" by looking at the crafted popular mythology surrounding westward expansion, discovery, and conquest. Disney invokes history here, but it is more often than not a mythic history that most academic historians rarely consider.[15]

In large part this is because Frontierland deals with the "West" of Hollywood, and thus the myths that Americans tell themselves about the West. As a genre, it is virtually impossible to escape the western in American cinema. It is also almost instantly familiar, despite the fact that most people have never personally experienced, say, riding a horse on the Great Plains. And while Hollywood's version is often far removed from actual historic events, and there are fewer movies made about it now than in the past, the power of the western remains. Director John Ford, when talking about the mythic versus historic West, argued that on film myth was always better.[16] Disney, then, was tapping into a myth that had become history, even more than history itself.

---

14 Worster, *Under Western Skies*, 6; Kent Ladd Steckmesser, *The Western Hero in History and Legend* (Norman: University of Oklahoma Press, 1965), vii, 6, 246, 249.

15 Kathy Merlock Jackson and Mark I. West, editors, *Disneyland and Culture: Essays on the Parks and Their Influence* (Jefferson, NC: McFarland and Company, 2011), 62–63, 74; Francaviglia, "Walt Disney's Frontierland as an Allegorical Map of the American West, " 158, 160, 181; Michael R. Real, *Mass-Mediated Culture* (Englewood Cliffs, New Jersey: Prentice-Hall, 1977), 61; "Luis Marin: Disneyland as Degenerate Utopia," http://lmc.gatech.edu/~broglio/1101/marin.html, 23 September 2014.

16 Richard A. Maynard, *The American West on Film: Myth and Reality* (Rochelle Park, New Jersey: Hayden Book Company, Incorporated, 1974), vi; Thomas Hine, *Populuxe* (New York: Alfred A. Knopf, 1986), 152; Worster, *Under Western Skies: Nature and History in the American West* (New York: Oxford University Press, 1992), 28, 34, 51; Will Wright, *Six Guns and Society: A Structural Study of the Western* (Los Angeles: University of California Press, 1975), 1–7.

Walt understood the mythic power of the frontier. While it was often difficult for pioneers, and "a genocidal nightmare for indigenous people who stood in their way," the mythos of moving west was part of the American experience since 1492, and it was also something that Walt himself had experienced to a degree personally, in coming from the Midwest to California. It was thus an idea easy to utilize both personally and culturally, and it made coming to the park an instant success with visitors.[17] Walt saw Frontierland as being about the "American pioneer spirit" and "the most distinctly American statement" in the parks. When linked to guests' experiences in what became Liberty Square and Main Street, it offered the sweep of American history from the colonial period to the late nineteenth and early twentieth centuries.[18]

The notion of the West fits Disney in other ways as well. During the period of settlement, boosters had used every medium available to try and entice those living in the eastern United States (as well as people from around the world) to come live in the new territories being opened to settlement. Just like boosters before him, Walt used every medium available to him to promote visitors to his park.[19] Additionally, the frontier has served as a mythic dividing line between settlement and wilderness. And while Americans have long seen settlement as promoting civilization, there is also an inherent tension in conquest, because they also saw something pure and wondrous in the untamed wilderness. With Frontierland, Walt was taming the wilderness, while keeping an aspect of adventure alive.[20] It became a place that was "safe for homesteaders—and suburbanites."[21]

Frontierland when Disneyland opened was conceived by Walt and his Imagineers as a place visited in the midst of settlement. It

---

17 Michael Steiner, "Frontierland as Tommorowland: Walt Disney and the Architectural Packaging of the Mythic West," *Montana: The Magazine of Western History*, 48(Spring 1998), 4–5.

18 *The Imagineering Field Guide to Disneyland: An Imagineer's Eye Tour* (New York: Disney Editions, 2008), 46, 51–52, 75.

19 David M. Wrobel, *Promised Lands: Promotion, Memory, and the Creation of the American West*, (Lawrence: University of Kansas Press, 2002), 6–7, 24–26.

20 Simon Schama, *Landscape and Memory* (New York: Vintage Books, 1995), 7; Denis E. Cosgrove, *Social Formation and Symbolic Landscape* (Madison: The University of Wisconsin Press, 1998), 162, 184, 186; Stephen F. Fjellman, *Vinyl Leaves: Walt Disney World and America* (Boulder: Westview Press, 1992), 73–75.

21 Steiner, "Frontierland as Tommorowland: Walt Disney and the Architectural Packaging of the Mythic West," 9; Francaviglia, "Walt Disney's Frontierland as an Allegorical Map of the American West, "155; Marling, "Disneyland, 1955: Just Take the Santa Ana Freeway to the American Dream," 200.

represented the United States in the 1830s and1840s. Frontierland's "décor," (its theming and architecture, its very look), "promotes a feeling of historically winning the West in heroic fashion," according to some observers. Guests are thus immersed in their surroundings and are able to immerse themselves thematically in the area. But Walt wanted more than that. He strove to make Frontierland as authentic an experience as possible. He wanted real wagons, which guests could ride in, pulled by real horses. He ordered that the entrance's stockade fence be made with "real logs and foot-long nails," invoking the string of forts that had once "linked the American frontiers" and "held our young country together." Walt said that "Frontierland is a tribute to the faith, courage, and ingenuity of the pioneers who blazed the trails across America." Disneyland's Frontierland was designed on such a scale as to make guests feel as though they are walking, if not back into the past, then onto a lavish movie set where they were going to be actors in an historical reenactment.[22] As the publicity noted: "Historical excitement unfolds in Frontierland where Indians, stage coaches and wagons, western sheriffs, keel boats and show boats all work together to bring you a glimpse of pioneer America." [23]

Walt was helped in this undertaking by the television shows he had made for ABC to promote the park. The Davy Crockett films had become a phenomenon, and for a generation, visually defined the frontier. Many of Disney's post-war live-action films invoke either the frontier as a theme or late nineteenth-century America. Though you will not find a *So Dear to My Heart* ride, the spirit of these films and the American values and folklore they embody permeates Frontierland.[24] As such, "to the public, Frontierland presented living history when Disneyland first opened, based on actual historical events and the Disney films in which these events were depicted," according to

---

22 Francaviglia, "Walt Disney's Frontierland as an Allegorical Map of the American West," 163, 165, 169, 172; Marling, editor, *Designing Disney's Theme Parks*, 103 ; "Luis Marin: Disneyland as Degenerate Utopia," http://lmc.gatech.edu/~broglio/1101/marin.html, 23 September 2014; Thomas, *Walt Disney*, 13, 266-267; Steiner, "Frontierland as Tommorowland: Walt Disney and the Architectural Packaging of the Mythic West," 6, 11; Dave Smith, *The Quotable Walt Disney* (New York: Disney Editions, 2001), 64.

23 1955-News from Disneyland folder. Public Relations, Walt Disney Studio Archives, Burbank, California.

24 J. G. O'Boyle, "'Be Sure You're Right, then Go Ahead': The Early Disney Westerns," *Journal of Popular Film & Television*, Summer96, Vol. 24 Issue 2. Accessed on 25 September 2014; Christopher Finch, *Walt Disney's America* (New York: Abbeville Press, 1978), 139; Steven Watts, *The Magic Kingdom: Walt Disney and the America Way of Life* (New York: Houghton Mifflin Company, 1997), 290–291.

Richard Francaviglia. And that was the intent. Walt said that part of his purpose with Frontierland was to "show today's youth the America of our great grandparents' day—and before." Not only might the guests learn a bit of history, but they might be instilled with some of the values (self-sufficiency, hard work, and self-reliance) he believed the frontier had instilled in Americans and their nation moving forward.[25]

King of the Wild Frontier

From the moment there was an American frontier, it produced larger-than-life heroes. The first was John Smith of Pocahontas fame.[26] But what Walt gravitated toward for Frontierland were the stories of Davy Crockett that were shaped by the earlier hero worship of Daniel Boone.[27] As historian James Atkins Shackford noted, "The frontiersman was history's agent for wresting land from the American Indian," and yet, he himself was "pursued by civilization ... [and] in front of him lay the rich wilderness and the trail of the retreating game upon which his very life depended. Pushed from behind, pulled from in front, he moved on inexorably into Indian territory."[28] Crockett's "greatest value," according to Shackford, was "as a symbol of the new man striking into this new and spiritual frontier," a symbol both the historian and Walt believed was still potent in the mid-twentieth century.[29]

Crockett was ready-made for Disney. Even before Walt's films, Davy Crockett was an American folk hero, who had both real history and mythic stories attached to him. Crockett was a frontiersman in Tennessee, who became a congressman (with a complicated relationship with his contemporary, Andrew Jackson), and a defender and martyr at the Alamo. The real Davy Crockett was an interesting and complicated person in his own right, whose death came at "the height of his greatest renown in a fight that itself seemed to symbolize the growing, expanding, liberating destiny of America, a death that seemed to be the final bravest act of which a brave man was capable."[30]

---

25 Francaviglia, "Walt Disney's Frontierland as an Allegorical Map of the American West, "166; Watts, *The Magic Kingdom*, 300; Neal Gabler, *Walt Disney: The Triumph of the American Imagination* (New York: Vintage Books, 2007), 517.

26 Kent Ladd Steckmesser, *The Western Hero in History and Legend* (Norman: University of Oklahoma Press, 1965), 3.

27 Steckmesser, *The Western Hero in History and Legend*, 8.

28 James Atkins Shackford, *David Crockett: The Man and the Legend* (Chapel Hill: The University of North Carolina Press, 1956), 3.

29 Shackford, *David Crockett*, 251–252.

30 Shackford, *David Crockett*, 62, 76–77, 163, 234–240, 247; James A.

Even if Disney's Davy Crockett was not like the real person, it was hardly surprising that Walt turned to Crockett for source material.[31] Walt had thought about doing a film about the legendary frontiersman since the late 1940s. The eventual product was five one-hour episodes, split into three segments and two segments (which were then released as two feature films) that aired on ABC between December 1954 and December 1955. The intention was to help spark interest in Disneyland's Frontierland.[32] The show was a huge success. Royalties from the sale of Davy Crockett merchandise expanded Disney's revenue stream in expected ways, but also were a foretaste of what was to come once the park opened.[33] Additionally, Disney had a massive musical hit on its hands with the show's theme song, *The Ballad of Davy Crockett*, which became a cultural phenomenon as well as a testament to the power of television.[34] Walt "struck a nerve" amongst Americans with the show, in part because of the Cold War (and the United States being in search of heroes who affirmed what the nation stood for) and in part because of Fess Parker's excellent portrayal. The show propelled Crockett back into the national spotlight.[35]

Davy Crockett became a triumph for Dis-History. Frontierland was also the most popular area when Disneyland opened in 1955, in large part due to the popularity of the television show. Indeed, guests on opening day were excited to learn that they had a chance to interact with Parker and some of the other actors (in character) from the show.[36] In many respects, Walt's efforts helped spark and built off of interest, including among scholars, of the real Davy Crockett. As Shackford, whose biography of Crockett was published in 1956 and remains one of the definitive accounts of the man, put it in his introduction, "The purpose of this work is to present an authentic biography

---

Shackford and Stanley J. Folmsbee, editors, *A Narrative Life of David Crockett of the State of Tennessee by David Crockett* (Knoxville: The University of Tennessee Press, 1973), v, x-xv, 4-5, 43, 179, 194.

31 Michael R. Real, *Mass-Mediated Culture* (Englewood Cliffs, New Jersey: Prentice-Hall, 1977), 61.

32 Barrier, *The Animated Man*, 249-251.

33 Eric Avila, *Popular Culture in the Age of White Flight: Fear and Fantasy in Suburban Los Angeles* (Los Angeles: University of California Press, 2004), 128.

34 Watts, *The Magic Kingdom*, 315; Thomas, *Walt Disney*, 256-257; Gabler, *Walt Disney*, 513-515.

35 Gabler, *Walt Disney*, 516; Watts, *The Magic Kingdom*, 313-322.

36 Marling, "Disneyland, 1955: Just Take the Santa Ana Freeway to the American Dream," 205; Steiner, "Frontierland as Tommorowland: Walt Disney and the Architectural Packaging of the Mythic West," 3.

of David Crockett against the background of his times, a new and creative period of American history, so that the reader may see him as an individual, as a type, and as an exponent of a type—a true pioneer not only of advancing geographical frontiers but also of the frontiers of a new democratic spirit."[37] Walt could not have put it better himself.

It is important to note when Shackford was writing: during 1953 to 1956. His book, in other words, arrived at the apex of Disney-fueled Crockett mania but was not influenced by it. Just as important, Shackford was writing to refute prior scholarship that had neglected Crockett or claimed that the historical man was so shrouded in myth that he was unknowable.[38] In some ways, then, Dis-History was working in concert with academic historians.

Davy Crockett's success also meant that there was pressure to repeat it. From 1957 to 1959, Dis-History was showcased via *Zorro*, with stories about Spanish California's masked hero. Left unsaid in the dramatic sword fights was that this was a fictional show set in America's (though not technically the United States) past, portraying what modern Americans would consider to be a minority (Hispanics), with a hero who was clearly representing modern American values and ideals. It was, in some respects, not just showing the universal nature of the American way of life, but also promoting assimilation of immigrants to that way of life. Disney followed *Zorro*, from 1959 to 1960, with a more blatant Dis-Historic appeal to American history, via a show about the Revolutionary War hero Francis "Swamp Fox" Marion. Not unlike Davy Crockett, Disney's choice of protagonist was larger than life in some respects (Marion waged a guerilla war against the British in South Carolina) who had largely been forgotten by the history books. And once again, Walt could draw on recent scholarship (in the form of Robert Duncan Bass' 1959 book on Marion) in informing the show. The successes of these shows not only cemented Dis-History (including giving rise to themes and areas within Disneyland) but also led to Walt moving his television presence from ABC to NBC in 1960, ending the partnership that had helped him build Disneyland to begin with.[39]

Frontierland, then, was the place Dis-History came to life, but also a place (somewhat revolutionary for the 1950s) where a multicultural America could be experienced all united by American values (as articulated by Walt). It included not just portions of a stockade fort and an area to encounter Davy Crockett, but also an area devoted to

---

37 Shackford, *David Crockett*, vii.

38 Shackford, *David Crockett*, vii–ix.

39 Christopher Finch, *Walt Disney's America* (New York: Abbeville Press, 1978), 142; Watts, *The Magic Kingdom*, 291–295.

the American Southwest (complete with appearances by Zorro), an area crafted around a Native American village (with actual Native Americans in traditional clothing), and even a restaurant built around Aunt Jemima, staffed by African Americans. In short, the original Frontierland, for all its flaws, was multi-ethnic, multi-racial, and incredibly diverse.[40] It was also a place where some of the "bumpier patches" of the past were at least hinted at if not fully explored, with Walt's treatment of Native Americans providing the clearest example. Native Americans were depicted as both potentially warlike (a settler's cabin on fire with the settler himself dead before it, struck down by Indian arrows, was one thing that could be viewed from the railroad in Disneyland), but also friendly. In Frontierland, even though there was mention of "hostile Indians," those that guests actually encountered in the Indian village area were friendly. All these groups and their stories helped Dis-History showcase an America that was transforming before the eyes of the guests into the nation they now lived in.[41] The frontier might be vanishing, but the end result was Disneyland.

It is interesting to speculate what this showcase meant at the time and what it might have meant for both Dis-History and to wider American culture had it continued. Guests were making mythical memories about a mythical past. But in Walt's Frontierland, Dis-History was playing out alongside the actual historic past in real ways. These areas existed and there was a sense of diversity in Disneyland's Frontierland, where stories that were peripheral to the largely white (or Anglo-American) narrative that most guests expected to encounter were told. And though critics, especially once Dis-History became a target of social historians, might claim these depictions as racially insensitive, culturally assimilationist, and a literal white washing of actual history (talking about the complicated relations between white settlers and Native Americans was something Disney was willing to do, talking about slavery was not), what was unprecedented was the

---

40 Steiner, "Frontierland as Tommorowland: Walt Disney and the Architectural Packaging of the Mythic West,"13.

41 Warren Leon and Roy Rosenzweig, editors, *History Museums in the United States: A Critical Assessment* (Chicago: University of Illinois Press, 1989), 163; Henry A. Giroux, *The Mouse that Roared: Disney and the End of Innocence* (New York: Rowman and Littlefield, 1999), 147–148; Francaviglia, "Walt Disney's Frontierland as an Allegorical Map of the American West, " 175–176; Eric Avila, *Popular Culture in the Age of White Flight: Fear and Fantasy in Suburban Los Angeles* (Los Angeles: University of California Press, 2004), 133; Finch, *Walt Disney's America*, 146; Kathy Merlock Jackson and Mark I. West, editors, *Disneyland and Culture: Essays on the Parks and Their Influence* (Jefferson, NC: McFarland and Company, 2011), 76.

degree of agency, the ability to tell largely white American guests these stories all within Frontierland's larger narrative framework.[42]

But that narrative, and Frontierland itself, began to change after Walt's death. Not only has much of the original Frontierland and its associated experiences vanished, but the concept was never fully replicated in Walt Disney World. Frontierland was the area of the park least changed during Walt's lifetime. After his death, changes came quickly. Real animals, which had been a mainstay at the park, including a trail ride, were sent into retirement as a means to cut costs. Davy Crockett (though his canoes remained in Disneyland) and Zorro disappeared from the park. Aunt Jemima's kitchen was displaced by New Orleans Square's expansion. And actual Native Americans were replaced by animatronics who no longer interacted with guests by 1972. Indeed, the changes with Native Americans are perhaps the starkest. While Disney might not have portrayed natives in the most politically correct light (one need only watch Peter Pan for an example), it had a long history of trying to show the complicated relationship between natives and white pioneers.[43] One could see this quite clearly with how Disney portrayed Native Americans in Fess Parker's *Davy Crockett* series: whites and natives could fight and become friends, and whites might not have always been right, nor the natives completely wrong. Now the Native American village is buried under Critter Country, and though Disney claimed (with *Pocahontas*) that it wanted to seriously engage with Native American stories, the sense of conflict between whites and natives has disappeared from Frontierland. Guests now see a native chief giving them a peace sign along the river banks, and though the settler's cabin is still on fire, it is now due to a lightning strike, not a war party.[44] Michael Steiner argues that whereas once Frontierland

---

42 Douglas Brode, *Multiculturalism and the Mouse: Race and Sex in Disney Entertainment* (Austin: University of Texas Press, 2005), 98; Francaviglia, "Walt Disney's Frontierland as an Allegorical Map of the American West, "177; Avila, *Popular Culture in the Age of White Flight*, 14; Mattey, Bob. Interviewed by George Sherman, Lectures and Transcripts, Walt Disney Studio Archives, Burbank, California.

43 Francaviglia, "Walt Disney's Frontierland as an Allegorical Map of the American West," 167; Joe Flower, *Prince of the Magic Kingdom: Michael Eisner and the Re-Making of Disney* (New York: John Wiley and Sons, Inc., 1991), Christian Moran, *Great Big Beautiful Tomorrow: Walt Disney and Technology* (Theme Park Press, 2015).

44 Leon and Rosenzweig, editors, *History Museums in the United States*, 163; Giroux, *The Mouse that Roared*, 147–148; Francaviglia, "Walt Disney's Frontierland as an Allegorical Map of the American West,"175–176; Avila, *Popular Culture in the Age of White Flight*, 133; Didier Ghez, editor, *Walt's People: Volume*

was a showplace of diversity, at a time when the suburbs promoted sameness, today it is "a calm refuge amid a cultural maelstrom."[45]

Even with these changes, Dis-History is still alive and well within Frontierland. But it is much more muted than when Walt first opened it in 1955. In Disneyland, not only have things been changed, but the area itself has seen portions taken away to become new lands such as Critter Country and the soon-to-open Star Wars land. Internationally, Frontierland remains one of the most popular areas of both Tokyo Disney and Disneyland Paris, in large part because of its Americaness. In Japan it is called "Westernland" rather than Frontierland, though in most respects it is an exact copy of the Disneyland original. In Europe, Frontierland was an almost immediate draw. For many Europeans, the Wild West was what they associated the most with the United States. As such, Frontierland was large, though its theming in Disneyland Paris is more the American Southwest, rather than the wooded forts of the eastern United States.[46]

Things are a bit different in Florida. Here guests to the Magic Kingdom, whose Frontierland was historically smaller to begin with, find the land wedged between Liberty Square and Adventureland. It has a condensed sign and only a portion of a stockade fence. Of the nine Frontierland attractions on the Disney map, three are food stations (including the replica of Disneyland's Diamond Horseshoe—whose signage proclaims it to be a saloon, thus meaning that Frontierland is a bit less reputable than Main Street) and one is a "trading post" where guests can buy merchandise. Of the remaining attractions, one is the Disney railroad station, one is Tom Sawyer Island, two others are rides (Splash Mountain and Big Thunder Mountain), and the final attraction is the Country Bear Jamboree. Here, American folk music, steeped in Appalachian culture, is sung by audio-animatronic bears. This is the only place a guest can still hear *The Ballad of Davy Crockett* being sung. It is a place where Dis-History triumphed over history.

4: *Talking Disney with the Artists Who Knew Him* (Theme Park Press, 2016), 291, 295; Brode, *Multiculturalism and the Mouse*, 26–35; Steiner, "Frontierland as Tommorowland: Walt Disney and the Architectural Packaging of the Mythic West," 13; *The Imagineering Field Guide to Disneyland: An Imagineer's Eye Tour* (New York: Disney Editions, 2008), 70.

45 Steiner, "Frontierland as Tommorowland: Walt Disney and the Architectural Packaging of the Mythic West," 13.

46 Steiner, "Frontierland as Tommorowland: Walt Disney and the Architectural Packaging of the Mythic West,"4; Andrew Lainsbury, *Once Upon an American Dream: The Story of Euro Disneyland* (Lawrence: University of Kansas Press, 2000), 59–61.

The Frontier Meets the World

Ultimately, the frontier for Walt was not just about the history it allowed him to draw from, but the adventure that produced that history. Of course, if you are going to have an amusement or theme park, it makes a good deal of sense to have some thrill rides. And that is what Adventureland is for. When coupled with Frontierland at the Magic Kingdom, Adventureland gives guests a taste of American manifest destiny overrunning the empires of old. It is a place (mythic in its construct) for Americans to experience the rest of the world. The blending of the two areas, where Dis-History interacts not just with other cultures but with the concept of adventure, was by design.[47] Disney's Imagineers hoped to create "tropical settings in Adventureland," a place where there "is a land of natural wonders and primitive savagery—a land of exotic beauty where the romance of the tropics prevails."[48] As Walt put it, "Here [Adventureland] is adventure, here is romance, here is mystery."[49]

Accepting that you are in Adventureland, however, is based in part on "cultural assumptions" as to what constitutes "adventure" and what you would expect to find there. Adventureland can blur the lines between reality and the audio-animatronic reality that the Imagineers have crafted. The idea of Adventureland was inspired, at least in part, by the True-Life Adventures series, but also by the Dis-Historic notion of cultural contact, themes that were present in the original Frontierland and in modern Epcot. And while that notion of contact has become muted in Frontierland, guests are still immersed in it when they visit Adventureland.[50]

Such contact and immersion in this area of the park is brought about by the attractions. Take the Enchanted Tiki Room, for example. Walt wanted guests to be able to enjoy a show (and for a time, the

---

47 Jackson and West, editors, *Disneyland and Culture*, 112; "Luis Marin: Disneyland as Degenerate Utopia," http://lmc.gatech.edu/~broglio/1101/marin.html, 23 September 2014; Alexander Moore, "Walt Disney World: Bounded Ritual Space and the Playful Pilgrimage Center," *Anthropological Quarterly*, 53(October 1980), 212; *The Imagineering Field Guide to the Magic Kingdom at Walt Disney World: An Imagineer's Eye Tour* (New York: Disney Editions, 2005), 38, 44.

48 1955 News from Disneyland folder, Walt Disney Studio Archives, Burbank, California.

49 Dave Smith, *The Quotable Walt Disney* (New York: Disney Editions, 2001), 63.

50 Jane Kuenz, Karen Klugman, Shelton Waldrep, and Susan Willis, editors, *Inside the Mouse: Work and Play at Disney World* (Durham: Duke University Press, 1995), 40; Eric Smoodin, editor, *Disney Discourse: Producing the Magic Kingdom* (New York: Routledge, 1994), 62–63; Michael R. Real, *Mass-Mediated Culture* (Englewood Cliffs, New Jersey: Prentice-Hall, 1977), 63.

thought was that there would be dinner as well) in Adventureland. The end result was the creation of an "enchanted" room, inspired by Polynesian stories and built around audio-animatronics. Originally constructed for Disneyland (and replicated in the Magic Kingdom), the Tiki Room can be seen as a type of "cultural appropriation," because of its use of songs and images from the South Pacific. But it also must be understood both within the cultural context of 1950s California (where "Polynesian décor and cuisine" was quite popular)[51] as well as a unique way for many guests to first experience Adventureland. Here was a chance to be physically removed from the world outside the park and immersed in this particular area of the park, by Disney magic (in the form of animatronic birds) and theming. If this is the point of entry for guests into Adventureland, they exit the show ready for more encounters which will both entertain and perhaps expose guests to new experiences.

And they can find it readily in the trees above them. In Magic Kingdom, guests encounter the Swiss Family Robinson Treehouse. Beyond simply a work of synergy for Disney, it is also Dis-Historic in its presentation. As Stephen Fjellman noted, there is a mind/time/genre-bending quality to walking into the treehouse. It is an amusement park attraction, based on a movie set piece, which is itself based on works of literature, which is a fictitious representation of actual historical occurrences or themes.[52] In short, it is a Dis-Historic amalgamation. At Disneyland, the treehouse is based around *Tarzan*, which carries with it many of the same connotations that Fjellman wrote about in connection to the Swiss Family house in Florida.[53] The houses, themed walk-through attractions, give a Dis-Historic glimpse at what Disney means by adventure in this land: Europeans exploring a place (whether the South Pacific or Africa) in which they encounter food, animals, and people that they consider to be exotic and different from what they have known at home. In some ways, it is a nice encapsulation of what Disney is doing with the parks for their guests.

In many ways, the capstone of the Adventureland rides is the Pirates of the Caribbean. Though it took Disney years to perfect the idea for the

---

51   Andi Stein, *Why We Love Disney: The Power of the Disney Brand* (New York: Peter Lang, 2011), 25; Jackson and West, editors, *Disneyland and Culture*, 108; Kevin Starr, *Golden Dreams: California in an Age of Abundance, 1950-1963* (New York: Oxford University Press, 2009), 50–51; Andrew Kiste, *A Historical Tour of Walt Disney World* (Theme Park Press, 2015); Moran, *Great Big Beautiful Tomorrow*.
52   Fjellman, *Vinyl Leaves*, 2.
53   Mark I. Pinsky, *The Gospel According to Disney: Faith, Trust, and Pixie Dust* (Louisville: Westminster John Knox Press, 2004), 185.

attraction, it has become a Dis-Historic masterpiece, in which guests take a boat ride in search of treasure and encounter death, destruction, battles, and plenty of adventure, all set to a sound track that includes song lyrics that are not always what they seem (a pirate's life seems to be, in a Hobbesian twist, rather solitary, nasty, brutal, and short, as well as being a catchy tune). It has also served as inspiration for a series of movies starring Johnny Depp (whose Captain Jack Sparrow character, in an act of corporate synergy, has been shoehorned into the ride and hosts a pirate experience outside) and in a Dis-Historic twist (along with a bit of utopian innocence and the belief of Imagineers that they can make anything fit a Disney storyline) have seemingly transformed pirates into heroes. Pirates is steeped in history, a sort of realistic fiction in many ways, that shows even serious (and perhaps disturbing) topics can still lead to family fun and a few thrills[54]—and if guests take a minute to ponder what they have been edu-tained with, perhaps spark further inquiry into what the age of pirates was really like.

Adventureland's size in California (it was "squeezed" into a smaller space, because of the size of Frontierland at Disneyland) has contributed to more consistent theming, regardless of which park a guest might visit. But that is not to say that all the parks are the same. In the Magic Kingdom, there was more room, which led to the creation of Agrabah Bazaar and an *Aladdin*-themed magic carpet ride. This *Aladdin* theme is enhanced even further in Disneyland Paris, where Adventureland's orientation was heavily influenced by the Imagineers understanding of French colonialism in the Far East and in North Africa.[55] And that Imagineering and synergistic thinking has led to Dis-Historic consequences for both how one interprets Adventureland and for Disney itself.

First is the decision to use Aladdin. Springing from folktales that range from modern India, Iran, Iraq, Syria, and Egypt, Aladdin first burst onto the European scene in the early 1700s (with some of the tales dating back to at least 900). The collection had been largely gathered and first translated into Arabic during the Caliphate period, with French and English translations arriving much later. The stories contained in *One Thousand and One Arabian Nights* helped Europeans of the eighteenth century form their opinion of the Islamic world after

---

54 Tison Pugh and Susan Aronstein, editors, *The Disney Middle Ages: A Fairy-Tale and Fantasy Past* (New York: Palgrave Macmillan, 2012), 10–11, 68–69; Didier Ghez, editor, *Walt's People: Volume 7: Talking Disney with the Artists Who Knew Him* (New York: Xlibris Corporation, 2008), 239; "Pirates of the Caribbean—Ship's Articles," http://pirates.hegewisch.net/articles_new.html, 13 October 2015.

55 Lainsbury, *Once Upon an American Dream*, 62–65.

centuries of conflict. Not surprisingly, given Dis-History's quest to create a common culture, eventually Disney's attention fell on the work as well. The animated film, *Aladdin*, released in 1992, was part of the second golden age of Disney animation, and so it was hardly a surprise when the company decided to synergize it in the parks. Critics allege that Disney was being both culturally appropriative (though this is an argument hard to support given the historical evidence) as well as Americanizing the story (with claims that it explains American involvement in the Gulf War as well as making Princess Jasmine "ethnically Arabian while culturally American"). But its use also forced Disney to deal with Islam as both a religious and a cultural force (mentioning Allah, changing anti-Arab dialog, and backing away from including Israel in Epcot).[56] Not even Disney is immune to geopolitics, especially those that potentially threaten its bottom line, even if it did little to Dis-History in the process.

The second thing *Aladdin* did was remind some critics of Dis-History's reliance on a colonial-themed worldview in Adventureland. As they are quick to point out, critics note that there was a good deal of racism that came with Western colonialism. But, while they might make mention of Aladdin (in particular the film) in this discussion, the critics inevitably turn to one of Adventureland's original attractions, the Jungle Cruise, for their full scorn. To detractors, the Jungle Cruise is built upon notions of Africa (and to an extent Asia) being a "dark continent" which only the light of European (and American) discovery opened up. These eighteenth- and nineteenth-century racial notions, they argue, infuse how visitors encounter the world's jungles and rivers on their trek.[57]

Disney, and thus Dis-History, see the Jungle Cruise in a different light. True, the attraction draws upon European colonial-era works ranging from Rudyard Kipling's *The Jungle Book* (which Disney has adapted as both an animated classic and more recently as a live-action/CGI film) and Henry Stanley's quest to find the missionary-doctor David Livingstone, as well as Hollywood films such as 1951's *The African Queen* (which surely influenced the conception of the ride at Disneyland) and Disney's own

---

56 Pugh and Aronstein, editors, *The Disney Middle Ages*, 214; Eleanor Byrne and Martin McQuillan, *Deconstructing Disney* (Sterling, Virginia: Pluto Press, 1999), 73, 76-82; Pinsky, *The Gospel According to Disney*, 150-153; Janet Wasko, *Understanding Disney: The Manufacture of Fantasy* (Cambridge: Polity Press, 2001), 140-141; Brenda Ayres, editor, *The Emperor's Old Groove: Decolonizing Disney's Magic Kingdom* (New York: Peter Lang, 2013), 8–10, 66–69, 105.

57 John Schultz, "The Fabulous Presumption of Disney World: Magic Kingdom in the Wilderness," *The Georgia Review*, 42(Summer 1988), 303-304; Ayres, editor, *The Emperor's Old Groove*, 18.

True-Life Adventures film, *African Lion*. But this "compressed safari" is much more than its critics give it credit for. Ultimately, the Jungle Cruise is about illusion.[58] It gives people not just the experience of traveling the world's rivers, but also encountering animals and people quite different from their fellow Disney guests (other than the skipper of their boat, all the other guest encounters are based upon audio-animatronics, since live animals and real head-hunters could simply not be trusted).[59] While at times it might run parallel to the colonialism/imperialism critique, it is more in the tone (adventure) rather than the plot (white people traversing the dark heart of Africa and Asia) of these works.

And for many guests, the idea that they can get a glimpse (through the lens of Dis-History), of the wider world is powerful. You could see a real crocodile at a zoo, but to see one in the water while on a cruise requires that you either travel to the Nile River or take a ride on Disney's Jungle Cruise. Walt wanted people to enjoy the ride, and take in the animals and the adventure. He wanted it to last longer than just four or five minutes. As technology has improved, Disney's Imagineers have attempted to make attractions like the Jungle Cruise more realistic. But they have also not lost sight of the goal that its purpose is to entertain. Indeed, for its power to inspire via the imagination, one of the Jungle Cruise's chief defenders was Ray Bradbury. Rather than join with critics who saw the attraction as yet another example of Disney replacing the real experiences with artificial ones, Bradbury noted that the Jungle Cruise was something most guests could actually do and be inspired by.[60] After all, people can afford a trip to a Disney park much easier than trips to Africa, Asia, and South America.

Ultimately, Disney and Dis-History is not really interested in academic debates about colonialism or imperialism. Rather, their focus is

---

58 Didier Ghez, editor, *Walt's People: Volume 5: Talking Disney with the Artists Who Knew Him* (Theme Park Press, 2016), 322; Kiste, *A Historical Tour of Walt Disney World*.

59 *The Imagineering Field Guide to Disneyland: An Imagineer's Eye Tour* (New York: Disney Editions, 2008), 36.

60 Marling, editor, *Designing Disney's Theme Parks*, 109, 111; Umberto Eco, *Travels in Hyper Reality* (New York: Harcourt Brace and Company, 1986), 44–45; Richard Schickel, *The Disney Version: The Life, Times, Art and Commerce of Walt Disney, Third Edition* (Chicago: Ivan R. Dee, 1997), 344; Marling, "Disneyland, 1955: Just Take the Santa Ana Freeway to the American Dream," 173; Michael R. Real, *Mass-Mediated Culture* (Englewood Cliffs, New Jersey: Prentice-Hall, 1977), 64–65; Kuenz, Klugman, Waldrep, and Willis, editors, *Inside the Mouse*, 184; Davis, Marc. Interviewed by Gabe Essoe, 1972, Walt Disney Studio Archives, Burbank, California; Mattey, Bob. Interviewed by George Sherman, Lectures and Transcripts, Walt Disney Studio Archives, Burbank, California.

on points of encounter—both in terms of bringing historical themes into contact with present-day guests to produce experiences, and to further the theme of adventure. Guests might encounter different cultures in Adventureland, but they are having fun while they do it. Dis-History has made sure that, as a result, they are more apt to remember and, it is hoped, seek out more information.

Standardizing American Folk Tales

The rivers of the Jungle Cruise are not the only bodies of water in these areas of the parks. In Frontierland, the area is dominated by the Rivers of America. At Disneyland, two boats take guests around: the Sailing Ship *Columbia* (a schooner of early America) and the *Mark Twain* riverboat, complementing the notion that Frontierland tells America's history from the colonial period through the mid-1800s. The Magic Kingdom's Frontierland boasts the *Liberty Belle* on its version of the waters, while Disneyland Paris has the *Molly Brown* Riverboat (named for the "unsinkable" Molly Brown of *Titanic* fame). Here guests can be reminded of adventure of another kind, the romance of sailing and getting lost in the moment as the ship navigates the water.

It is hardly surprising, given Dis-History, that in the middle of this river system in both California and Florida, there is an island named for one of Mark Twain's most famous characters, Tom Sawyer. Considering their shared Missouri past, their fictitious explorations (and love affair) with the West, and their understanding of the power of transportation (whether river or rail), it would be more surprising if Twain's greatest characters did not appear in a Disney park. As a child, Walt read all he could find on Mark Twain, and drew inspiration from both author and stories for his park. The buildings and caves on the island are to scale, as is the fort (which feeds into the theming of Frontierland). Not only does this reflect Dis-History, but the island reminded Disney of his own childhood. It is a place where he would have liked to have played as a child and is a secluded sanctuary in the midst of the park.[61]

As the swirling waters around Tom Sawyer Island mythically merge America's rivers into one, so too does Disney have an interest in not just using, but crafting a standard narrative out of a wide variety of versions. Such cultural creation is at the heart of Dis-History. One could argue that Frontierland and Adventureland are the best places to see this phenomenon. But so, too, is New Orleans Square.

The inclusion of New Orleans Square at Disneyland fit with the construction of the bend in the Rivers of America, with its planned paddle

---

61 Thomas, *Walt Disney*, 36; Fjellman, *Vinyl Leaves*, 77; Schickel, *The Disney Version*, 324; Jackson and West, editors, *Disneyland and Culture*, 101–103.

wheeler. Here was a sign of civilization in the midst of the frontier experience. From a historical perspective, New Orleans was one of, if not the, premier river city in America, sitting as it does where the Mississippi River empties into the Gulf of Mexico. It also fit with wider design ideas for the park, of bringing something different (the South) into the midst of southern California, while expanding the sweep of American history that guests encounter in Frontierland.[62] And while Walt enjoyed pointing out that his New Orleans was cleaner than the real thing (including to the mayor of the city),[63] by bringing the South into his park he was doing something else as well. He was raising the specter of race relations.[64]

Such a discussion, steeped in Dis-History, was present in how the square was dedicated on July 24, 1966, and in how Disney described the area to the press in the years since. Walt said:

> Disneyland, as you know, is sort of made up of the various things that represent our country. As Main Street is, you know, it's the turn of the century. It represents the kind of life that was changing then from the horse and buggy on into the electrical area now the electronic and things. And we have our Adventureland, we have our Frontierland. Frontierland is a—is representing the hearty pioneers and things that really made this country in the last hundred years what it is. And New Orleans comes into this thing in this way. That it was a very important acquisition that we made at the time that we purchased New Orleans from the French and I don't know if many of you are familiar with that deal. That was the biggest real estate deal ever, I think, consummated. The real reason that we wanted to—we wanted to buy New Orleans port. We had no interest in anything but the city of New Orleans. But in negotiating with Napoleon, Napoleon had his hands full over in Europe with the wars and things and he could only get them up to a certain price for the city. So he told his negotiators, he said, "Well, throw in the peripheral area and see if you can get another couple of million out of them," and so they did and it made a good deal. And the peripheral area took us clear up to the Canadian border and that is what is known as the Louisiana Purchase. So it was a great—what you might call—not a political maneuver. It was statesmanship. Now also you know, the Gadsden Purchase

---

62 *The Imagineering Field Guide to Disneyland: An Imagineer's Eye Tour* (New York: Disney Editions, 2008), 58.

63 Avila, *Popular Culture in the Age of White Flight*, 134–135; Gabler, *Walt Disney*, 619.

64 Avila, *Popular Culture in the Age of White Flight*, 132.

was another part of the expansion of our country and that is what will be known, and developed later on, as the Mexican area over here, because that is when we purchased all of Arizona, and the New Mexico territory. And remember we *purchased*, we purchased, we didn't acquire it by any other means. We went out and we paid for it and we bought it. We bought Alaska. And we bought the land from Mexico. And it wasn't by conquest that we acquired it. And I think we should be proud of that. Anyway, that what New Orleans Square means in this land of Disneyland. Which again, this entire theme is based on Americana.[65]

While long on history, there was no mention of slavery in Walt's words (nor, for that matter, the war with Mexico). Nor was there any from New Orleans' mayor, Victor Schiro, though he did praise Walt, saying, "You have done more than any man in the world that I know of for the children of our great country."[66] The press release that went along with the speeches show this was a conscious omission: "The time is the 1860s ... the place is New Orleans where cotton was king and the Good Life was his decree."[67] The timing means slavery has to be part of the historic conversation. But Dis-History offers only silence. Subsequent reimagining by 1971 placed the square in the 1850s, which does little for the lack of mention of slavery. Indeed, in some ways it is even worse. This "bygone era"[68] is described as one with well-dressed ladies and gentlemen (presumably white planters), "Indian squaws," and "hawkers." But there remains no mention of slaves.[69]

As we have seen, critics often fault Dis-History for not talking about difficult historical issues. But with the silences in New Orleans Square, Disney is raising it directly, even when they are not mentioned overtly. Whether with the original Aunt Jemima's kitchen or with today's references to *Princess and the Frog*, Disney is opening the door for guests to raise questions about what it means to think about the Old South,

---

65 Disney, Walt. "Speech at opening of New Orleans Square at Disneyland" folder, Disney, Walt—Lectures and Transcripts, Walt Disney Studio Archives, Burbank, California.

66 Disney, Walt. "Speech at opening of New Orleans Square at Disneyland" folder, Disney, Walt—Lectures and Transcripts, Walt Disney Studio Archives, Burbank, California.

67 New Orleans Square-General (DL). "Welcome to New Orleans Square 1966." Walt Disney Studio Archives, Burbank, California.

68 New Orleans Square-General (DL). "New Orleans Square 24 July 1966-24 July 1971." Walt Disney Studio Archives, Burbank, California.

69 New Orleans Square-General (DL). "WED Imagineering, Disneyland 1966." Walt Disney Studio Archives, Burbank, California.

and even of slavery. Where does slavery fit into the American past? What does it mean for present-day race relations? How can/should it be discussed? What does/did the Civil War mean/do for the nation? And if guests turn to the nearby Splash Mountain (a log ride that is almost assured to end in at least one person in the log getting wet), those issues go to the next level.[70]

Few who make the journey down the mountain have probably ever seen the movie that inspired it, and fewer still have read the stories that Walt based the movie off of. The theming is of Br'er Rabbit, Br'er Fox, Br'er Bear, and their friends. The movie is *Song of the South*. And the origins of the stories are found in Joel Chandler Harris' collection of Uncle Remus tales. Taken together, not only are they another example of Dis-History's standardization, but we also have discussion of race at nearly unprecedented levels.

In November 1946, Disney released *Song of the South*, a movie that harkened back to Walt's early years of mixing animation with live-action sequences. The stated goal was to introduce a portion of Harris' stories to a new generation because "of their place in the heritage of this country" and because there was some "ambivalence" (according to scholars) about them.[71] Walt had always loved the stories, and was drawn to them as a project because of the animals that acted like people. From a business standpoint, *Song of the South* was attractive because the mixture of live action and animation would help keep costs down and provide Disney with a diverse product. Most of the live-action sequences were filmed before World War II, and the animation afterward (to the great joy of the animators, who were pleased to work on something that was not war related). Walt had high hopes for the movie.[72]

But almost immediately there were problems. To begin with, Dis-History was employed to standardize the stories, which had been collected by Harris (who was white) from blacks both before and after the Civil War, with some of the stories in his collection having distinctly African roots. Disney then created a narrative for the film that used Harris' characters and setting, but created essentially an original

---

70 Marty Sklar, *Dream It! Do It!: My Half-Century Creating Disney's Magic Kingdoms* (New York: Disney Editions, 2013), 232.

71 Jason Sperb, *Disney's Most Notorious Film: Race, Convergence, and the Hidden Histories of Song of the South* (Austin: University of Texas Press, 2012), 37.

72 Sperb, *Disney's Most Notorious Film*, 83; Jim Korkis, *Who's Afraid of the Song of the South? And Other Forbidden Disney Stories* (Orlando: Theme Park Press, 2012), 21, 25, 77; Thomas, *Walt Disney*, 204-205; Gabler, *Walt Disney*, 437; Watts, *The Magic Kingdom*, 273–275.

story.[73] On the surface, that is fairly standard. But in reality, Disney had to contend with the issue of race. Uncle Remus is an elderly black man and the stories Harris captured were first told in the United States by slaves. Should Disney set the story in the Old South, and attempt to cash in on the Lost Cause/*Gone with the Wind* mentality, or should they set the story after the war, perhaps even explicitly during Reconstruction? With neither being a perfect solution, the company opted to blur the historical fabric of the stories (Dis-History trumping history) in order to avoid directly having to talk about slavery at all.[74] By having the film told largely from the perspective of the children, Disney was able to be vague about events happening outside of the main story arc, reasoning that they did not know what was going on in the wider world.[75]

Blurring the historical era may have allowed Disney to not deal with slavery, but the issue of race was always going to be front and center. The character of Uncle Remus is black after all. In Harris' stories, Remus is a moral educator in the vein of Aesop, using stories about animals to dispense folk wisdom to his listeners. However, as critics saw Uncle Remus on film, he was little more than a stereotypical minstrel, singing, dancing, and telling humorous stories—all character traits for blacks in film that Hollywood was beginning to move away from, but that Disney seemed to be reaffirming.[76] Maurice Rapf, who worked on *Song of the South*, believed that the problem was not in the script, but rather how the characters were portrayed in the film. When he saw an early cut of the movie, he anticipated a backlash against it.[77]

The premiere, held in Atlanta to much fanfare, was a segregated one, and without its star. This was hardly a surprise, as even during shooting of the live-action sequences, most of which took place in Phoenix, Arizona, the man portraying Uncle Remus, James Baskett, had been unable to find a hotel room. He was able to rent a room in the

---

73 Peggy A. Russo, "Uncle Walt's Uncle Remus: Disney's Distortion of Harris's Hero," *The Southern Literary Journal*, 25(Fall, 1992), 19–32; Korkis, *Who's Afraid of the Song of the South?*, 94.

74 Korkis, *Who's Afraid of the Song of the South?*, 32; Didier Ghez, editor, *Walt's People: Volume 3: Talking Disney with the Artists Who Knew Him* (Theme Park Press, 2015), 236.

75 Ghez, editor, *Walt's People: Volume 6*, 137.

76 Sperb, *Disney's Most Notorious Film*, 13–15; Russo, "Uncle Walt's Uncle Remus: Disney's Distortion of Harris's Hero," 19–32; Elizabeth Bell, Lynda Haas, and Laura Sells, editors, *From Mouse to Mermaid: The Politics of Film, Gender, and Culture* (Indianapolis: Indiana University Press, 1995), 88–91.

77 Ghez, editor, *Walt's People: Volume 6*, 136-137. Rapf was a Communist, who later was blacklisted.

back of a laundry, where a car picked him up each day for shooting. But a segregated premiere was the least of Disney's worries. While there are many more films that are blatantly racist than *Song of the South*, the movie was coming at the same time as the post-war civil rights movement was beginning to take shape. Film critics, though largely praising the animation and Baskett's acting, also attacked Disney (and in some cases Baskett) for the way blacks were portrayed in the film. Indeed, the film launched a debate over race and Hollywood, with critics alleging that *Song of the South* was incredibly racist because its use of animation tricked children (and adults) into thinking that such representations of African Americans were correct. Other critics believed that only educated blacks (perhaps once again reflecting the old anti-Disney bias that high culturalists could find no redeeming value in anything the studio produced) were likely to take offence while lower-class African-Americans would enjoy the film. And despite blacks being portrayed so prominently, the movie was also seen as "safe" for white adults to take their children to see.[78] According to Peggy Russo, the latter group, whites, were exactly the audience Disney had in mind all along for the film. It was never designed to appeal to a racially diverse audience.[79]

And yet, there is something inconsistent with at least some of the criticism. Disney may very well have been aiming at a white audience, but they were doing so with an African-American actor as the lead, and many African-Americans in the film and as voice talent. Walt may have used iconic figures ("Tom" and "Mammy"), but those figures were still expected by white audiences, even if public opinion about them was starting to shift. He may have standardized the Remus stories, but he was telling a largely white audience stories that originated within black circles. Moreover, the villains in *Song of the South* are clearly "the white redneck children," while the protagonists (other than Remus) are two little boys, one black and the other white, who form an interracial friendship. According to Douglas Brode, "in Walt's vision of the world, only when blacks and whites exist in a state of total equality do we discover a proper sense of order in the universe."[80] Beyond that, we do not really know what Walt's view on race relations were. He used

---

78 Eric Smoodin, *Animating Culture: Hollywood Cartoons from the Sound Era* (New Brunswick, NJ: Rutgers University Press, 1993), 107–108; Korkis, *Who's Afraid of the Song of the South?*, 19, 64–65, 75, 80; Sperb, *Disney's Most Notorious Film*, 71, 82, 154–155; Didier Ghez, editor, *Walt's People: Volume 7: Talking Disney with the Artists Who Knew Him* (New York: Xlibris Corporation, 2008), 220.

79 Russo, "Uncle Walt's Uncle Remus: Disney's Distortion of Harris's Hero," 19–32.

80 Brode, *Multiculturalism and the Mouse*, 54–55, 59–61, 77.

mildly racist language from time to time, but that was not uncommon considering his own background and when he lived. Even if shocking to modern ears considering the Walt mythos, it proves more he was an average white American who had flaws. The studio had depicted Africans in overtly racists ways in some of its cartoons and comic books, to be sure. Yet, Walt worked to promote the careers of blacks who did work for him, including Baskett (without whose support, *Song of the South* could not have been made). Walt pushed to get Baskett an honorary Academy Award, in part because the man who had portrayed Uncle Remus was in ill health, and in part because he carried the film— including singing and doing some voice work as well. When he received it at the 1948 Academy Awards, mere months before his death, Baskett was the first African-American male to be awarded an Oscar. None of this is to say that Walt was a civil rights champion, but with *Song of the South* neither was he trying to "write history with lightening" either.[81]

Despite winning an Academy Award in its own right (for Best Song), *Song of the South* was not a commercial success (in part because of the accusations of racism), and remained the only Disney film with an black protagonist until *Princess and the Frog* in 2009. Though it has not been released since the 1980s (it is the only film permanently locked away in the Disney vaults), *Song of the South* lives on, in large part thanks to Splash Mountain and the nearly seventy years of controversy. It also remains a film (for those who have seen it) with a richly contested legacy that is open to multiple levels of interpretation.[82] But this kind of debate is lost in Frontierland. Even as Disney's Uncle Remus displaced Harris' (in a way, the ultimate act of standardization) in the minds of both the general population and (as Russo notes, even) academics,[83] it is not Uncle Remus who takes center stage on Splash Mountain. In a Dis-Historic triumph, it is the animals (Br'er Rabbit, Br'er Fox, and Br'er Bear) who narrate the ride's action. And for those who stand in line on a hot day to journey through the briar patch, that is all that matters.

Though racism might not be present at Splash Mountain, the questions raised by *Song of the South* still linger around Disney. While some film critics note that stereotypes are needed in movies, because they can be used to hasten character development without necessarily being

---

81 Watts, *The Magic Kingdom*, 275–280; Korkis, *Who's Afraid of the Song of the South?*, 42–43; Bell, Haas, and Sells, editors, *From Mouse to Mermaid*, 88–91; Ghez, editor, *Walt's People: Volume 7*, 49.

82 Sperb, *Disney's Most Notorious Film*, 6–7. Sperb, for example, sees the movie's continued relevance as part of white backlash against the civil rights movement.

83 Russo, "Uncle Walt's Uncle Remus: Disney's Distortion of Harris's Hero," 27–29.

racist, utilizing them as a device opens a filmmaker up to charges of racism. Looking historically at films can lead to new analysis that resurrect charges of racism as well.[84] In the case of other Disney movies, *Dumbo*, the 1941 animated classic (about a flying elephant), is a good example. Though the narrative is about a young elephant calf with large ears who becomes a circus star after learning how to fly, the movie includes minstrel-like black crows (who are clearly caricatures of African-Americans) that help him along the way.[85] Alternatively, one might also look at Disney and the issue of racism via 1955's *Lady and the Tramp*. Here there are enough racial stereotypes or caricatures than perhaps in any other film: the Siamese cats are villains (showcasing a fear of Asians, or at least some variant of the "Yellow Peril"), there are dogs that represent England, Scotland, Russia, Mexico, Germany, Italy, and the American South—all of which are used in the context of showing early twentieth-century America as a land of immigrants and diversity. Then, of course, there are Lady and the Tramp themselves: two very different kinds of Americans (one upper class, the other working class and a mutt to boot) who bring an element of classism to the discussion as well.[86] Unlike *Dumbo*, *Lady and the Tramp* has no ride in the Magic Kingdom—though Tony's Italian restaurant is a mainstay of Main Street, but its cinematic use of stereotypes seem to provide plenty of evidence of prejudice indeed.

However, while these might be (in the opinion of some) rather damning proof positive, it is instructive to remember that what critics allege and what Dis-History actually does do not always match up with one another. In the case of *Song of the South*, for example, Floyd Norman, an African-American Disney animator, has argued that "Walt Disney had no racial agenda in his 1948 motion picture ... the stories, thankfully preserved by Joel Chandler Harris are part of our American heritage even though a part of it deals with a period in our history we would rather forget. However, forgetting history is never a good idea. Walt Disney understood that, and so should the rest of us."[87] Or one could look at whether Walt and his company were anti-Semitic. The

---

84 Korkis, *Who's Afraid of the Song of the South?*, xi-xii; Janet Wasko, *Understanding Disney: The Manufacture of Fantasy* (Cambridge: Polity Press, 2001), 139.
85 Brode, *Multiculturalism and the Mouse*, 51; Pinsky, *The Gospel According to Disney*, 43.
86 Byrne and McQuillan, *Deconstructing Disney*, 98–99; Pinsky, *The Gospel According to Disney*, 69, 73.
87 "Forgetting History is Never a Good Idea—Mr. Fun's Journal," http://floydnormancom.squarespace.com/blog/2016/8/8/forgetting-history-is-never-a-good-idea, 11 August 2016.

allegations were first heard during the 1941 strike by Disney workers, levied by former employees who were fired as a result and some of their union allies (both groups of which contained men who were Jewish). Disney's supporters are quick to point out that disgruntled workers and union officials (some of whom also happened to either be or whom Walt believed to be communists) are not, perhaps, the best witnesses to bring against Walt. Nor should he and the company be labeled as anti-Semitic simply because he happened to be in competition with other studios (who were headed by Jews) and against whom he said derogatory things, any more than there is proof in the fact that he was a wealthy Protestant who lived in an exclusive community proves he hated Jews. Critics, some of whom argue that all these things fit into a pattern of anti-Semitism, will inevitably point to Disney's 1933 and 1934 short masterpieces, *The Three Little Pigs* and *The Big Bad Wolf*, respectively, as cinematic proof of their charges. In particular, they argue that the Big Bad Wolf adopting a "peddler persona" is blatantly anti-Semitic. Up against this, Walt's defenders will point to Walt and his company hiring many Jews (including, eventually, Michael Eisner) and the fact that the *Three Little Pigs* was an early foray into Dis-History, the creation of a common literary heritage for all Americans out of various European stories (including Jewish sources).[88]

Ultimately, raising discussions about race or anti-Semitism or some other issue does more to help Dis-History than deter it. While critics might believe they have Disney figured out, what they are actually helping to show is just how complicated and important what Disney is doing with their attempt to create a common American culture. By engaging it, raising issues with it, and even in trying to debunk it, critics are not only validating Dis-History but also advancing and refining its mission, by forcing the company and its defenders to engage in a spirited debate over what, say, a rabbit in a briar patch or a flying elephant who clutches a feather actually mean for Americans.[89]

Helping guests begin to start wrestling with big issues like there are exactly what Frontierland and Adventureland accomplish. Confronting, even in small ways, such issues is something that these lands help to foster. These areas of the parks give guests a visual rendering of America's "creation myth," one that is nurtured by an individualism (the guest, the citizen) in service to the public good (having

---

88 Wasko, *Understanding Disney*, 139; Pinsky, *The Gospel According to Disney*, 111–113; Gabler, *Walt Disney*, 456-457; Eisner, *Work in Progress*, 33; Sklar, *Dream It! Do It!*, 44–45; Didier Ghez, editor, *Walt's People: Volume 2: Talking Disney with the Artists Who Knew Him* (Theme Park Press, 2015), 122–123.

89 Watts, *The Magic Kingdom*, xvii, 33.

fun, being patriotic). If suburbia created a "geography of nowhere" that needed something, including a common past, to center it, then lessons learned on the frontier and various adventures provided by Disney stoked the fires to make that happen.[90] And as the 1990s dawned, Michael Eisner believed he was firmly in position to keep those efforts going for years to come.[91]

---

90 Pugh and Aronstein, editors, *The Disney Middle Ages*, 60-62; Watts, *The Magic Kingdom*, 299, 302; Andrea Carosso, "America's Disneylands and the end-of-century American Cityscape," *Revue francaise d'etudes americaines* 83(January 2000), 66.

91 Joe Flower, *Prince of the Magic Kingdom: Michael Eisner and the Re-Making of Disney* (New York: John Wiley and Sons, Inc., 1991), 1.

CHAPTER SEVEN

A Great Big Beautiful Tomorrow(land)

Experience the Carousel of Progress

How do we experience the past? Can we anticipate the future? Should we see history as the advancement of progress to a better tomorrow? Walt Disney answered "yes" to all these questions and sought to prove it with the Carousel of Progress. Housed today at Walt Disney World's Magic Kingdom, the Carousel is a Dis-Historic glimpse into the past and the future, both in terms of Disney's own history as well as that of people who experienced the arc of twentieth-century history.

The Carousel allows guests to witness "how industrial advances over the past century have changed everyday living for an American family." The show "follows a typical American family—narrated by patriarch, John—through 4 generations of the past 100 years" with each generation showcasing the technological advances of the past and how they build toward the future. The attraction is no simple walk-through, however. To make it interesting and entertaining, the Carousel rotates its seated guests around the staged scenes.[1] It is a unique means of display and a nice Disney take on a theater in the round, which can be as captivating a concept as the scenes themselves. The first act, set at the dawn of the twentieth century, shows such artifacts as gas lamps, a hand-cranked washing machine, and a gramophone. The second act, set in the 1920s, showcases new electric conveniences including an iron, radio, sewing machine, and light bulbs. The late 1940s, where the third act is set, offers an automatic dishwasher, an exercise machine, and television. The final act, set in the near present, has a virtual reality video game, high-definition television, and voice-activated appliances. The intention with the last scene, since the attraction

---

1 "Carousel of Progress," https://disneyworld.disney.go.com/attractions/magic-kingdom/walt-disney-carousel-of-progress/, 20 February 2014.

became part of the Disney park system, is to always keep it updated (though this is followed in principle more than in practice), so that it continues to anticipate "a dream come true for you and me."[2]

Walt's vision for Tomorrowland, perhaps more so than any other land in the parks, was shaped by the 1964 World's Fair. As we have seen, Walt had long been influenced by World's Fairs, but as the park system came into being, he became more active with them. For the 1958 fair, in Brussels, Belgium, Disney created a film entitled *America the Beautiful*, which became the hit of the exposition.[3] As planning began for a World's Fair to be held in New York City, fair organizers wanted Disney to be a part, believing it would drive up attendance. Walt agreed, but planned on going a step further than he had in Brussels. Armed with a list of corporations who were being asked to underwrite the fair, Walt began to pitch the idea of Disney-designed pavilions, themed to showcase the corporations involved. He asked only for a $1 million fee and the right to use what was produced (after the fair) in his park. He believed this was win/win/win—companies would get world class attractions for the fair, Disneyland would get new attractions at virtually no cost, and Walt could test out the possibility of building an East Coast park.[4]

Walt went ahead with the World's Fair projects, even though he only had a year to design and build attractions, and despite some on his staff doubting if it could be done.[5] He found four sponsors for his WED Imagineers to build pavilions for, each with their own demands—both from the sponsors and from the space allocated them by the World's

---

[2] John Hench with Peggy Van Pelt, *Designing Disney: Imagineering and the Art of the Show* (New York: Disney Editions, 2008), 10–11; "Carousel of Progress," https://disneyworld.disney.go.com/attractions/magic-kingdom/walt-disney-carousel-of-progress/, 20 February 2014.

[3] Neal Gabler, *Walt Disney: The Triumph of the American Imagination* (New York: Vintage Books, 2007), 574.

[4] Michael Barrier, *The Animated Man: A Life of Walt Disney* (Los Angeles: University of California Press, 2007), 291; Bob Thomas, *Walt Disney: An American Original* (New York: Disney Editions, 1994), 307–311; Gabler, *Walt Disney*, 575–576; Bob Thomas, *Building a Company: Roy O. Disney and the Creation of an Entertainment Empire* (New York: Hyperion, 1998), 251; Marty Sklar, *Dream It! Do It!: My Half-Century Creating Disney's Magic Kingdoms* (New York: Disney Editions, 2013), 108; Joseph Tirella, *Tomorrow-Land: The 1964–1965 World's Fair and the Transformation of America* (Guilford, Connecticut: Lyons Press, 2014), 49–50; Robert A. Caro, *The Power Broker: Robert Moses and the Fall of New York* (New York: Alfred A. Knopf, 1974), 1092; "Walt Disney and World's Fairs," http://www.expomuseum.com/disney/, 15 November 2015.

[5] Joe Flower, *Prince of the Magic Kingdom: Michael Eisner and the Re-Making of Disney* (New York: John Wiley and Sons, Inc., 1991), 23.

Fair board. As we have seen, Great Moments with Mr. Lincoln was built for the State of Illinois. Ford Motor Company sponsored Disney's Magic Skyway which used PeopleMover technology to transport guests from pre-historic times to a futuristic city. Pepsi and UNICEF were the sponsors of It's A Small World, while Carousel of Progress was built for General Electric. By the end of the fair, the four Disney-built pavilions were among the most popular and most visited by fair goers.[6]

Considering what he hoped to gain, most observers believe that of all the World's Fair attractions, Walt put the most of himself into Carousel of Progress. The attraction blends two of his favorite things, family and progress, into its presentation—in large part because of his insistence and attention. He asked the Sherman brothers, already acclaimed at the studio for producing catchy songs for both movies and the parks (and who were also composing a song for It's a Small World), to craft what became "A Great Big Beautiful Tomorrow" for the Carousel. Eventually, his Imagineers produced a concept that showed the march of progress (as largely told through General Electric products), using audio-animatronics and a catchy jingle. Walt was well on his way to creating a show that was destined to break the record for most staged performances in American history.[7]

The only problem was that the pavilion's sponsor, General Electric, initially balked at the idea of using historic nostalgia to showcase their products. In a meeting ahead of the fair, one GE vice president expressed serious doubts. Walt, who had already disposed of internal Disney criticisms that the Carousel was little more than a "refrigerator commercial," now turned his fury on his corporate partner. Noting that he had built an entire company around nostalgia, Walt told the GE delegation that he knew his idea would reach people and if they did not want to go forward with it, he was willing to not create a pavilion for them. When the CEO of G.E., Gerald Philippi, learned of Walt's investment in the concept, he quickly approved the Carousel project. Ultimately, the Carousel of Progress cost G.E. $10 million and when the company's board of directors saw the finished show, they loved it.[8]

---

6   Sklar, *Dream It! Do It!*, 104; Karal Ann Marling, editor, *Designing Disney's Theme Parks: The Architecture of Reassurance* (New York: Flammarion, 1997), 22; Hench with Van Pelt, *Designing Disney*, 10; Andi Stein, *Why We Love Disney: The Power of the Disney Brand* (New York: Peter Lang, 2011), 26.

7   "Q&A: Vanessa Hunt and Tony Baxter," http://www.waltdisney.org/storyboard/qa-vanessa-hunt-and-tony-baxter, 5 June 2014; Steven Watts, *The Magic Kingdom: Walt Disney and the America Way of Life* (New York: Houghton Mifflin Company, 1997), 415.

8   Gabler, *Walt Disney*, 577, 602; ; Tirella, *Tomorrow-Land*, 54.

When the fair was over, Disney packed up the Carousel and shipped it back to California. Originally, it was to go to Disneyland, for an area called "Edison Square." Imagineers planned to build a new portion of the park that would "dramatically present the story of the way in which one invention by Thomas A. Edison has influenced the growth and development of America and the world"—the lightbulb. It was to be a "residential expansion" of Main Street, with electricity replacing gas, and national exteriors, including New York brownstones, Philadelphia red brick, Chicago graystone, wood buildings pulled from San Francisco and St. Louis, colonial Boston buildings.[9] But when Edison Square was scrapped, the Carousel stayed in the park only until 1975, when it moved to Florida and the Magic Kingdom, where it remains as "a tribute to nostalgia."[10]

For historians, there is something very Whigish about the Carousel. Of course, there is the notion of progress, and surely there are parallels to be drawn to the Progressive Era that Walt came of age in—with its belief that if a problem was worked on long enough, a solution (often governmental) could be found. But there is something deeper going on here, a belief not just in progress and technology, but that these are things in the American context that have a unique, historical inevitability about them. Walt and his Imagineers infused the Carousel with a sense of pride that is unmistakable.[11]

The Carousel of Progress is perhaps the best representation possible of Dis-History as an attraction. There is no debate about the historical action that is on display. Each set is minutely accurate in both its words, staging, and props. But the narrative thread, that progress is linked to both technology and consumerism (coming as it does from an audio-animatronic narrator), also opens it up to critics. Among the criticism (beyond just the storyline of progress), there are charges that guests are passive (as they are seated) and that Disney is lecturing (or indoctrinating) a captive audience. The latter point is interesting, if only because one does not see similar criticisms about the Hall of

---

9 *Edison Square (Misc. DL) file, Walt Disney Studio Archives, Burbank, California.*

10 "Carousel of Progress," https://disneyworld.disney.go.com/attractions/magic-kingdom/walt-disney-carousel-of-progress/, 20 February 2014.

11 Hench with Van Pelt, *Designing Disney*, 10; Warren Leon and Roy Rosenzweig, editors, *History Museums in the United States: A Critical Assessment* (Chicago: University of Illinois Press, 1989), 165; Jane Kuenz, Karen Klugman, Shelton Waldrep, and Susan Willis, editors, *Inside the Mouse: Work and Play at Disney World* (Durham: Duke University Press, 1995), 59; Cher Krause Knight, *Power and Paradise in Walt Disney's World* (Gainesville: University Press of Florida, 2014), 129.

Presidents, for example. Perhaps we can explain that simply because the Carousel's narrative is about consumerism, instead of patriotism—though, as we will see, there are critics who would argue that Disney attempts to link those two forces as well, in a vast corporate conspiracy to dominate both America and the world's popular culture.[12] But the Carousel highlights something else: Dis-History anticipates the future based on the past.

Critics have also interpreted the Carousel as being a means to convey to visitors that the traditional nuclear family is the norm and can survive the currents of history. As Henry Giroux puts it, Disney "renders history as an affirmation of a Norman Rockwell painting."[13] Of course, the family is merely the means to a narrative end, and it is not just a nuclear (mom, dad, brother, sister) family either, as other relatives live at the house. But considering Walt's belief that his company embodied family values, it is not a stretch to imagine this scenario, or Walt's embrace of it as an observation (rather than a critique) either.

The familial scenes guests witness as part of the Carousel of Progress are hardly revolutionary themselves. John and his family live in "average" middle-class homes in each time period.[14] In that respect, the Carousel represents historic reality. Though it is a reality that "blatantly promotes corporate ideals" and links them to park themes,[15] what is revolutionary is the march of progress that history, those ideals, and the park itself showcase. It takes the guests from the past, to the present,and right on to a great, big, beautiful tomorrow.

Visions and Reality

Perhaps, befittingly, the Carousel of Progress is part of Tomorrowland. According to Christian Moran, when Disneyland opened the goal was to create a land that was "science-factual," and give guests a glimpse of what the future held. It is the area of the park in which Dis-History (because it deals with the future) has the hardest time finding its footing. But it shows the inevitable conclusion of Dis-History, a future firmly rooted in the past and yet (optimistically) has transcended it. If a guest ends their day in Tomorrowland, they will have traversed

---

12 "Luis Marin: Disneyland as Degenerate Utopia," http://lmc.gatech.edu/~broglio/1101/marin.html, 23 September 2014.

13 Henry A. Giroux, *The Mouse that Roared: Disney and the End of Innocence* (New York: Rowman and Littlefield, 1999), 40–41.

14 Andrew Kiste, *A Historical Tour of Walt Disney World* (Theme Park Press, 2015).

15 Janet Wasko, *Understanding Disney: The Manufacture of Fantasy* (Cambridge: Polity Press, 2001), 160.

lands of myth and history and arrived ready to face the future that lies before them. And, as we will see, Dis-History also was a means to transform the land into something workable as the years progressed.

Tomorrowland, like Disneyland itself, was conceived in the 1950s, when optimism about the future and America's role in the world were high. At the park, Walt wanted people to see the world not just in terms of the mythic past and fantasy, but also get a glimpse of the future. And considering what some commentators argue is America's "preoccupation with the future," the land also made a good deal of sense. Guests get to see potential implications of the future might be for themselves and for the United States, but Tomorrowland also asked the most of guests, that this is what the future was going to hold in store.[16]

The land was also problematic for Disney from the start. Walt announced its existence on the television show that allowed him to build Disneyland, without having a plan for what was to actually go into the area—unlike the rollout for Fantasyland, Frontierland, and Adventureland. Indeed, the company had never really engaged the concept of the future before.[17] Now they had to be.

Luckily, the 1950s provided Disney with the material they needed to develop Tomorrowland: outer space. If Frontierland could draw upon manifest destiny and the railroad for inspiration, then Tomorrowland was going to draw upon the notion that space was a new frontier, just waiting to be conquered by American know-how. Considering the influence that railroads had on Walt, it is little wonder that space travel also captured his imagination as the middle of the twentieth century began.[18] As he said at the opening, "tomorrow offers new frontiers in science, adventure, and ideals. The Atomic Age, the challenge of outer space ... and the hope for a peaceful and unified world."[19]

---

16   "Q&A: Vanessa Hunt and Tony Baxter," http://www.waltdisney.org/storyboard/qa-vanessa-hunt-and-tony-baxter, 5 June 2014; Christopher Finch, *Walt Disney's America* (New York: Abbeville Press, 1978), 181; Thomas Hine, *Populuxe* (New York: Alfred A. Knopf, 1986), 152; Scott Bukatman, "There's Always Tomorrowland: Disney and the Hypercinematic Experience," *October* (Summer, 1991), 57; Michael R. Real, *Mass-Mediated Culture* (Englewood Cliffs, New Jersey: Prentice-Hall, 1977), 56.

17   J. P. Telotte (2005) Disney in Science Fiction Land, *Journal of Popular Film and Television*, 33:1, 12–21, DOI: 10.3200/JPFT.33.1.12-21.

18   Bruce Mazlish, editor, *The Railroad and the Space Program: An Exploration in Historical Analogy* (Cambridge, Massachusetts: The M.I.T. Press, 1965); Dave Smith and Steven Clark, *Disney: The First 100 Years* (New York: Hyperion, 1999), 78.

19   Dave Smith, *The Quotable Walt Disney* (New York: Disney Editions, 2001), 68.

In 1955, Disney began work on a series of three features for television, built around the idea of putting men into space. The first two installments, *Man in Space* (in March) and *Man and the Moon* (in December) aired in 1955. The third film, *Mars and Beyond*, aired at the end of 1957.[20] Disney turned to experts for help. They worked with Willy Ley, Wernher von Braun, and Fritz Haber, allowing the scientists to convey ideas about rockets and manned space flight to the American public that at times was complicated by their Nazi past.[21] Many of the things the Disney films portrayed on television were quite similar to how the United States actually pulled off the moon landing over a decade later.[22] When coupled with the January 1957 film *Our Friend the Atom* (which talked about the benefits of nuclear energy), Disney was unleashing an array of science-based films that made new concepts and technology familiar to the average American, while also touting an American "can do" spirit and pushing the nation toward a bright future.[23]

The 1950s saw another angle when it came to America, Disney, and space: Sputnik. While Walt was painting a picture of what was possible, and the American public was confident that the United States, under President Eisenhower, could get us there, America's Cold War nemesis, the Soviet Union, was actually working on a rocket program. In October 1957, to the surprise of virtually the entire world, the U.S.S.R. launched the first man-made satellite, Sputnik, into outer space. The launch cast a pall of pessimism over the Western world. People began demanding proof that the United States could do such things and more, and do them quickly. The space race was on, and Walt's films had not only shown the way, but had also made possible a park where guests could come and be reassured. In Disneyland, Dis-History was able to make a convincing argument that Americans could make history in the future, just as they had in the past.[24]

Disney Imagineer Ward Kimball later argued that after Sputnik, Disney's Man in Space films were the most influential component in

---

20 Watts, *The Magic Kingdom*, 308–313; Tison Pugh and Susan Aronstein, editors, *The Disney Middle Ages: A Fairy-Tale and Fantasy Past* (New York: Palgrave Macmillan, 2012), 153, 156; Christian Moran, *Great Big Beautiful Tomorrow: Walt Disney and Technology* (Theme Park Press, 2015).

21 Pugh and Aronstein, editors, *The Disney Middle Ages*, 156–157.

22 Didier Ghez, editor, *Walt's People: Volume 2: Talking Disney with the Artists Who Knew Him* (Theme Park Press, 2015), 95.

23 Pugh and Aronstein, editors, *The Disney Middle Ages*, 154–155; Watts, *The Magic Kingdom*, 308-313; Moran, *Great Big Beautiful Tomorrow*.

24 Nicholas Michael Sambaluk, *The Other Space Race: Eisenhower and the Quest for Aerospace Security* (Annapolis: Naval Institute Press, 2015).

spurring the United States to build rockets of its own.²⁵ As such, space travel and rockets were a constant in the theming of Tomorrowland, including (eventually) a Saturn V rocket and a flight simulator that took guests to first the moon and later to Mars).²⁶ In 1956, Disney opened what would become (today) the Astro Orbiter, at the time known as Star Jets, which allowed guests to "fly" space rockets of their own.²⁷ In 1959, Space Mountain (an indoor, dark thrill ride) was launched, with obvious ties to both the Cold War space race as well as the Man in Space films. And as the years went on, Disney continued to invest in ways to show the public realistic interpretations of what manned space flight was and could be.²⁸

Walt could sense trouble with Tomorrowland. As he put it in an interview, "Now, when we opened Disneyland, outer space was Buck Rogers. I did put in a trip to the moon. And I got Wernher von Braun to help me plan the thing. And, of course, we were going up to the moon long before Sputnik. And since then has come Sputnik and then has come our great program in outer space. So I had to tear down my Tomorrowland that I built eleven years ago and rebuild it to keep pace."²⁹

Beyond space, though, Disney was unsure about what else Tomorrowland might hold. Due to the time and monetary crunch of getting Disneyland opened, the area remained the least developed and the most open for the Imagineers once guests began visiting.³⁰ The original concept was to give guests a glimpse at a possible future. The Imagineers decided to theme much of the rest of the area around the future thirty years hence, or the mid-1980s, coinciding with 1986 and the return of Halley's Comet, which Walt witnessed as a boy. It was conceived at a time of optimism in the post-war period.³¹ Doing so required a good dose of Dis-History, and banking heavily

---

25   Didier Ghez, editor, *Walt's People: Volume 5: Talking Disney with the Artists Who Knew Him* (Theme Park Press, 2015), 29.

26   Irvine, Dick. "Disney Biography: Bob Thomas' Interview with Dick Irvine 1968", Lectures and Transcripts, Walt Disney Studio Archives, Burbank, California.

27   "Astro Orbiter," disneyparkhistory.com/astro-orbiter.html, 13 March 2015.

28   *The Imagineering Field Guide to Disneyland: An Imagineer's Eye Tour* (New York: Disney Editions, 2008), 114; Moran, *Great Big Beautiful Tomorrow*; Christopher Finch, *Walt Disney's America* (New York: Abbeville Press, 1978), 181.

29   Smith, *The Quotable Walt Disney*, 69.

30   *The Imagineering Field Guide to Disneyland: An Imagineer's Eye Tour* (New York: Disney Editions, 2008), 110.

31   Tomorrowland General 1970s-1980s folder, Attraction File, Walt Disney Studio Archives, Burbank, California.

on collective knowledge of the past and present. Because the future is unknown, the past acts to balance out that uncertainty with what is already know—right up to the present.[32]

Nowhere was this attempted more systematically than the Monsanto House of the Future. A concept that dated back to the 1930s in home-building circles, Disney's house was open from 1957–1967, was designed by MIT architecture professors, and had corporate sponsorship from General Electric and General Motors. A plastic-reinforced-by-fiberglass home, it was visited by some 20 million guests during its decade of existence. Redecorated twice, the house was a showcase for possibilities, not a blueprint for futuristic home construction. As an attraction, though, it continually lost its luster as the new devices that filled it rapidly became consumer goods and common place.[33]

Another area where Disney contemplated the future was in new ways that technology and mechanization might be employed. Tomorrowland "identifies with conventional industrial and scientific progress through its glorification of the machine." One does not find "nature" here—and very little about "human welfare" either.[34] That being said, appreciation for the "purely practical part of science" and of modernization has long been an American trait, with the parks being a testament to technology and innovation in and of themselves. In Tomorrowland, Walt wanted to show guests all the things machines could do and how new technology might be applied in an urban environment. One of the areas he hoped to showcase was the transformative nature of transportation brought about by new technology. Tomorrowland became a place where Disney was "predicting the future of transportation."[35] Walt had already largely removed the automobile from his parks, and by showing the PeopleMover, he hoped to convince people that this new form of public transportation was a real possibility for cities.[36] When he learned of a Swiss company that was creating a transportation system based off of ropes and pulleys,

---

32 Hench with Van Pelt, *Designing Disney*, 41; Kuenz, Klugman, Waldrep, and Willis, editors, *Inside the Mouse*, 65.

33 Beth Dunlop, *Building a Dream: The Art of Disney Architecture* (New York: Harry N. Abrams, 1996), 134–135; Moran, *Great Big Beautiful Tomorrow*; Steve Manheim, *Walt Disney and the Quest for Community* (Burlington, Vermont: Ashgate, 2002), 52; Gary Cross, *Consumed Nostalgia: Memory in the Age of Fast Capitalism* (New York: Columbia University Press, 2015), 96.

34 Real, *Mass-Mediated Culture*, 57.

35 1959, News from Disneyland folder, Walt Disney Studio Archives, Burbank, California.

36 Alexis de Tocqueville, *Democracy in America* (New York: Mentor, 1984), 164;

he wanted what became the Skyway (essentially a cable-car system) as a showcase of this technology for Tomorrowland as well.[37] Here, personal history (experiences) were to be forged based on a fantastical future, proving what Walt had once said, "Science and technology have already given us the tools we need to build the world of the future."[38]

Despite these innovations, the future has proven to be a very illusive muse and Tomorrowland has gone through numerous overhauls and re-Imagineerings. As Karal Ann Marling notes, "Tomorrow has a distressing habit of catching up with daydreams about it. Or the daydreams prove wildly wrong. Either way, building a simulated future is a risky business."[39] A bit more harshly, one critic labeled Tomorrowland a "pathetic" place where vehicular modes of transportation are worshiped and "yesterday's version of the future" stands in all its "silliness."[40] Disney decided that the best way to deal with the future was to break with its mission statement. While the early Tomorrowland programs were steeped in aspiration and education as the parks continued, Disney took a much more "cinematic" or "fantasy future" approach to dealing with the land as it undertook several successive overhauls of the area as time passed.[41]

In 1998, after over forty years of trying, the original Tomorrowland in Disneyland was almost completely reinvented. At last there was an acknowledgement that despite updates in the 1960s and 1970s, the future that Walt was trying to capture, where space was the next great American frontier, was finally gutted, reimagined, and transformed (when it was not outright replaced). Disney's Imagineers brought in science-fiction-themed rides, inspired (as Lawrence Culver points out,

---

"Luis Marin: Disneyland as Degenerate Utopia," http://lmc.gatech.edu/~broglio/1101/marin.html, 23 September 2014; Watts, *The Magic Kingdom*, 393, 396; Scott Bukatman, "There's Always Tomorrowland: Disney and the Hypercinematic Experience," *October* (Summer, 1991), 62; Leon and Rosenzweig, editors, *History Museums in the United States:*, 173.

37 "Skyway to Fantasyland," http://www.disneyparkhistory.com/skyway-to-fantasyland.html, 13 March 2015; 1967, News from Disneyland folder, Walt Disney Studio Archives, Burbank, California.

38 Tomorrowland General 1950s–1960s folder, Attraction File, Walt Disney Studio Archives, Burbank, California.

39 Karal Ann Marling, editor, *Designing Disney's Theme Parks: The Architecture of Reassurance* (New York: Flammarion, 1997), 140.

40 James Howard Kunstler, *The Geography of Nowhere: The Rise and Decline of America's Man-Made Landscape* (New York: Touchstone Book, 1993), 226.

41 Telotte, "Disney in Science Fiction Land", 12–21; Dave Smith and Steven Clark, *Disney: The First 100 Years* (New York: Hyperion, 1999), 184.

in a very Dis-Historic way) by Jules Verne and H.G. Wells, and that pioneered at Disneyland Paris—where Tomorrowland's very name was replaced. There the area is known as Discoveryland, and its Space Mountain was rethemed around Jules Verne's *From the Earth to the Moon*.[42] A retro-futuristic look, it was determined, was better than trying to keep pace with the future itself.[43] Back in the United States, there was Disneyland's 20,000 Leagues Under the Sea submarine ride was reworked into a Finding Nemo Submarine Voyage (interestingly, Disneyland Paris kept a walk-through of the *Nautilus*), along with Star Tours, a refurbished Autopia, and Innoventions (which has been used as a rotating gallery for props from the Marvel and Star Wars franchises). The Imagineers had learned that keeping up with the future was too difficult a task.[44]

The modern attractions have largely left the edutainment dictum of the original behind. Though flashes remain in the Carousel of Progress, the Astro-Orbiter, the People Mover (at the Magic Kingdom), and even Space Mountain, Dis-History has become marginalized, because the future is too difficult to organize around. Instead, rides like Buzz Lightyear Space Ranger Spin, Stitch's Great Escape, and Monster, Inc Laugh Floor all represent both corporate synergy and Disney's attempt to get around the ever-unfolding future by utilizing its characters. This fit into Michael Eisner's idea that what guests at the parks really wanted was to "ride the movies,"[45] a business idea that was at odds with much of the Dis-Historic narrative crafted by Walt.

In many ways, the addition of Buzz Lightyear makes a good deal of sense. The Pixar character from *Toy Story* is a bridge between Tomorrowland's past (space) with Disney's new approach toward Tomorrowland. The laser-blaster game is housed in one of Tomorrowland's areas which was once home to an attraction that simulated flight. Furthermore, in the original *Toy Story*, Buzz was seen as desirable by Andy because he was new and represented technology.

---

42 Andrew Lainsbury, *Once Upon an American Dream: The Story of Euro Disneyland* (Lawrence: University of Kansas Press, 2000), 166; Lawrence Culver, *The Frontier of Leisure: Southern California and the Shaping of Modern America* (New York: Oxford University Press, 2010), 239.

43 "Disney Should Have Closed This Attraction Years Ago: Here's Why," http://www.themeparktourist.com/features/20160710/32052/stitchs-great-escape, 10 August 2016.

44 Lainsbury, *Once Upon an American Dream*, 72-73.

45 "Disney Should Have Closed This Attraction Years Ago: Here's Why," http://www.themeparktourist.com/features/20160710/32052/stitchs-great-escape, 10 August 2016.

While Buzz's *Toy Story* counterpart, Woody (a cowboy who represents the past, both from an historic perspective and as Andy's old favorite toy), can be found as a character meet-and-greet in Frontierland, Buzz has both an attraction and a character meeting spot in Tomorrowland. Again, we can see a sort of Dis-Historic synergy at work between the past and future. But their separation might also be seen as an example of the distance that by the 1990s was driving some of Disney's best animators to Pixar, and Pixar further away from the Disney corporate fold (as we will see below).[46]

Stitch's Great Escape, which gives guests the chance to try and recapture Disney's most famous alien, also conjures up an association with space, and thus Tomorrowland's past. And like Buzz's attraction, it also occupies historic Tomorrowland real estate. It is housed in a building that started life as home to a movie about flying to the moon. But it is also not the first replacement Disney attempted to craft here. After the United States actually accomplished the goal of reaching the moon, a new simulation was created about a space mission to Mars, again befitting Tomorrowland's original plan. But with Epcot's opening (complete with its Mission: SPACE attraction), Disney again retooled the building for ExtraTERRORestrial, an attraction similar to Stitch's Great Escape in theming (and thus, easily converted), but more of a thrilling dark ride than Stitch, which ends with the escaped "Experiment 626" trying to get a kiss from Cinderella.[47]

While Stitch's future is in doubt, the rumored replacement attraction (based around *Wreck-It Ralph*)[48] also fits more with the direction Tomorrowland seems to be moving toward. Dis-History, it seemed, could only take the park so far into the future. Unlike the other two attractions, Monster, Inc Laugh Floor has virtually nothing to do with space or Tomorrowland's past. Rather than screams, the monsters now need laughter to produce energy, and the crowd participation in the comedy routine is always a fun time (especially if you are "that

---

46 Eleanor Byrne and Martin McQuillan, *Deconstructing Disney* (Sterling, Virginia: Pluto Press, 1999), 128-129; James B. Stewart, *Disney War* (New York: Simon and Schuster, 2005), 241; "Buzz Lightyear Space Ranger Spin," http://www.disneyparkhistory.com/buzz-lightyears-space-ranger-spin.html, 13 March 2015.

47 "Stitch's Great Escape," http://www.disneyparkhistory.com/stitchs-great-escape.html, 13 March 2015.

48 In October 2016, Stitch went to "seasonal" as an attraction, meaning that it was only open at certain times and days. As we noticed during our time on the PeopleMover, the narration no longer mentions Stitch at all, even if the signage remains a part of the Tomorrowland infrastructure.

guy"). But the building it occupies illustrates just how difficult a time Disney had with trying to capture the future in Tomorrowland. Long before monsters garnered human laughter there, it was home to patriotic films in CircleVision. *America the Beautiful* was shown at both parks, depicting various aspects of life in America, from landmarks, to natural wonders, to cities. Its closing statement included the line, "This, then, has been our American portrait, a glimpse of a nation's splendor, infinite in its variety, rich in its tradition, and blessed in its heritage." The film was changed in the mid-1970s to *Magic Carpet Ride Around the World*, similar in tone to its American cousin, and then changed again during the bicentennial to *American Journeys*, an updated and reworking of *America the Beautiful*, which itself was replaced in the mid-1990s by a time-travel adventure starring the Time Keeper, an attraction that debuted in Disneyland Paris. In some ways, all of these attractions were "fillers" for the space, having nothing to do with Tomorrowland as a concept. The Time Keeper was replaced by Laugh Floor in the 2000s.[49]

Even with the changes (and change is a constant when contemplating the future[50]), on Disney maps Tomorrowland continues to look sleek and modern, as opposed to the other lands that are part of the Magic Kingdom. And the changes have prompted something else as well, along with the new attractions: the old ones that remain in Tomorrowland have generated nostalgia of their own. Christopher Finch has called it "nostalgia for the future,"[51] but not the actual future, rather "the future that never was" as depicted in Tomorrowland. Here even memories have become commodities, which in turn can be turned into retro merchandise. Or, in the minds of critics, all Disney is doing is delivering consumers directly to corporations, who are given a venue in the parks to showcase their work and not just advertise to consumers but also get them to purchase their products. Indeed, guests are shown consumerism the moment they walk down Main Street. In some ways, by walking through the past to get to the future while being awash in products for purchase, consumerism is argued to be the norm, with the past just one more product that can be bought.[52]

---

49 "Monster, Inc. Laugh Floor," http://www.disneyparkhistory.com/monsters-inc-laugh-floor.html, 13 March 2015.

50 *The Imagineering Field Guide to the Magic Kingdom at Walt Disney World: An Imagineer's Eye Tour* (New York: Disney Editions, 2005), 21, 108.

51 Bukatman, "There's Always Tomorrowland" 56; Finch, *Walt Disney's America*, 179.

52 Kuenz, Klugman, Waldrep, and Willis, editors, *Inside the Mouse*, 191; Alan Bryman, *Disney and His Worlds* (New York: Routledge, 1995; ebook version), 191;

The concept of the future was important to Walt, but it always vexed him.[53] As he put it, "The only problem with anything of tomorrow is that at the pace we're going right now, tomorrow would catch up with us before we got it built."[54] If anything, the changes to Tomorrowland are testament to the fact that while Disney remains "fascinated" by the future, it is virtually impossible for the parks to keep up with it.[55] As Imagineer Dick Irvine put it, "Tomorrowland was the hardest land to get hold of and we always called it 'The Land of Tomorrow.' It was never called Tomorrowland in those days."[56]

Though Tomorrowland is billed as a place "on the move," and its signage proclaims it to be "the future that never was is finally here," the question of whether you can truly capture the future remains—as well as whether this new Tomorrowland is truly the future we want it to be.[57] As noted above, Tomorrowland has proven "difficult to sustain." The future may not be of one of progress; there are fears associated with change and uncertainty as to what can be achieved.[58] Furthermore, what happens when the future catches up to Tomorrowland and predictions about it are wrong? Tomorrowland, when it was conceived in the 1950s, was set in the 1980s. It was believed that by then, people would regularly be traveling to the moon. But the modern future is not dominated by outer space. Rather, ours is a future that seemingly is defined by cyberspace.[59] Other than the technology surrounding a guest, Tomorrowland has very little to say about that.

Others understood what Walt was attempting. One of Disney's biggest supporters was science-fiction writer Ray Bradbury. The author of *Fahrenheit 451* believed that Disney was giving mankind a "look

---

"Luis Marin: Disneyland as Degenerate Utopia," http://lmc.gatech.edu/~broglio/1101/marin.html, 23 September 2014.

53 Thomas, *Walt Disney*, 290.

54 Smith, *The Quotable Walt Disney*, 250.

55 Beth Dunlop, *Building a Dream: The Art of Disney Architecture* (New York: Harry N. Abrams, 1996), 131.

56 Irvine, Dick. "Disney Biography: Bob Thomas' Interview with Dick Irvine 1968", Lectures and Transcripts, Walt Disney Studio Archives, Burbank, California.

57 Stephen F. Fjellman, *Vinyl Leaves: Walt Disney World and America* (Boulder: Westview Press, 1992), 320.

58 Michael Steiner, "Frontierland as Tomorrowland: Walt Disney and the Architectural Packaging of the Mythic West," *Montana: The Magazine of Western History*, 48(Spring 1998), 15.

59 Svetlana Boym, *The Future of Nostalgia* (New York: Basic Books, 2001), 346–347.

at the world of the future."⁶⁰ Bradbury's support is perhaps not that surprising, once one considers the author's background. Like Walt, Bradbury was a product of the Midwest (in his case, Illinois) who had early in life "immersed himself in popular culture, from cinema to comic strips to traveling circuses." And like Disney, he did not always find critical acclaim (because, he believed, he did not share in "the terrible creative negativism admired by New York critics"). Bradbury believed "science fiction is the fiction of ideas" and was a wonderful way to ponder present issues, while pretending to deal only in the future. In Walt, he found a kindred spirit.⁶¹

Walt always had a spirit of optimism. He believed the future would be better than the past, even if we remembered fondly what once was. He told one interviewer, who asked him to comment on the Baby Boomers, that while that generation had been "maligned by the communications media, hunting for things and giving them a spotlight they don't deserve," he still had "great faith in them." If he were offering them advice it would be "believe in the future, the world is getting better; there still is plenty of opportunity. Why, would you believe it, when I was a kid I thought it was already too late for me to make good at anything."⁶²

A Future Full of Synergy and Consumerism

At both Disneyland and Magic Kingdom, there are two entrances into Tomorrowland. For many of Disney's guests in Florida, who find their way in from Fantasyland directly, the gateway attraction is the Tomorrowland Speedway. Nothing futuristic in that: the go-karts (crafted to look like racecars) allow drivers to go around a track (*on* a track—the cars all go the same speed, and drivers have little actual control other than starting and stopping, though as any parent knows who has let their child behind the steering wheel, it can make you rethink allowing them to get their driver's license). It is similar to Disneyland's Autopia, though the California models have a more retro, less race-car, look.⁶³ At first, the speedway might seem an odd point of departure into the world of tomorrow, until you realize that this

---

60   *USA Today*, 7 June 2012.
61   "Ray Bradbury, The Art of Fiction No. 203—The Paris Review," http://www.theparisreview.org/interviews/6012/the-art-of-fiction-no-203-ray-bradbury, 15 August 2014.
62   Kathy Merlock Jackson, editor, *Walt Disney: Conversations* (Jackson: University of Mississippi Press, 2006), 137.
63   Bukatman, "There's Always Tomorrowland," 55.

is really the first time that Disney has acknowledged the automobile within the Magic Kingdom itself. When compared to other modes of transportation within the park, the speedway's cars are the very definition of cutting-edge technology. However, if a guest comes into Tomorrowland from the castle/Main Street hub, they are greeted with a different experience altogether. At Disneyland there is a large display denoting the land guests are about to enter, but there is also an interesting juxtaposition of Dis-History that takes place as they do. The Plaza Restaurant borders Main Street and Tomorrowland. Officially a part of Main Street, the restaurant invokes a degree of nineteenth-century opulence. And yet it is mere steps away from Tomorrowland and one can gaze out its windows and see the rockets of the Astro-Orbiter. Here, the past is quite literally looking at the future and intergenerational experiences can happen.

Perhaps, given Walt Disney's own future-centric optimism and love of nostalgia, such (eventual) placement of pieces of the park should not be surprising. As the twenty-first century approached, the company still clung to the promises of the Carousel of Progress, that there was "a great big beautiful tomorrow, shining at the end of every day." It could still count on Dis-History, even in its evolved form, to pave the way for future successes. But what was concerning to some observers was where the company was headed in the immediate present.

As Michael Eisner prepared to start his second decade as the head of the company, thoughts on the future abounded. Though still upset about the failure of Disney's America and still watching over the shaky establishment of Disneyland Paris, Eisner was already thinking of expanding the parks presence both at home (Animal Kingdom, California Adventure) and abroad (Hong Kong). Tomorrowland would soon be updated, but Eisner turned his attention about what shape the future might hold by putting his attention on Epcot (rather than where Walt had envisioned) and further distancing (when he could) attractions from Dis-History altogether.[64]

Even his triumphs aided these tendencies. In July 1995, Disney announced plans to purchase Capital Cities-ABC, a multimedia entertainment conglomerate that included music, radio, broadcast, and cable stations. While critics worried about an entertainment giant like Disney now owning so many media outlets and controlling their content (including the news they provided), Eisner believed the business move made a good deal of sense. Obviously, it would help with the distribution of Disney's wide variety of programing, but if

---

64 Flower, *Prince of the Magic Kingdom*, 280.

it also scared some of their rivals, so much the better.⁶⁵ One of the problems that developed, however, was that after Disney purchased ABC, Eisner increasingly turned his attention toward television, and was less concerned about the core of the Disney empire he had taken over a decade before.⁶⁶

That being said, though Disney's America had been a failure, Eisner still had hopes for reimagining Disney's theme parks. Throughout the 1990s he worked to open a second gate for Disneyland, a park that became known as California Adventure (to be constructed atop the original Disneyland parking lot). Eisner believed that Disneyland remained largely a "local theme park," and that this second park would help draw in guests from outside California. But construction came with an additional Eisner caveat: California Adventure was to be an "un-Disneyland." It was to be more adult-centric, with nicer restaurants, more traditional amusement park rides, and very few Disney characters or theming.⁶⁷ Dis-History was to be jettisoned, and a park quite similar to what Walt had rejected building was to be constructed in its place. Eisner only backtracked after public opinion (both in the form of poor reviews and lack of ticket sales) became readily apparent after the park opened in February 2001. The Imagineers were then brought in to re-theme and rework a virtually brand-new park.⁶⁸

Still, even with these missteps, Eisner was comfortable in his position and secure in his power. Not unlike Walt, Eisner was creative and hardnosed when it came to business.⁶⁹ The problem became that Walt was checked by his own history of building the company into what Eisner took over (Eisner expanded and enriched upon ideas that either already existed or were already in development) and that Walt had Roy to check him. When Frank Wells died in a tragic helicopter accident in 1994, Eisner suddenly had no one to check him, and diminished personal ties both to the Hollywood establishment (his connections were often more professional) and to the Disney family (while Roy E. Disney had helped bring Eisner into power, Disney and Wells had been friends since their college days). As Eisner's power grew after Wells' death, his creativity started to dwindle.⁷⁰

---

65 Lainsbury, *Once Upon an American Dream*, 184–190.
66 Stewart, *Disney War*, 280–281.
67 Michael D. Eisner, *Work in Progress* (New York: Random House, 1998), 201; Stein, *Why We Love Disney*, 113–114.
68 "Theme Park History: A Short History of Disney's California Adventure," http://www.themeparkinsider.com/flume/201309/3665/, 29 June 2016.
69 Flower, *Prince of the Magic Kingdom*, 232–233, 249–250.
70 Stewart, *Disney War*, 530–531; *Los Angeles Times*, 4 April 1994; Eisner,

Eisner's power grew so large because of the power struggle that developed shortly after Wells' funeral. Jeffrey Katzenberg, who had come in with Eisner and Wells (and who helped lead the resurgence of Disney's animation department), felt Eisner had promised him Wells' position. When Eisner refused to promote Katzenberg, because he believed him more interested in furthering a personal agenda than the company's, and because he thought that Katzenberg lacked the "maturity and judgement needed to be the president of a company that served as many constituencies as Disney did," Katzenberg resigned in protest. He then sued Disney for compensation and benefits (in what turned into a nasty legal battle) and helped form a new studio (with director/producer Steven Spielberg and music mogul David Geffen), DreamWorks SKG. For his part, Eisner simply assumed much of Wells' old responsibilities and brought in Hollywood's most powerful talent agent, Michael Ovitz, to serve as his de-facto second in command.[71]

Ovitz, however, did not work out. Though many industry insiders really thought it was a good idea for the agent, with all of his industry connections, to join with Disney, many of his ideas did not make economic sense for the company. Hired with much fanfare in 1995, Ovitz was fired after just fifteen months as president. His compensation package, of $130 million, did not sit well with some stockholders, who by the late 1990s were beginning to wonder if Eisner had too much power and if the board of directors was more interested in enriching themselves rather than putting the interests of the company first.[72]

Dissatisfaction was growing within the company. While Eisner had done much in his time as the leader of Disney, and he had supporters (especially among the Imagineers whose responsibilities were growing as the park system expanded), there was a sense that good people were leaving Disney and their replacements were not always of the same caliber.[73] Critics pointed perhaps most notably to Paul Pressler, who many believed was squeezing short-term profits out of first the Disney Stores and then Disneyland itself, by cutting the budgets for things like maintenance.[74] Then there was the exodus of Disney-trained animators

---

Work in Progress, 4, 294–295.

71 Eisner, *Work in Progress*, 198–200, 298–299; *The Hollywood Reporter*, 18 April 2014.

72 Eisner, *Work in Progress*, 4–5, 380, 384–385; Stewart, *Disney War*, 231, 253, 268–269, 278–279; "Judge Rules in Favor of Disney in Ovitz Case, But Criticizes Eisner," http://articles.latimes.com/2005/aug/10/business/fi-disney10, 29 June 2016.

73 Sklar, *Dream It! Do It!*, 292–295.

74 Sklar, *Dream It! Do It!*, 305.

to rivals (like Katzenberg's DreamWorks) or to computer animation at Pixar (co-owned by Steve Jobs, the co-founder of Apple), which was only made worse when Eisner and Jobs clashed, and the latter threatened to end Pixar's distribution deal with Disney—and thus cut Disney off from what was becoming its chief source of animated hits.[75]

The Pixar threat, in particular, was real. While Jobs' company was producing innovative films (largely along the Disney model), Disney's own animation division was starting to flounder again. Katzenberg's departure, in many ways, left them without a powerful voice (though they could still count on Roy E. Disney for support) and as the 1990s progressed, hits became few and far between. To cut costs, the old storyboard process for animated movies was scrapped, making it more difficult (in the short term) to chart out the traditionally hand-drawn films. The creative process began to stymy, the once-thriving pipeline began to slow up, and Eisner's team became known to make "creative choices" with the films. For example, in a seemingly Dis-Historic move, Disney announced that it would release *Treasure Planet* in 2002, a space-based version of the Robert Louis Stevenson classic *Treasure Island*. Despite being a story that involved pirates and sword fights, with a movie that was supposed to be aimed toward boys (after a string of princess movies in the early 1990s aimed at girls, Disney attempted to create movies for young boys; *Hercules* in 1997 and *The Emperor's New Groove* in 2000 were part of this attempt as well), Eisner ordered that the movie have no swords and the adventure and violence be toned down. In the case of *Treasure Planet*, these decisions may have led to the movie being a box-office and merchandising flop.[76]

Eisner made other mistakes as well. His team was not as careful as they might have been to keep and cultivate good relations with the Orlando area. Disney as a corporate giant became notorious for protecting its trademark, sometimes (at least from a public relation's standpoint) in rather ridiculous ways. The building of a statue in the Canadian town of White River to honor Winnie the Pooh, for example (a soldier during World War I had taken a bear from that area as his brigade's mascot, and the bear ended up in the London Zoo, where A.A. Miline saw it), or when some day-care centers used classic children's characters (including Mickey) as part of their murals. Disney objected to and litigated both of these cases.[77] But considering the nature of

---

75 "The End: Pixar Breaks Up With Its Distribution Partner Disney," http://www.wsj.com/articles/SB107541081328315628, 29 June 2016.

76 Didier Ghez, editor, *Walt's People: Volume 4: Talking Disney with the Artists Who Knew Him* (Theme Park Press, 2016),279–281.

77 Flower, *Prince of the Magic Kingdom*, 251–255.

copyright, and the notion of commodification, it is hardly surprising either. And then there were the problems the company had no control over, such as the terrorist attacks of September 11, 2001, which shut down the nation's airports for several days and prompted all sorts of travel and vacation cancellations, many of which impacted Disney. If people could not fly, they could not come to Disney's parks.[78]

All of these issues were contributing to Eisner's alienation of both wings of the Disney family as well. By 1999, Walt's nephew Roy and others were growing tired of Eisner's leadership. They questioned some of the acquisitions and corporate decisions.[79] The culmination came in late 2003, when Roy was informed (on Eisner's orders) that he would not be re-nominated to the company's board, officially because of age. Roy believed that the company was still, in some respects, his family's company, and retained strong support within the animation division as well. He was prepared to go to war for the heart of the Walt Disney company. Roy decided to publicly resign, stating in his letter that Eisner had had a good first ten years, but had now increasingly lost his vision for the company. Eisner initially believed that all Roy really had was the Disney name. The problem for Eisner was that Roy's last name was going to prove to be worth quite a bit. Roy and his business partner Stanley Gold formed a group, Save Disney, and held a meeting ahead of the annual stockholder's meeting in Philadelphia in 2004.[80]

Roy found unexpected aid from his cousin Diane. The two had not been close since the early 1980s, when Roy had forced her husband Ron Miller out as head of the company and replaced him with Eisner. In the midst of Roy's campaign, the Comcast Cable Company made a bid to purchase Disney. Diane Miller was determined to make sure this did not come to pass, because Comcast had soft-core pornography channels, which were at odds with the family-centered entertainment company her father had created. With that, she became convinced that Eisner had to go and threw her support behind Roy.[81]

The corporate infighting highlighted how far things had come in the fifty years since Walt laid the ground for the park. Disney had gone from a small studio that dealt chiefly in cartoon shorts to a multi-faceted corporation with international reach and presence. In the process, it had validated the notion of corporate consumption,

---

78 Stewart, *Disney War*, 356–357, 370–373.
79 Stewart, *Disney War*, 1, 414–417, 428.
80 David A. Bossert, *Remembering Roy E. Disney: Memories and Photos of a Storied Life* (New York: Disney Editions, 2013), 147–149; Stewart, *Disney War*, 465–473, 480–481.
81 Stewart, *Disney War*, 490–493.

and by the early twenty-first century was itself in danger of being consumed.[82] As stockholders gathered in Philadelphia, no one could be sure of what the future held for the company started by a little mouse over seventy years before.

And as the struggles with Tomorrowland attest, it is much easier to deal with the past, via Dis-History, than it is to predict the future. In its best light, perhaps Tomorrowland is preparing guests for the future by grounding it in "traditional forms," for even in the future, there is "the smell of history," as Richard Snow put it. However, historic silences grow louder the closer we get to the present in Dis-History, and the concept is all but swallowed up by those silences in Tomorrowland.[83]

Historians love George Santayana's maxim that "those who do not remember the past are condemned to repeat it." And yet, no historical situation is ever exactly the same as previous ones, and, though history can inform our present it is not always a reliable guide to the future. While these issues are present within Dis-History, as Eisner prepared for the 2004 stockholder's meeting, the past may have been threatening to repeat itself.

---

82   Kuenz, Klugman, Waldrep, and Willis, editors, *Inside the Mouse*, 188.

83   Bukatman, "There's Always Tomorrowland," 75; Wasko, *Understanding Disney*, 175; Alexander Moore, "Walt Disney World: Bounded Ritual Space and the Playful Pilgrimage Center," *Anthropological Quarterly*, 53(October 1980), 217; Richard Snow, "Disney: Coast to Coast, "http://www.americanheritage.com/content/disney-coast-coast, 2 June 2014; Fjellman, *Vinyl Leaves*, 80.

CHAPTER EIGHT

A Dis-Historic Showcase at Home and Abroad

Experience Epcot's World Showcase

Would you like to visit an ancient Mexican temple? Travel through Norwegian mythology and history (as well as dine with princesses)? Drink in a German beer hall? Go to a Moroccan bazaar? Stand with legendary Chinese warriors? Have dessert in a Parisian café? Eat fish and chips in an English pub? And do all this and more in a single day? If so, then welcome to Epcot's World Showcase.

The World Showcase is the least "Disney" area of the parks. Guests walk through shops, dine in restaurants, interact with cast members from the respective countries, and perhaps see a princess or two. But the Disney branding has tended to be more low key. If that is changing, it does not belittle the Dis-Historic roots of the area, nor its original intent. Next to Disneyland under Walt and the Magic Kingdom itself, few areas of the parks have come as close as the World Showcase (and perhaps Epcot as it was built) to fulfilling various Dis-Historic goals.

We have already encountered Epcot briefly, with our earlier discussion of Spaceship Earth. The home of the World Showcase was the "second gate park" of Walt Disney World. If Dis-History does have a streak of actual education (as opposed to just edu-tainment), it can be found here. The map given guests in 2014 encouraged people to "immerse yourself in a world of history and heritage." To some critics such statements reek of superficiality.[1] However, the reality here is at least a chance to taste and encounter, if only for a few moments, the history and culture of a wide variety of nations.

And it is an impressive assembly of nationalities and cultures. When the idea was pitched in the late 1970s and early 1980s, Disney

---

1 Theodor W. Adorno, *The Culture Industry: Selected Essays on Mass Culture* (New York: Routledge, 1991), 174.

had no problem finding nations willing to finance and staff its World Showcase.² Today there are eleven nations represented in this massive undertaking: Mexico, Norway, China, Germany, Italy, the United States, Japan, Morocco, France, the United Kingdom, and Canada. And there is plenty of room to either add six to eight more nations, or to expand existing national footprints, should Disney ever wish to do so. In addition to these eleven nations, there is an "African outpost," the only area not directly sponsored by a single nation in Epcot.³ And while each nation took a different approach to their theming (some have movies, a few have rides, and all have shops), what guests see is an artistic representation of the nations, as the nations want to be seen—to help spark tourism, with very few Disney flourishes (in the main) and lots of history and culture invoked for guests to experience.

What guests encounter is not exactly what Walt Disney himself pitched to the world in his final year of life. Walt's public vision for Epcot was to be "a living blueprint of the future." He was "confident we can create a world showcase for American free enterprise" in Florida.⁴ Indeed, Walt often said that the second area he planned to develop in Florida, his "experimental city," was not going to be so much a park but a "weenie" for both development and to get people to stay in central Florida longer than just for a trip to Disney World.⁵ But after Walt's death the design for Epcot's World Showcase evolved into a sort of "permanent world's fair," grounded in that tradition rather than Walt's dream.⁶

---

2 Warren Leon and Roy Rosenzweig, editors, *History Museums in the United States: A Critical Assessment* (Chicago: University of Illinois Press, 1989), 169.

3 Marty Sklar, *Dream It! Do It!: My Half-Century Creating Disney's Magic Kingdoms* (New York: Disney Editions, 2013), 208; EPCOT General File. According to Sklar, Disney had also entered into negotiations with Costa Rica, Denmark, Iran, Israel, Spain, Switzerland, and Venezuela at different times, and the corporate archives include the United Arab Emirates as a potential addition as well, but for a wide variety of reasons these pavilions were never constructed.

4 Stephen F. Fjellman, *Vinyl Leaves: Walt Disney World and America* (Boulder: Westview Press, 1992), 115.

5 Bob Thomas, *Building a Company: Roy O. Disney and the Creation of an Entertainment Empire* (New York: Hyperion, 1998), 274.

6 Jane Kuenz, Karen Klugman, Shelton Waldrep, and Susan Willis, editors, *Inside the Mouse: Work and Play at Disney World* (Durham: Duke University Press, 1995), 227; Judith A. Adams, *The American Amusement Park Industry: A History of Technology and Thrills* (Boston: Twayne Publishers, 1991), 148; Fjellman, *Vinyl Leaves*, 232–233; Steve Nelson, "Walt Disney's EPCOT and the World's Fair Performance Tradition," *The Drama Review* (Winter, 1986), 106–146; Cher Krause Knight, *Power and Paradise in Walt Disney's World* (Gainesville:

None of that deters from the fact that the World Showcase provides a fun alternative to the normal Disney experience and a strong Dis-Historic glimpse at the world. Here, travel of foreign lands is "rendered safe while remaining absurdly picturesque."[7] And though it is not the real world[8] (the World Showcase is much too urban, for example), Epcot does give the "essence" of the countries that are represented.[9] Whatever its flaws might be, the World Showcase is a place where people from all over the world actually interact.[10] And it is a place where Dis-History is alive and well.

Epcot's Dis-Historic Origins

Epcot, though focused on the future, is where Disney took all the lessons it had learned at Disneyland and the Magic Kingdom about utilizing Dis-History to craft a narrative and put them to good use. With some 600 acres to work with, Imagineers were able to create a "seamless environment" where guests' views of the park are controlled—not just from the parking lot but also from the various portions of the park itself.[11] It is also a park with two halves and a history all its own.

Epcot as it exists today is not how it was first proposed. Indeed, Epcot is actually an acronym for Experimental Prototype City of Tomorrow, and the concept of building a model city likely intrigued Walt as much (if not more) than just building a clone of Disneyland in Florida. As Steve Manheim notes, Epcot was conceptualized in the midst of the Great Society and federal initiatives to create "model cities. It also happened during the Civil Rights movement and the nation's growing involvement in Vietnam." With American society both increasingly affluent and rapidly changing, with urban centers suffering as suburbs blossomed, it is little wonder that the man who was so interested in forging a common American culture and had revolutionized theme parks also started to wonder if he could transform cities, before they

---

University Press of Florida, 2014), 119.

7 Scott Bukatman, "There's Always Tomorrowland: Disney and the Hypercinematic Experience," *October* (Summer, 1991), 66.

8 Fjellman, *Vinyl Leaves*, 389.

9 Eric Smoodin, editor, *Disney Discourse: Producing the Magic Kingdom* (New York: Routledge, 1994), 123; Kuenz, Klugman, Waldrep, and Willis, editors, *Inside the Mouse*, 77; Fjellman, *Vinyl Leaves*, 224.

10 Knight, *Power and Paradise in Walt Disney's World*, 138.

11 Warren Leon and Roy Rosenzweig, editors, *History Museums in the United States: A Critical Assessment* (Chicago: University of Illinois Press, 1989), 167; Smoodin, editor, *Disney Discourse*, 119, 122; Adams, *The American Amusement Park Industry*, 149; Fjellman, *Vinyl Leaves*, 213.

fell apart completely.[12] Walt believed Epcot could solve urban problems and serve as an example for how to renew America's cities.[13] [14]

And so, Walt began to read up on city and urban planning.[15] Ever since Disneyland opened in 1955, urban planners and architects had been among his biggest fans. They seemed to be in awe of how Disney was able to construct emotion and convey feelings to so many guests, as well as how the park's infrastructure handled the sheer daily volume of feet and hands.[16] Walt knew men like the urban designer Jim Rouse, who believed spaces and places should matter. Rouse also did not like unplanned growth or urban slums, saying of the latter "bad housing must not be tolerated." He also believed that old cities could be remade, slums revitalized, and that urban problems were solvable.[17] Walt was also sought out (and influenced by) Victor Gruen—the man who pioneered the concept of malls as anchors to suburban communities. Gruen argued that malls were places where people could "come together, enjoying themselves, and shop," and that if they could act as both a "civic attraction" and as shopping centers for scattered suburbanites then they could do the same thing for decaying urban cores. Both Disney and Gruen wanted cities to be more pedestrian friendly, believed that corporations could solve America's social problems, and that careful planning was the only thing needed to make this dream come true.[18]

---

12 Steve Manheim, *Walt Disney and the Quest for Community* (Burlington, Vermont: Ashgate, 2002), 17, 112–113, 118; Paul Boyer, *Urban Masses and Moral Order in America, 1820–1920* (Cambridge, Massachusetts: Harvard University Press, 1997); M. Jeffrey Hardwick, *Mall Maker: Victor Gruen, Architect of an American Dream* (Philadelphia: The University of Pennsylvania Press, 2004), 180–185.

13 Hench, John (1). "Interviewed by Gabe Essoe 1972," Lectures and Transcripts, Walt Disney Studio Archives, Burbank, California.

14 Hench, John (1). December 1974 Interview, Lectures and Transcripts, Walt Disney Studio Archives, Burbank, California.

15 Stacy Warren, "The Corporate-Sponsored City: The Evolution of Walt Disney World's EPCOT Theme Park," paper delivered at Association of American Geographers, April 2014; Jeff Kurtti, *Walt Disney's Imagineering Legends and the Genesis of the Disney Theme Park* (New York: Disney Editions, 2008), 38.

16 Mark Gottdiener, *The Theming of America: Dreams, Visions, and Commercial Spaces* (New York: Westview Press, 1997), 110.

17 Paul Marx, *Jim Rouse: Capitalist/Idealist* (New York: University Press of America, 2008), 8, 56, 84, 119–120, 215.

18 Hardwick, *Mall Maker*, 2–6, 82, 86, 115, 121, 130–131, 140–141, 151, 163, 166, 175–177. Hardwick calls Disney Gruen's "dream client."

In some ways Walt had been preparing for this moment his entire life. He had come of age in the midst of the Progressive Era, which had seen the "city beautiful" movement grow out of the 1893 Columbian World's Fair in Chicago. Landscape architects like George Kessler then set to work across the Midwest (including in Walt's own Kansas City) building parks and boulevard streets to combat urban and industrial grime.[19] Additionally, Walt had spent the better part of four summers in the late 1940s and early 1950s in England, shooting live-action films that used British actors and crews (for monetary purposes). There he was likely exposed to the New Town movement, which itself was inspired by earlier urban planners, such as Ebenezer Howard. Most famous for his "garden city concept" inscribed in his 1898 tome *To-Morrow: A Peaceful Path to Real Reform*, Howard wrote of creating a well-planned (with ideas being guidelines that could be altered in reality) model city, laid out in a circular pattern, tied together by rapid transportation, and buttressed by a greenbelt from other communities.[20] Many of Howard's ideas found fertile ground in the mind of Walt Disney.

The idea of Epcot was "exciting" to Walt.[21] He viewed it as a chance give people a true "city of tomorrow," one that would be full of the latest technology, and largely be based on pedestrian living.[22] So, when Project X was announced in 1965, Walt told reporters and government leaders in Florida that the Disney company planned to build another theme park, complete with hotels, but that it also would be constructing a model city. Epcot was going to be built in concentric circles, with linked industrial zones, a nearby airport, and plenty of land between it and other urban centers. Homes would be equipped with the latest in appliances and technology, as well as their own renewable energy source, schools would utilize the latest in innovative teaching techniques, and there would be no need for cars (though there would be adequate underground parking for residents and visitors) because of

---

19 Eric Avila, *Popular Culture in the Age of White Flight: Fear and Fantasy in Suburban Los Angeles* (Los Angeles: University of California Press, 2004), 114 ; "City Beautiful, " http://www.nypap.org/content/city-beautiful-movement, 13 October 2014 ; "George Kessler," http://www.georgekessler.org/index.php?option=com_content&view=category&id=45&Itemid=73, 13 October 2014.

20 Manheim, *Walt Disney and the Quest for Community*, xviii; "Garden Cities of To-Morrow," http://urbanplanning.library.cornell.edu/DOCS/howard.htm, 24 September 2015.

21 Dave Smith, *The Quotable Walt Disney* (New York: Disney Editions, 2001), 70.

22 Smith, *The Quotable Walt Disney*, 72; Hench, John (1). December 1974 Interview, Lectures and Transcripts, Walt Disney Studio Archives, Burbank, California.

public transportation systems like the PeopleMover. Epcot would also be easily accessible to the planned Disney World park, which would serve as an instant source of jobs and revenue to help sustain Epcot in its early years. As such, there would be no fear that slums would or could develop. Epcot, not Disney World, was going to be the main attraction of what Disney was building.[23]

To pull Epcot off, to fill those homes with the latest technology, Walt was going to need the help of other American corporations. He believed he could pitch the idea to companies, and that they would be eager to fill his model city with "prototype concepts" (not unlike what they had done on a smaller scale for the Monsanto House of the Future in Tomorrowland) that could be displayed and tested in a real-world environment. Epcot would serve as "an on-going forum of the future" where "industry, government, and academia" could discuss the needs of citizens. It would be an example to the rest of the world of American ingenuity, "industry and research," and those ideas could span not just the United States, but also the globe (as Walt always intended for there to be a World Showcase at either the park or in Epcot).[24] As Walt predicted, Disney was able to find (and keep in the years to come) a bevy of corporate sponsors.[25]

Walt's vision for Epcot was clear: he was applying Dis-History (the past, memories, myth, and belief in an optimistic future) to the real world.[26] Walt was convinced that suburbs could not replace cities, but that his model city would be an example for how cities could be

---

23 Manheim, *Walt Disney and the Quest for Community*, 31, 36–38, 41, 89; Leonard E. Zehnder, *Florida's Disney World: Promises and Problems* (Tallahassee: The Peninsular Publishing Company, 1975), 63, 86–87, 182; Neal Gabler, *Walt Disney: The Triumph of the American Imagination* (New York: Vintage Books, 2007), 608–609; Bob Thomas, *Walt Disney: An American Original* (New York: Disney Editions, 1994), 338-339; Richard E. Foglesong, *Married to the Mouse: Walt Disney World and Orlando* (New Haven: Yale University Press, 2001), xi, 51, 59 ; Michael Barrier, *The Animated Man: A Life of Walt Disney* (Los Angeles: University of California Press, 2007), 303, 310; Sharon Zukin, *Landscapes of Power: From Detroit to Disney World* (Los Angeles: University of California Press, 1993), 224.

24 Christopher Finch, *Walt Disney's America* (New York: Abbeville Press, 1978), 191-193; Leon and Rosenzweig, editors, *History Museums in the United States*, 167; Sklar, *Dream It! Do It!*, 130; Manheim, *Walt Disney and the Quest for Community*, 7; Hench, John and Dick Irvine. "Walt Disney Biography 1968" Lectures and Transcripts, Walt Disney Studio Archives, Burbank, California.

25 Knight, *Power and Paradise*, 123.

26 Kurtti, *Walt Disney's Imagineering Legends and the Genesis of the Disney Theme Park*, 104.

a functioning place to live and work,[27] a showcase for the future, always twenty to thirty years ahead while also demonstrating how urban problems could be solved.[28] As Steve Manheim notes, "While Epcot would be the community of tomorrow, the word *community* undoubtedly held Midwestern meanings for Disney." Epcot would be a place where people came together.[29] Built "on virgin land," it would be "a special kind of new community" that would embody progress.[30] As Elting Morison said in 1983, Walt's rhetoric envisioned construction of "a new sort of city on a hill"—invoking the stirring words of the Puritans when they arrived to found the Massachusetts Bay Colony in the mid-1600s—a place where the American dream could flourish.[31] Ray Bradbury simply labeled Epcot as a "contemporary Renaissance," a place from which American society could be continually reborn and renewed.[32]

Accomplishing Walt's vision was another task entirely. In order to transform the land he had purchased into both a city and a park, he needed to convince Florida officials to let him have complete control over the area that spread over two counties.[33] Disney ultimately got what it wanted with special legislation that created the Reedy Creek Improvement District. Florida officials apparently did not read what they approved, literally handing Disney the keys to the kingdom, granting the company "total autonomy" to build the park as it saw fit. Disney now had "complete control in the production and regulation of water use, power generation, waste disposal, environmental preservation, and all other issues of infrastructure on their territory," and rivals are kept at bay. The promise of Epcot, an experimental city of the future, and thus people living there, probably sealed the deal.[34]

---

27 Avila, *Popular Culture in the Age of White Flight*, 140; Joseph Tirella, *Tomorrow-Land: The 1964–1965 World's Fair and the Transformation of America* (Guilford, Connecticut: Lyons Press, 2014), 53; James Howard Kunstler, *The Geography of Nowhere* (New York: Touchstone Book, 1993), 189.

28 Didier Ghez, editor, *Walt's People: Volume 6: Talking Disney with the Artists Who Knew Him* (New York: Xlibris Corporation, 2008), 205–206, 210.

29 Manheim, *Walt Disney and the Quest for Community*, 19.

30 Sklar, *Dream It! Do It!*, 3, 212–213

31 Elting E. Morison, "What Went Wrong with Disney's World's Fair," http://www.americanheritage.com, 2 June 2014.

32 Sklar, *Dream It! Do It!*, 361.

33 Leonard E. Zehnder, *Florida's Disney World: Promises and Problems* (Tallahassee: The Peninsular Publishing Company, 1975), 200–201; Beth Dunlop, *Building a Dream: The Art of Disney Architecture* (New York: Harry N. Abrams, 1996), 46.

34 T.D. Allman, *Finding Florida: The True History of the Sunshine State* (New York: Atlantic Monthly Press, 2013), 376–379.

For all his optimism, Walt doubted that Epcot would actually be built the way he envisioned if he was not alive to do it.[35] And so, he began working extremely hard designing his model city and the advantages to society he believed it would produce.[36] Walt literally worked on Epcot his last day at the studio, filming presentations in late October 1966 for both public distribution and corporate sponsors for the Florida Project.[37] And while Epcot may have been his "dying dream" as the cancer claimed his life, his earlier premonition was also correct. It was not long after his death that his brother Roy announced that Disney would be focusing on opening its second park, not a model city. Epcot, as Walt had pitched it, simply did not fit with the company's edu-tainment model of business.[38] But it did fit within Dis-History's goal of forging an American common culture.

As subsequent events proved, Roy's decision may have been one that Walt himself would have ultimately agreed to. In the mid-1990s, Disney under Michael Eisner launched the model community of Celebration on 4,900 acres of Disney's holdings in Florida. The community was laid out not as a subdivision, but rather as a small town, with strict home designs that attempted to replicate classic American architecture. The problem with residents, though, was that they, ultimately, would want a say in how their community was governed—not trusting a corporate home-owner's association to actually take care of their interests. No sooner was Celebration established as a viable community than Disney excluded it from the Reedy Creek Improvement District.[39] Even Walt had recognized this issue prior to his death. In

---

35 Knight, *Power and Paradise in Walt Disney's World*, 116.

36 Didier Ghez, editor, *Walt's People: Volume 5: Talking Disney with the Artists Who Knew Him* (New York: Xlibris Corporation, 2007), 52; Manheim, *Walt Disney and the Quest for Community*, 116–117.

37 Sklar, *Dream It! Do It!*, 9.

38 Didier Ghez, editor, *Walt's People: Volume 7: Talking Disney with the Artists Who Knew Him* (New York: Xlibris Corporation, 2008), 254-255; Gabler, *Walt Disney*, 622–623; John Taylor, *Storming the Magic Kingdom: Wall Street, the Raiders, and the Battle for Disney* (New York: Alfred A. Knopf, 1987), 11; Thomas, *Building a Company*, 296-297;Marling, editor, *Designing Disney's Theme Parks*, 154; Michael Barrier, *The Animated Man: A Life of Walt Disney* (Los Angeles: University of California Press, 2007), 319.

39 Foglesong, *Married to the Mouse*, 67-68, 75, 153; Kathy Merlock Jackson and Mark I. West, editors, *Disneyland and Culture: Essays on the Parks and Their Influence* (Jefferson, NC: McFarland and Company, 2011), 159; Michael D. Eisner, *Work in Progress* (New York: Random House, 1998), 408–410; Janet Wasko, *Understanding Disney: The Manufacture of Fantasy* (Cambridge: Polity Press, 2001), 178–182; Andi Stein, *Why We Love Disney: The Power of the Disney*

a memo found in his desk, he had expressed reluctance to consider those who lived at Epcot as residents, preferring a plan where they would be temporary guests in the city instead. The legal ramifications and risks of having voters living within Disney's property were too great for the corporation's larger plans.[40]

So, the Epcot that was constructed does not look like Walt's vision. It is another park within the Disney system. Like its cousins, it is well laid out and always clean. Though it is a park and not a living community, it incorporated a good deal of Dis-History into its make-up. In that regard, it is Disney's World's Fair, complete with pavilions that showcase industry and technology, as well as those that highlight eleven nations of the world.[41] And because it is heavily infused with the idea that it would be a showcase for edu-tainment, its attractions' backstories were carefully constructed.[42]

The assumption underlying Epcot is that the park seeks to educate its guests about global cultures, history, science, and industry. Thus, Dis-History is employed in how attractions are positioned within the park and when and where guests might encounter them. Think again to the first attraction we encountered, Spaceship Earth, where the past is employed to show that progress is on the march and that the daily lives of people around the world, thanks in no small part to technology (and the corporations that produce it), are getting better.[43] While there might be lapses in the historic record as displayed in Epcot, and the past itself is sometimes shown in a humorous way, today is much better than yesterday, and tomorrow is sure to be better still.[44]

For critics, this is why Dis-History is so problematic at Epcot. As Michael Wallace notes, what it opts not to mention, or omits, is even

---

Brand (New York: Peter Lang, 2011), 128; Andrew Lainsbury, *Once Upon an American Dream: The Story of Euro Disneyland* (Lawrence: University Press of Kansas, 2000), 192–193; Watts, *The Magic Kingdom*, 444; Allman, *Finding Florida*, 383, 387; Knight, *Power and Paradise in Walt Disney's World*, 85-90; Manheim, *Walt Disney and the Quest for Community*, 135–138.

40 Barrier, *The Animated Man*, 303; Zukin, *Landscapes of Power*, 224; Knight, *Power and Paradise in Walt Disney's World*, 142.

41 Morison, "What Went Wrong with Disney's World's Fair," http://www.americanheritage.com, 2 June 2014; Dunlop, *Building a Dream*, 55.

42 Sklar, *Dream It! Do It!*, 170–171.

43 Leon and Rosenzweig, editors, *History Museums in the United States*, 170; Judith A. Adams, *The American Amusement Park Industry: A History of Technology and Thrills* (Boston: Twayne Publishers, 1991), 150–152.

44 Morison, "What Went Wrong with Disney's World's Fair," http://www.americanheritage.com, 2 June 2014.

more telling than what it actually talks about (whether in the World Showcase or at an attraction like Mission to Mars—where Disney once again enters the frontier that Tomorrowland pioneered). As Wallace argues, at Epcot war is rarely mentioned, even in passing. But Wallace saves his most scathing attacks for Epcot's Future World, where he charges that Dis-History has been used to dull historical understanding to the point where the pavilions promote acceptance of the corporate story and are "historicidal" toward the education they claim to be advancing.[45] Other critics see the entire park as an "anachronistic nightmare," whose theming was almost outdated the moment it opened, and simply has not aged well, if it has been continued at all.[46] They are seemingly befuddled by Epcot's very existence.

What critics fail to recognize is that Dis-History has evolved. It is no longer just a storyteller's technique and a framework for consulting theme-park lands and attractions. During the Eisner years and continuing to the present, it has become enhanced by helping guests create their own memories as well as by reliance on Disney's history (especially its animated films). This shift has led Dis-History to embrace consumerism, hegemony, and globalism/colonialism/imperialism in ways that it never did when Walt first created the concept. It is now all encompassing and global in its vision for what the company can accomplish.

Be Our Guest

Of the new concepts Dis-History has come to embrace, consumerism is perhaps the least surprising of the lot. It was, after all, originally crafted as a story-telling technique to help the company harness history for use in the parks. And while doing so may have been toward the goal of creating a common American culture, it also was designed to make money for Disney. Dis-History, in other words, was always intended to be a tool to help the company's bottom line—it is a means for a corporation (Disney) to engage consumers (guests) in new ways and generate more revenue as a result.

While today most people accept Epcot as a second gate—an additional park that prompts guests to spend additional time and money

---

45 Morison, "What Went Wrong with Disney's World's Fair," http://www.americanheritage.com, 2 June 2014; Leon and Rosenzweig, editors, *History Museums in the United States*, 173; Geoffrey M. White, "Disney's Pearl Harbor: National Memory at the Movies," *The Public Historian*, 24(Fall 2002), 114; Wallace, "Mickey Mouse History," 149.

46 Kuenz, Klugman, Waldrep, and Willis, editors, *Inside the Mouse*, 42, 82–83, 133; Karal Ann Marling, editor, *Designing Disney's Theme Parks: The Architecture of Reassurance* (New York: Flammarion, 1997), 168.

at Disney—when the park was proposed in the late 1970s, we must remember what a radical notion that was. After all, while Epcot differed from Walt's original vision, it was still designed to appeal to "grown-up Mouseketeers" via its stress on science, industry, technology, history, and culture, which was a new market for Disney.[47] It represented a certain degree of financial risk for the company, at a time when it was undergoing external and internal threats to its future.[48] That the gamble paid off ultimately has much to do with both the power of the Disney brand and the strength of Dis-History as both a concept and a tool for the company.

That being said, Epcot could not have opened in October 1982 if not for other corporations partnering with Disney.[49] While these corporate sponsorships are perhaps most explicit at Epcot, they have been a part of the park idea from the moment Disneyland was conceived and Walt made his television deal with ABC in the early 1950s. Corporate sponsors like Kraft, Coca-Cola, Kodak, General Motors, and General Electric all signed on and sponsored attractions and pavilions around the basic organizing idea that corporations gave consumers technology that made everyone's life better. Even as corporate sponsors change, the notion of corporate contribution and responsibility to the world around them, in areas like energy, environmental stewardship, ecology, food production, and space travel, remains strong.[50]

Epcot, then, is a place full of both Dis-History and a "corporate view of history." In some respects, the marriage of these two concepts is merely a reflection of Disney's own corporate power. Its various arms mean that it is an incredibly diverse corporation with a global reach, and immense influence—which of course tells a story itself. Walt believed that corporations had much to contribute when it came to making America what it was and what it could be. It is also a means of "self-affirmation," whereby corporations get to tout their own accomplishments and contributions. And while this kind of corporate sponsorship highlights American capitalism, critics worry that all too often the corporation's version of the facts becomes

---

47   Leon and Rosenzweig, editors, *History Museums in the United States*, 168.

48   James B. Stewart, *Disney War* (New York: Simon and Schuster, 2005), 61; Joe Flower, *Prince of the Magic Kingdom: Michael Eisner and the Re-Making of Disney* (New York: John Wiley and Sons, Inc., 1991), 91.

49   Sklar, *Dream It! Do It!*, 161.

50   Leon and Rosenzweig, editors, *History Museums in the United States*, 159, 172–173; Morison, "What Went Wrong with Disney's World's Fair," http://www.americanheritage.com, 2 June 2014; Alan Bryman, *Disney and His Worlds* (New York: Routledge, 1995; ebook version), 71–72

the visitor's version once they exit the parks.[51] Here, then, is a new critique of Dis-History. There is no doubt that corporate-sponsored history needs more study than it has received. As Henry Giroux, who is among Disney's critics, argues, corporations like Disney, because of their cultural influence, political sway, and economic clout, pose real dangers to democracies.[52] Whether or not Disney alone should be singled out, however, is another matter. Corporate conglomerates like Disney, despite their branding, size, and influence, run a fine line between exerting influence and angering the consumers they rely on for revenue.[53] They are also but one agent in the field of corporations seeking public influence. And, as we will see, critics are often too quick to dismiss the agency that the individual consumer still exerts.

By opting to become Disney's guest, there is little doubt that consumers witness an onslaught of corporate history (shaped by Dis-History) that urges them to consume. Indeed, that it is almost un-American not to shop. We have seen this in Main Street, where the buildings invoke an historic town, but the inside is a modern shopping experience. We saw this emerging in Tomorrowland, as Dis-History's narrative gave way to corporate-themed attractions. We have seen both nostalgia and fantasy itself become a commodity in large part because of Disney. And now at Epcot, the narrative becomes, especially as guests tour the World Showcase, that "global capitalism" is the norm.[54]

As a corporation, Disney is ultimately interested in making money, and thus, to having consumers purchase their products. The revolutionary thing about Disney as a business is, thanks in large part to Dis-History, for the first time a company views every potential

---

51   Fjellman, *Vinyl Leaves*, 85-87; Henry A. Giroux, *The Mouse that Roared: Disney and the End of Innocence* (New York: Rowman and Littlefield, 1999), 44-45; Kuenz, Klugman, Waldrep, and Willis, editors, *Inside the Mouse*, 84–85; Watts, *The Magic Kingdom*, 441-442; Leon and Rosenzweig, editors, *History Museums in the United States:*, 168–169, 174, 178; Eric Smoodin, editor, *Disney Discourse: Producing the Magic Kingdom* (New York: Routledge, 1994), 126; William F. Van Wert, "Disney World and Posthistory," *Cultural Critique*, 32(Winter, 1995–1996), 202–203.

52   Leon and Rosenzweig, editors, *History Museums in the United States*, 179; Giroux, *The Mouse that Roared*, 4.

53   Douglas Brode, *Multiculturalism and the Mouse: Race and Sex in Disney Entertainment* (Austin: University of Texas Press, 2005), 259.

54   Umberto Eco, *Travels in Hyper Reality* (New York: Harcourt Brace and Company, 1986), 43; Wasko, *Understanding Disney*, 223; Kuenz, Klugman, Waldrep, and Willis, editors, *Inside the Mouse*, 43; Giroux, *The Mouse that Roared: Disney*, 39; Alan Bryman, *Disney and His Worlds* (New York: Routledge, 1995; ebook version), 158; Adams, *The American Amusement Park Industry*, 153.

demographic (children, their parents, their grandparents, even teenagers and adults) as its customer base. Simply put, they want to be able to convince every group, every category of person, to experience Disney magic for themselves. Furthermore, they view potential guests as both an "audience" (those who pay to view artistry in a variety of forms) and as "consumers" (those who purchase things because there are things to purchase). Disney has proven willing to invest to get both groups to come to its movies and parks.⁵⁵

Consumerism does not just drive Disney. Lizabeth Cohen argues, rather convincingly, that the concept needs to be put at the center of the American experience during the twentieth century. Cohen is even more explicit that we cannot understand post-World War II American history at all without doing so.⁵⁶ And, it just so happens, the second half of the twentieth century saw both the rise of Disney and the establishment of its theme parks. Furthermore, modern American society mirrors the Disney parks in the way that consumerism is themed: Items must be given at least the veneer of meaning so that people will buy them. But Disney has pioneered other facets of consumerism as well: hybrid consumption (everything that has to be purchased, most often from providers, in order to achieve a single result), merchandising (goods with logos), and performance labor (work as theater).⁵⁷ If consumerism is the American Way, Americans learned about it from Disney.

Because consumerism has become so ingrained in American life, Disney faces competition from other companies and entities for consumers' money. This list of rivals, of course, includes other theme and amusement parks (such as Universal Studios), entertainment venues, as well as museums and other historic sites.⁵⁸ This competition has forced Disney to push to diversify its revenue streams. While the Disney brothers had movies, merchandising, television, and the parks, in the years after Walt and Roy's deaths, the company launched retail

---

55 Alice Y. Kaplan, Myriam Herve-Gil, and Jean-Philippe Mazzia, "Diamond Lil at Euro-Disneyland: A Conversation," *SubStance*, 24(Special Issue: France's Identity Crises, 1995), 161, 164; Lizabeth Cohen, *A Consumer's Republic: The Politics of Mass Consumption in Postwar America* (New York: Alfred A. Knopf, 2003), 121; Wasko, *Understanding Disney*, 158–159, 184–187, 205, 208; Giroux, *The Mouse that Roared*, 158–159.

56 Cohen, *A Consumer's Republic*, 7–8.

57 Bryman, *The Disneyization of Society*, 2, 15, 57–58, 79, 103; Adams, *The American Amusement Park Industry*, 100.

58 John Terrell, "Disneyland and the Future of Museum Anthropology," *American Anthropologist*, 93(March 1991), 149, 151.

stores in malls, the Disney Vacation Club, Broadway musicals, and a cruise line of its own. Michael Eisner was instrumental in pushing for many of these new ventures, recognizing that consumers needed to be able to have touch points with Disney beyond just the parks and the occasional movie. The inclusion of Disney in attempts to reinvent Times Square in New York City, with its rehabilitation of the New Amsterdam Theater for the production of musicals based on its animated classics (the first of which was *Beauty and the Beast*), was a means for Disney to return to the city that had hosted the 1964 World's Fair and had helped make "Disneyland East" a reality. While the retail stores have faced increased competition from internet sales (as well as overexpansion), they have also allowed Disney to enter new markets (such as China) ahead of some of the other branches of the company.[59]

Consumerism has become ubiquitous and has helped enhance Disney's profits, but it has altered Dis-History in significant ways. What started as a means to find and tell stories in order to forge a usable past and culture for guests at Disney parks has also become a means to advance consumerism—indeed, it has equated consumerism with progress itself for individuals and the United States. But this definition of what constitutes progress for Americans is at odds with what many historians might label as progress for wider American society. How, for example, can we see progress when it comes to civil rights as being the same as having multiple places to purchase Disney t-shirts?[60] Such questions raise issues about the narrative power of Dis-History as well as its longevity into the twenty-first century.

Dis-History and the Natural World

Even as Disney and Dis-History has evolved, its dominance as both an entertainment company and as a provider of edu-tainment in its parks has remained unparalleled. Indeed, despite an increase in competition, Disney has maintained a degree of hegemony nearly unprecedented. As we have discussed when considering Adventureland, Disney's dominant place in entertainment culture is mirrored and tied to America's role in the world. And while this has usually been extended to talking about imperialism or colonialism, Disney has sought to extend its hegemony to the natural world as well.[61] No place is this seen better than the fourth park in the Walt Disney World system, Animal Kingdom.

---

59 Stein, *Why We Love Disney*, 147–149, 231–232, 248; Eisner, *Work in Progress*, 418.
60 Avila, *Popular Culture in the Age of White Flight*, 136–137.
61 Alexander Moore, "Walt Disney World: Bounded Ritual Space and the Playful Pilgrimage Center," *Anthropological Quarterly*, 53(October 1980), 215.

Walt had been interested in dealing with the natural world at least since 1942's *Bambi*. The story of a young fawn who grows to take his place beside the Great Prince of the Forest (a large buck/great stag, who is likely also his father), *Bambi* presented a simple maxim about nature alongside the coming of age tale: "Nature undisturbed is good—if not ideal. Man disrupts and destroys" according to Mark Pinsky. The loss of Bambi's mother to a hunter and the forest fire (sparked by a campfire) that consumes much of the idyllic setting in the final act reinforces that message to viewers young and old alike.[62]

After World War II, Walt was ready to explore the natural world in more detail. In what became the True-Life Adventures series of fourteen films between the years 1948 to 1960, Walt argued that "we have our own approach to wildlife nature as entertainment. We are not telling the dry academic natural history of bird and beast and reptile in these dramas seen from the animals' standpoint," capturing moments most people had never seen before. Instead, Disney used musical cues to build drama, accentuate a theme, and make things like baby animals taking flight or their first steps into comedic moments. Critics called such edited scenes "patronizing" to the animals and a form of "sham nature," but even they were forced to admit that Walt had found a way to not only capture the moments that usually only naturalists got to see, but find an audience willing to watch such documentaries.[63]

Despite winning eight Academy Awards, the nature films do not fit neatly into Dis-History. But they are its cousins in many respects. Walt insisted that the True-Life Adventures have a narrative arc, that they tell a story. He also wanted to prove that he could make educational films, so in that respect, they fit into the wider pattern Dis-History established of edu-tainment as a directive for the Disney company.[64]

But eventually, the company that Walt had once led wanted more. In April 1998, Animal Kingdom opened to the public. Disney argued

---

62 Eisner, *Work in Progress*, 402–403; Pinsky, *The Gospel According to Disney*, 51; Kathy Merlock Jackson, editor, *Walt Disney: Conversations* (Jackson: University of Mississippi Press, 2006), 110.

63 Jackson, editor, *Walt Disney: Conversations*, 70; Richard Schickel, *The Disney Version, Third Edition* (Chicago: Ivan R. Dee Publisher, 1997), 288–291; Richard Shale, *Donald Duck Joins Up: The Walt Disney Studio During World War II* (Ann Arbor: UMI Research Press, 1982), 110; Christopher Finch, *Walt Disney's America* (New York: Abbeville Press, 1978), 166; Watts, *The Magic Kingdom*, 304-308; Siegfried Kracauer, *Theory of Film: The Redemption of Physical Reality* (Princeton, New Jersey: Princeton University Press, 1997), 90, 141.

64 Gabler, *Walt Disney*, 444–445; Barrier, *The Animated Man*, 208; Finch, *Walt Disney's America*, 167; Ghez, editor, *Walt's People: Volume 5*, 100.

that it was not a zoo, going so far as to create a word, "nahtazu," to describe the park. A zoo, after all, was a place to showcase animals. Disney, thanks to Dis-History, promised guests a look at the mythic and prehistoric pasts in addition to the present, with a good dose of culture and preservation thrown in as well. At Animal Kingdom, guests can visit the jungles of India and see tigers and birds. They can take a safari in Africa. Or they can visit the mountains of Asia. And everywhere, they can see nature and animals.[65] For many guests, the zoo-like quality is exactly why they make plans to visit. But in building the park, Disney had shown it had learned from the Disney's America debacle: from the outset, the company worked with leading zoologists, biologists, and other experts. For Roy E. Disney, who did some of his first work for his family's company on the True-Life Adventures films, Animal Kingdom was worth the effort.[66]

One of the goals of Animal Kingdom (beyond being yet another gate for Walt Disney World) was to live up to one of Disney's original Florida promises. Shortly after the company had purchased the property in Florida in the mid-1960s, Disney set aside over 7000 acres as a nature preserve. Part of this was to show the people of Florida that the company was capable of good stewardship of the immense land it had purchased. Part of it was to try and sway conservationist groups, including the Sierra Club, that Disney understood their concerns about the environment and protecting wildlife, since, after all, building a park in a wetlands/wilderness is hardly environmentally friendly.[67] In theming much of the park, Disney sought to harken back to ideas advanced not just in True-Life Adventures but in Bambi as well: human activity (if not people themselves) is almost always seen as the largest problem facing the natural world. Guests find this to be true at attractions as varied as It's Tough to Be a Bug (a 3-D film, housed in the Tree of Life and based on the Disney-Pixar movie *A Bug's Life*), Flights of Wonder (an attraction that uses live birds in the Asia area of the park, and which discusses at length the harmful effects of DDT), and Kilimanjaro Safaris, where guests are warned about poachers in the

---

65 "Disney's Animal Kingdom History," http://www.disneyparkhistory.com/animal-kingdom.html, 13 August 2014.

66 "Disney's Animal Kingdom History," http://www.disneyparkhistory.com/animal-kingdom.html, 13 August 2014; David A. Bossert, *Remembering Roy E. Disney: Memories and Photos of a Storied Life* (New York: Disney Editions, 2013), 167.

67 Finch, *Walt Disney's America*, 153; Manheim, *Walt Disney and the Quest for Community*, 110; Tison Pugh and Susan Aronstein, editors, *The Disney Middle Ages: A Fairy-Tale and Fantasy Past* (New York: Palgrave Macmillan, 2012), 201.

park.⁶⁸ There is little doubt that the Imagineers have done their homework and that at Animal Kingdom, there is at least some education going into a guest's day as there is entertainment.⁶⁹

Dis-History is not lost in all the environmental messages that guests can find at Animal Kingdom. As mentioned above, along with attractions there are several cultural outposts where guests can learn more about Asia and Africa. Not surprisingly, the *Lion King* is part of the entertainment, environmental, and cultural (especially at the show) aspects, as well as reminding guests of its Dis-Historic origins (with some critics calling the film Disney's version of Shakespeare's *Hamlet*, set against the backdrop of apartheid-era South Africa) of being a literary work reimagined.⁷⁰ Interestingly enough, the most obvious Dis-Historic attraction at the park is DINOSAUR, a dark ride that whisks guests back to the age of dinosaurs via "time travel." Housed at the Dino Institute, guests are surrounded by real fossils and reminded repeatedly (ahead of their mission) that "the future is in the past."⁷¹

When Animal Kingdom opened, there was thought of a fantasy area, where guests might have encountered animals such as dragons and unicorns. One can imagine perhaps a castle in Animal Kingdom, where knights might have done battle on fantastic beasts of mythology. From a Dis-Historic perspective, such an area could have then moved toward the pre-historic period of the Dino Institute area, before giving way to the animals we know today in the Asia and Africa areas. The progression would have been akin to guests in the Magic Kingdom moving from Fantasyland to Liberty Square, and then on to Frontierland and Adventureland. But for the first twenty years of the park's existence little has been done to make the Imagineers' dreams a reality. Only in the 2010s has Disney moved toward addressing this missed area, but it does not neatly fit the Dis-Historic pattern. Pandora, the newest land in Animal Kingdom, and based off the 2009 film *Avatar* and its planned sequels, introduces guests to a fantastic world, but one built much more on science fiction than classic mythology. And while there

---

68 Leonard E. Zehnder, *Florida's Disney World: Promises and Problems* (Tallahassee: The Peninsular Publishing Company, 1975), 350.

69 Bron Taylor, *Dark Green Religion: Nature, Spirituality, and the Planetary Future* (Los Angeles: University of California Press, 2010), 132–133, 137; Sklar, *Dream It! Do It!*, 300–301.

70 Eleanor Byrne and Martin McQuillan, *Deconstructing Disney* (Sterling, Virginia: Pluto Press, 1999), 82–93, 102–103; Brenda Ayres, editor, *The Emperor's Old Groove: Decolonizing Disney's Magic Kingdom* (New York: Peter Lang, 2013), 123; Taylor, *Dark Green Religion*, 133–136.

71 Jackson and West, editors, *Disneyland and Culture*, 176.

may be talk of environmental preservation attached to it, the new land also seems an odd addition to both Animal Kingdom and a new development for Dis-History.

The arrival of Pandora raises questions about Dis-History's future as well. While never a perfect fit for such a park, there is still enough of it in the theming of Animal Kingdom to recognize Dis-History's influence and to see how it helped take a complex topic (nature) and used it to advance Disney's hegemony when it comes to theme parks. But Animal Kingdom also stands as a park that needed very little Dis-History to begin with.[72] And yet, it is also a place where we see Dis-History further evolve as a means to reference Disney's own (corporate) history. In 2008, Bob Iger, by then the man leading Disney, announced the creation of Disneynature, a documentary arm of film division. In doing so, the company was harkening directly back to Walt's True Life Adventures films.[73] Perhaps, then, Dis-History is not quite ready to fade away after all.

The Global Reach of Dis-History

If consumerism and hegemony showcase the ability of Dis-History to meet new demands for the company, then considering the global Disney parks offers a way to see that even as many aspects about Dis-History change, the core remains firmly intact. Disney is a global company with an equally global reach, highlighted by parks in Japan, France, Hong Kong, and China.[74] For some critics, these parks look a good deal like Alfred Thayer Mahon's (the military theorist who helped convince American political elites in the late nineteenth and early twentieth centuries to embark on overseas colonization) "strategic outposts"—bases for Disney (and thus American) imperialism.[75] As we have noted, Epcot gives its guests a taste of globalized Dis-History, but with the global parks guests from around the world are able to sample the concept (to varying degrees) without having to travel to

---

72 Knight, *Power and Paradise in Walt Disney's World*, 68.

73 Taylor, *Dark Green Religion*, 138.

74 Michael Wallace, *Mickey Mouse History and Other Essays on American Memory* (Philadelphia: Temple University Press, 1996), 162–163; John Taylor, *Storming the Magic Kingdom: Wall Street, the Raiders, and the Battle for Disney* (New York: Alfred A. Knopf, 1987), 211; Bryman, *Disney and His Worlds*, 46.

75 William A. Covino, "Walt Disney Meets Mary Daly: Invention, Imagination, and the Construction of Community," *JAC* 20(Winter 2000), 154; Zukin, *Landscapes of Power*, 257; Ingolf Bogeler and Anthony R. De Souza, editors, *Dialectics of Third World Development* (Montclair, NJ: Allanheld, Osmun & Company, 1980), 134.

the United States. And while cultural imperialism is a charge we have already seen levied against the parks,[76] if we stipulate to Disney's critics that its animated films "are at the center of its ideological hegemony and capitalist expansion,"[77] then these overseas parks are the physical representations of the same. And perhaps they are then what some critics have called "the latest wave of U.S. cultural imperialism in an increasingly Americanized world."[78]

Michael Eisner often gets credit for creating Disney's global parks, but well before he came to the company, Disney was casting its gaze to places around the world where it believed it could enhance its revenue streams. While "franchise" is perhaps the wrong word to use, the early forays into a global theme park presence are not far from that metaphor, making Disney a slightly different version of, say, McDonalds. The first place to land its own version of Disneyland was Tokyo, in 1983. The park is a product of late twentieth-century Japanese "high consumerism" and Disney's desire (and need) to reach more guests. The chief issue to crafting the park was needing to balance the requests of the Japanese investors (who said they wanted an exact replica of Disneyland—complete with the Disney experience one would find in the United States) with the realization that in order to be a success, Dis-History was going to need to adapt to its new surroundings. Japanese towns, after all, had nothing like Main Street, U.S.A. to spark any sort of collective memory or attachment. Disneyland Tokyo is a wonderful mixture of both the California and Florida parks, with strong referential points to Dis-History, perhaps best seen in Westernland (the park's version of Frontierland). Its eventual second gate, Disney Sea (which may remind many American guests of a nautically themed World Showcase), has proven to be even more popular than the Japanese version of Disneyland itself. In many ways, the park "is a case of cultural adaptation rather than cultural imperialism," and is successful because of shared consumer values about merchandise and brand loyalty between Japan and the United States, which trumps the need for a shared past.[79] Here is where the evolution of Dis-History perhaps began.

---

76 Pinsky, *The Gospel According to Disney*, 194.

77 Brenda Ayres, editor, *The Emperor's Old Groove: Decolonizing Disney's Magic Kingdom* (New York: Peter Lang, 2013), 3.

78 Stephen F. Mills, "Disney and the Promotions of Synthetic Worlds," *American Studies International*, 28(October 1990), 66.

79 Eric Smoodin, editor, *Disney Discourse: Producing the Magic Kingdom* (New York: Routledge, 1994), 189–190, 194–197; Aviad E. Raz, *Riding the Black Ship: Japan and Tokyo Disneyland* (Cambridge: Harvard University Press, 1999), 66, 194–195, 198; Jackson and West, editors, *Disneyland and Culture*, 140; Bryman,

From a corporate Dis-Historic view, the Tokyo park carried with it all sorts of lessons. For starters, the deal had been delayed (at least in part) because of Card Walker. One of the Disney executives Roy Disney had selected to help run the company after Walt's death, Walker had been in the U.S. Navy during World War II, and his ship (the USS *Bunker Hill*) had been hit by Japanese kamikaze pilots, killing nearly 400 men on board. He had been on leave at the time, narrowly missing the attack that killed so many of his shipmates, and the animosity (plus survivor's remorse) lingered on nearly forty years later. In addition to Walker's reluctance to go ahead with the park, Disney was also engaged in building Epcot at the exact same time. The company simply did not have the money to build two parks at once. As a result, Disney had to enter into a partnership with Japanese investors, who owned a controlling percentage. For much of its existence, then, Disney received only a percentage of the park's revenues (a funding statistic that only started to change with the opening of the second gate). While Disneyland Tokyo excited the company about the possibilities of overseas parks as revenue streams, nearly everyone involved wanted to make sure that the next park would be directly controlled by Disney itself.[80]

Even as the park in Tokyo was welcoming its first guests, Walker and Walt's son-in-law Ron Miller began entertaining offers to put a park somewhere in Europe. The move made a good deal of sense. Europeans loved Disney, and had almost since the beginning of the company. They knew the characters and the films almost as well as their American peers. By the 1980s, when negotiations got serious, Walt Disney World was the number-three travel destination for Europeans in the world. That alone was reason enough to put a park there. The company could build on this good will and attraction, and add to its financial bottom line. Walker and Miller, however, would not be the ones to do so. It was up to Michael Eisner and Frank Wells to make the dream a reality.[81]

The Disneyization of Society, 163; Stein, *Why We Love Disney*, 120–122; Sklar, *Dream It! Do It!*, 222–223.

80   Sklar, *Dream It! Do It!*, 220–221; Aircraft Carrier USS *Bunker Hill*," http://ww2db.com/ship_spec.php?ship_id=164, 12 May 2015; Adams, *The American Amusement Park Industry*, 170–171; Joe Flower, *Prince of the Magic Kingdom: Michael Eisner and the Re-Making of Disney* (New York: John Wiley and Sons, Inc., 1991), 88; Janet Wasko, *Understanding Disney: The Manufacture of Fantasy* (Cambridge: Polity Press, 2001), 66.

81   Eisner, *Work in Progress*, 262; Lainsbury, *Once Upon an American Dream*, 6, 17–18, 86; Sharon Zukin, *Point of Purchase: How Shopping Changed American Culture* (New York: Routledge, 2005), 207, 219.

The finalists for what was then known as Euro-Disney were Spain and France. Both nations worked very hard to lure Disney, but as Eisner and Wells considered their proposals a clear frontrunner developed: France. The problem for the incredibly disappointed Spanish, ultimately, was that despite better weather, they were not as centrally located as France was to the rest of Europe. On August 12, 1985, Disney announced that sugar beet fields just 15 miles from Paris were to be the future home of its European theme park. Already near major highways (which made for easy driving for guests from Germany, Belgium, and the Netherlands), what sealed the deal from a transportation standpoint was the promise by the French government to ensure that the Paris Metro and the TGV (the bullet train) would have their lines extended to the park area as well.[82]

All of those things were important factors, but the best part of the deal for Disney was the price they got for the land. The French government arraigned for the sale of over 4,800 acres at 1971 farmland prices, "a mere fraction of its then market value." Disney was then given the right of first refusal on an additional 10,000 acres. Eisner constantly compared what was negotiated in Europe to the deal for Tokyo Disneyland. Here, Disney got creative control and the majority of the profits.[83]

While the deal might be done, not everyone was happy about it. Many of those who lived near the proposed park, in the small villages in Marne-la-Vallee, were upset at the park's chosen location. Not only would they have to suffer from noise and outside visitors, but they also were giving up land that their families had farmed for generations.[84] French cultural elites also weighed in. Some found it difficult to accept the concept of Dis-History: how could an American park, a park that was inspired by real places (many of them European), be placed in France in the midst of real European castles and towns? While most disavowed any (intentional) anti-American sentiment, the core of their argument was the Disney park brought little of value to France, and was itself the product of a mass-culture industry that had no redeeming value. As Jennifer James noted, "Europe has its own [myths] and America's myths simply don't work there."[85] Other European critics

---

82 Lainsbury, *Once Upon an American Dream*, 15, 19–22; Eisner, *Work in Progress*, 264–267; Sklar, *Dream It! Do It!*, 266.

83 Lainsbury, *Once Upon an American Dream*, 29–31; Eisner, *Work in Progress*, 263.

84 Lainsbury, *Once Upon an American Dream*, 24.

85 Lainsbury, *Once Upon an American Dream*, 23, 34–41; Jackson and West, editors, *Disneyland and Culture*, 126–127; Tom Gaughan, "Manifest Destiny at

and intellectuals were more explicit and talked of their concern that the park represented the "Americanization" of Europe—that this was American imperialism run amok, with Disney representing "the latest landings of the barbarian longboats on the shores of Europe," laying "siege to the cultural and historical heart of Europe."[86] Some even predicted that the park, because of its Americanness and outside advances in technology, would soon be surpassed and abandoned.[87]

Disney tried its best to deal with the critics head-on.[88] The company made a compelling argument that many of the stories it was seeking to bring to the park were actually European in origin—that rather than cultural imperialism, it was a Dis-Historic opportunity to share in a common culture. Disney (and its defenders) also pointed out that just because a park is built does not mean that other cultural institutions or traditions needed to suffer. It also empowered the Imagineers, tasked with the park's construction, to be inspired by, but not in competition with, historic European architecture and to collaborate with experts from Europe about designing and theming the park.[89] The end result was a park that made guests completely marvel that they are a mere 20 miles outside of Paris.[90]

Eisner wanted everything to be as perfect as possible once the park opened.[91] When that day arrived in 1992, there was a great deal of Disney fanfare and pageantry, all captured in a television special that was broadcast back in the United States. The park was visibly similar and yet different (beyond the name changes and altered theming

---

Disney World," *American Libraries* 26(January 1995), 84.

86 Byrne and McQuillan, *Deconstructing Disney*, 20–36, 45–56.

87 Lainsbury, *Once Upon an American Dream*, 194.

88 Eisner, *Work in Progress*, 269–272, 283; Lainsbury, *Once Upon an American Dream*, 16, 52; Alice Y. Kaplan, Myriam Herve-Gil, and Jean-Philippe Mazzia, "Diamond Lil at Euro-Disneyland: A Conversation," *SubStance*, 24(Special Issue: France's Identity Crises, 1995), 154–159.

89 Sklar, *Dream It! Do It!*, 281; Robin Allan, *Walt Disney and Europe: European Influences on the Animated Feature Films of Walt Disney* (Indianapolis: Indiana University Press, 1999), 258; Anne-Marie d'Hautesserre, "Constructing Alterity in Ile De France?", *Urban Geography*, published online,21 June 2013; Lainsbury, *Once Upon an American Dream*, 36–37, 42, 105, 181–183; Harrison Price, *Walt's Revolution! By the Numbers* (Orlando: Ripley Entertainment Incorporated, 2004), 159.

90 Beth Dunlop, *Building a Dream: The Art of Disney Architecture* (New York: Harry N. Abrams, 1996), 168.

91 Deyan Sudjic, *The Edifice Complex: How the Rich and Powerful Shape the World* (New York: Penguin Press, 2005), 8.

of some attractions) to make it a unique addition to the Disney park family.[92] And though some French critics called it a "cultural Chernobyl," many of their fellow countrymen and women were willing to give the park a chance. Disney had reason for optimism. Their polls showed that the park was very popular within France already. Just as important, Disney had the full support of the French government.[93]

Still, it was soon obvious that despite their attempts, Disney had miscalculated in several areas when it came to the new park. The company had not done enough research to discover the differences between European and American guests: the former were more unwilling to spend money in the Disney-owned hotels (which had greater guest capacity than was initially needed) and gift shops than the latter were in California or Florida.[94] Despite an extensive hiring and training process, Disney's expectations for their cast members were not always met.[95] Disney had also failed to tailor its marketing rollout of the park to different nations/regions of Europe, instead employing a sort of "one size fits all" campaign.[96] There were areas for improvement and it seemed obvious that Dis-History needed to adapt.

Eisner did not like to hear bad news, particularly when it was brought about by decisions he had made. In the case of Euro-Disney, he had made all the big decisions, and then let Frank Wells (who was "overextended" and not detail-oriented, according to James B. Stewart) try and make it work.[97] The park had, of course, cost more to build than originally budgeted, and its financial success was largely predicated on unrealistic attendance figures (based in large part on Disney's experiences in California and Florida, and not accounting for a financial

---

92   Lainsbury, *Once Upon an American Dream*, 1; James B. Stewart, *Disney War* (New York: Simon and Schuster, 2005), 127; Jackson and West, editors, *Disneyland and Culture*, 132–133; Eric Smoodin, editor, *Disney Discourse: Producing the Magic Kingdom* (New York: Routledge, 1994), 14–15.

93   Kaplan, Herve-Gil, and Mazzia, "Diamond Lil at Euro-Disneyland: A Conversation," 165; Lainsbury, *Once Upon an American Dream*, 4, 38; Benjamin R. Barber, *Jihad vs. McWorld* (New York: Ballantine Books, 1996), 18, 132.

94   Sklar, *Dream It! Do It!*, 272–273; William F. Van Wert, "Disney World and Posthistory," *Cultural Critique*, 32(Winter, 1995–1996), 212; Jackson and West, editors, *Disneyland and Culture*, 125; Stewart, *Disney War*, 128–129.

95   Lainsbury, *Once Upon an American Dream*, 94–95, 106. During our trip in 2015, we witnessed that living up to Disney standards is still something the park struggles with. Trash was allowed to visibly pile up and there was even graffiti in some of the queues.

96   Stein, *Why We Love Disney*, 123.

97   Stewart, *Disney War*, 130–131.

situation where it was less expensive for many Europeans to travel to the United States rather than to France). As a result, for the first two years it was open, the park was "hemorrhaging money," to the tune of over $921 million in its first year alone. The company was slow to react, as it was dealing with the failed attempt to open Disney's America in Virginia, and Wells' death, and the subsequent battle between Eisner and Jeffrey Katzenberg over the latter's promotion. The short-term answer was to find funding from banks. But everyone realized that to save the park, a new strategy was going to be needed.[98]

The year 1994 was the turning point. Disney unveiled a new advertising plan (centered around Aladdin), as well as a name change. The company had discovered that to Europeans, the prefix "Euro" had a financial and business connotation to it, which was off-putting to many. Henceforth, the park would be known as "Disneyland Paris" instead. The company was also able to secure funding, via Saudi Prince Al-Waleed, to inject more money into the park's operations. Disney had also discovered that guests, like in Tokyo Disneyland, enjoyed those areas of the park that were the most "American." Additions to the park accentuated these areas and themes.[99] But perhaps best of all, former U.S. President George H.W. Bush visited France that year. He took his friend, French president Francois Mitterrand, to dinner at L'Auberge de Cendrillion at the park. As the two men left the restaurant, Bush prodded Mitterrand to smile for the cameras, an image (and thus endorsement of the park) that appeared on newspapers across France. It was approval of the park at the highest levels.[100]

Three years after it opened, in July 1995, Disney was able to announce that the park turned a profit. The company put more money into the park to make changes and to add attractions because they were sure it would eventually succeed. Though it struggled into the 2000s, another financial restructuring (which put Disney as the majority stockholder) allowed the park to gain its footing. In 2002, Disney opened a second gate, Walt Disney Studios (a smaller version of its Florida Hollywood Studios park), in an effort to get Europeans to

---

98 Stewart, *Disney War*, 126; Kaplan, Herve-Gil, and Mazzia, "Diamond Lil at Euro-Disneyland: A Conversation," 154; Eisner, *Work in Progress*, 284–291; Lainsbury, *Once Upon an American Dream*, 123, 127, 138–139, 148–149, 157–158, 161; Roger Mills, "Euro-Disney: A Mickey Mouse Project?", *European Management Journal*, 12(September 1994), 306–314.

99 Alan Bryman, *The Disneyization of Society* (Thousand Oaks, California: Sage, 2004), 164; Lainsbury, *Once Upon an American Dream*, 75–77, 82–83, 130–131, 134–135.

100 Lainsbury, *Once Upon an American Dream*, 146–148, 154–155, 158–159.

stay longer. In 2014, Disney announced a plan to further shore up the finances of Disneyland Paris. Speculation mounted that the company was working on a plan to own the park outright.[101]

Disneyland Paris in 2015 was everything Eisner and the company could have hoped for in the 1990s. Americanization, the great fear of so many of the park's opponents, has been largely embraced (there are too many people on the streets of Paris walking around with either English language shirts or American sports-team apparel for them all to be tourists). It is easy to get to, either by car or train, and there is a sense of excitement when you arrive. Main Street, though slightly different, is familiar if you have been to a Disney park before (and like an old friend if you are an American traveling in Europe). Le Chateau de la Belle au Bois Dormant (the French park's version of Sleeping Beauty Castle) is truly spectacular—in part because it includes a slumbering dragon. Like Main Street, Fantasyland is full of the familiar, but guests can also encounter (if they make their way through it) Alice's Curious Labyrinth, whose Queen of Hearts castle provides spectacular views of the park. Frontierland evokes "the conquest of the West," a story told perhaps just as well outside of Paris as at either of the parks in the United States. Adventureland can be entered through Aladdin's Agrabah (which is truly impressive) and a place where guests can experience time with both pirates and Indiana Jones—truly a "world of explorers and adventurers." Discoveryland (the reimagined Tomorrowland) is a place where "dreams of the future from the past and present" emerge for guests to experience. And the second gate, Walt Disney Studios, contains not just a Toy Story land, but also two of the greatest attractions ever Imagineered: Crush's Coaster and Ratatouille: The Adventure. All in all, it is a very nice break from Paris—with plenty of Disney magic.

Rides and attractions translated well from Disneyland and Walt Disney World, but what about Dis-History? While the parks may be proof of the power and attractiveness of Americanization (even more so with the two parks in China) they are not examples of the transmutability of Dis-History. If Walt had hoped to create a common American culture, even with much of that culture originating in Europe, that does not mean Dis-History arrived outside of Paris as well. The nostalgia, for guests who know Disney and have visited the American parks, is based in the parks' Disneyness, not history. Disneyland Paris has a Statue of

---

101 Stewart, *Disney War*, 386-388; Lainsbury, *Once Upon an American Dream*, 132–133, 163; Stein, *Why We Love Disney*, 124 ; "Disney looks to bail out Disneyland Paris," http://www.talkdisney.com/forums/disney-front-page-news/52156-disney-looks-bail-out-disneyland-paris.html#.VDslOBZnT9h, 6 October 2014.

Liberty tableau, a connection between the U.S. and France, but it is also in an arcade, largely hidden from direct view. It has to be discovered. In Disneyland Paris' Frontierland there is a Pocahontas Indian Village. But rather than a throwback to the original Native American area in Disneyland, it serves as a children's play area, with historic theming that is a mix of tribes, chiefly eastern woodlands and southwestern adobe. They are thematic touches more than Dis-History in action.

While Tokyo Disneyland and Disneyland Paris were, in many ways, copies of Walt's Disneyland, the two other parks in Asia have followed the example of Disneyland Paris and adapted themselves (and Dis-History) to their surroundings. In 1998, just a year after Great Britain transferred sovereignty of the island back to the People's Republic of China, Disney announced plans to open a park in Hong Kong. Due to the island's small size, this park would be the smallest Disney had ever built, but the company was confident it had learned from opening parks in Japan and France that it could avoid past mistakes and successfully bring the Disney experience to China. Opening in 2005, the park is an "eclectic" mix of American, Disney, and Chinese themes. Despite the plans, the park ultimately ran into two problems: there was not enough land to truly develop the park experience and the company already had eyes on the mainland.[102]

For Disney, Hong Kong was always seen as a first step toward building a park in China. In 2000, the company negotiated a deal with the government of the People's Republic of China to build a park in Shanghai (with at least an eight-year pause to give the Hong Kong park a chance to become established).[103] In 2016, when Shanghai Disneyland finally opened, it did so with all the ceremony and pageantry Disney could bring about. There was a television special in which Bob Iger welcomed China (and the world) to the new park. As guests reported, the park had room to grow, was culturally sensitive to the expectations of its Chinese guests, and included some tremendous Imagineered attractions, such as a reimagined pirate adventure with cutting-edge audio-animatronics) and the Enchanted Storybook Castle. It also showed how far the concept of the parks had come since Walt built Disneyland. In place of Dis-History, there is simply Disney. There is no Main Street here, rather the park has Mickey Avenue—a place where guests (who have little history with Disney's characters or stories) can

---

102   Jackson and West, editors, *Disneyland and Culture*, 139; Pinsky, *The Gospel According to Disney*, 183; Stein, *Why We Love Disney*, 125–126; Knight, *Power and Paradise in Walt Disney's World*, 146.

103   Jackson and West, editors, *Disneyland and Culture*, 139; Pinsky, *The Gospel According to Disney*, 183; Stein, *Why We Love Disney*, 125–126.

be introduced to Mickey, Minnie, and the rest of the gang, as the characters—not cast members—operate themed stores along the street.[104] And though some have worried that the Shanghai park threatens the long-term stability of the parks, if not the company itself,[105] the grand opening (at least for the moment) suppressed those fears.

For critics, the three Disney parks in Asia prove the imperialistic (and capitalistic) tendencies of the Disney corporation—reminiscent of the scrambles for colonies by European powers (and the United States as well) during the late nineteenth and early twentieth centuries.[106] Obviously, they are examples of the global reach and appeal of the Disney brand, but not, out of hand, of the power of Dis-History as Walt conceived it. Rather, it shows the continued evolution of the concept, where Disney's history alone, not Dis-History's version of the past, is highlighted. We should also remember that corporate imperialism is hardly unique to Disney, nor is it the domain just of American companies.[107] But unlike the colonial powers of the past, Disney has not arrived unannounced on a foreign shore. They have been invited.

America's Story at the Center of the World

Ultimately, we must return to Epcot's World Showcase, for while Dis-History has been altered globally, when pondering how Dis-History sees the world, our attention must shift again to Walt Disney World. Here, at the center of the World Showcase, stands the American Pavilion. Mexico, Norway, China, Germany, and Italy flank one side of it. To the other stands Japan, Morocco, France, the United Kingdom, and Canada. While some critics have pondered what this might mean geographically or politically (arguing, in part, that it is proof that Disney sees itself remaking the globe in its image),[108] for Dis-History the answer is simple: America is at the center of all it does.

Such a conclusion is hardly surprising. As Cher Krause Knight notes, the U.S. World's Fairs tended to promote manifest destiny and place

---

104   Disney Tourist Blob, "Shanghai Disney Opening Trip Report," http://www.disneytouristblog.com/shanghai-disneyland-grand-opening-trip-report/, 10 October 2016.

105   "MiceAge Disneyland Update: Shanghai Surprise," http://micechat.com/122782-disneyland-cutbacks/, 29 March 2016.

106   Benedict Anderson, *Imagined Communities: Reflections on the Origin and Spread of Nationalism* (New York: Verso Press, 1998), 142.

107   Lainsbury, *Once Upon an American Dream*, 9-10.

108   William F. Van Wert, "Disney World and Posthistory," *Cultural Critique*, 32(Winter, 1995–1996), 204–206.

other cultures beneath the American story.[109] The idea of American exceptionalism was never far off from the fairs that the showcase is modeled after. Indeed, elements of that kind of thinking can be found within the showcase itself. Of the eleven nations represented in the World Showcase, five of them have movies. And while Norway, China, France, and Canada each have unique offerings, they pale in comparison to the film (and show) that are part of the United States pavilion, whose American Adventure includes not just a film but audio-animatronics.[110]

The American Pavilion "is the castle of the World Showcase." Both the physical building and the show it houses were massive undertakings on the part of the Imagineers. The pavilion's architecture is meant to invoke history and was not just inspired by colonial architecture (it is in the classic Georgian style, similar to "Colonial Williamsburg, Independence Hall, Thomas Jefferson's Monticello, and the Old State House in Boston") and colors (all 110,000 bricks are made from red Georgia clay), but built to provide a "consistent silhouette to make it easy to identify," even at a distance. The show it houses, the American Adventure, took Disney's team of Imagineers five years to complete.[111]

Much like the Hall of Presidents or the Mr. Lincoln attractions, guests who enter the pavilion must wait for the show in an area steeped in patriotism. There are quotes on the walls from Wendell Willkie, Jane Addams, Walt Disney, Charles Lindbergh, Ayn Rand, Sam Foss, Althea Gibson, and Thomas Wolfe. Paintings adorn the waiting area, depicting such scenes as World War II industrial production, a one-room school under construction, immigrants arriving under the careful gaze of the Statue of Liberty, a nineteenth-century political stump speech, sailing ships, the space race, industrialization, westward migration, a family eating Thanksgiving dinner together, and Squanto helping the Pilgrims. Each of these paintings was conceived by an Imagineer. There is also an American Heritage gallery, which is home to an exhibit entitled "Hope," which deals with African-American history.

The theater is a space much grander (though less intimate) than the Hall of Presidents. In a Parthenon to American virtues, there are

---

109 Knight, *Power and Paradise in Walt Disney's World*, 110.

110 Elizabeth Bell, Lynda Haas, and Laura Sells, editors, *From Mouse to Mermaid: The Politics of Film, Gender, and Culture* (Indianapolis: Indiana University Press, 1995), 242.

111 Sklar, *Dream It! Do It!*, 177–178, 206–207; Eric Smoodin, editor, *Disney Discourse: Producing the Magic Kingdom* (New York: Routledge, 1994), 127; John Hench, *Designing Disney: Imagineering and the Art of the Show* (New York: Disney Editions, 2008), 110; "American Adventure," https://disneyworld.disney.go.com/attractions/epcot/american-adventure/, 19 February 2014.

twelve statues, four of which are represented by a female sculpture, each in its own alcove. If it were to be compared to Statutory Hall in the United States Capitol, one would be hard-pressed not to find Disney's presentation better. There are statues dedicated to the American ideals of Heritage, Freedom, Knowledge, Adventure, Pioneering, Compassion, Discovery, Tomorrow, Individualism, Innovation, Independence, and Self-Reliance, all in an orderly display.[112] But guests only have a few moments to take them in, for the show is about to start.

And what a show it is! Benjamin Franklin and Mark Twain are the guides for the guests, as they encounter ten different scenes that showcase key events like "the landing of the Mayflower, the Boston Tea Party, the winter at Valley Forge, the penning of the Declaration of Independence, the Civil War, Industrialization, and the Great Depression," among others.[113] Its cast of audio-animatronic characters is also more diverse than the Americans represented in the Hall of Presidents. Here, guests meet Frederick Douglass, Rosie the Riveter, Chief Joseph, Susan B. Anthony, and John Muir. It is not the "wartless" history that Dis-History is often accused of being and in many ways is much more "sophisticated" than critics have come to expect.[114]

The American Adventure encapsulates and showcases the Dis-History in Liberty Square, Frontierland, and Main Street.[115] Originally conceived under the direction of Card Walker and Ron Miller's leadership, the show highlights a grand sweep of American history. The progress of the American ideals (seen on the walls and statues of the pavilion) are the narrative thread holding the show together, and so, while influenced by trends within social history, it is more akin to traditional historic interpretation. That being said, it does present a more complicated view of what that progress might mean (and the lengths some groups had to go in order to achieve it) than other portions of Dis-Historic interpretation. The past is still, ultimately, upbeat and moving directly toward the present, which is better than the past ever was.[116]

---

112   "American Adventure," https://disneyworld.disney.go.com/attractions/epcot/american-adventure/, 19 February 2014.

113   "American Adventure," https://disneyworld.disney.go.com/attractions/epcot/american-adventure/, 19 February 2014.

114   Michael Wallace, "Serious Fun," *The Public Historian*, 17 (Autumn 1995), 83; Richard Snow, "Disney: Coast to Coast," http://www.americanheritage.com/content/disney-coast-coast, 2 June 2014.

115   Fjellman, *Vinyl Leaves*, 93–106.

116   Flower, *Prince of the Magic Kingdom*, 84; Leon and Rosenzweig, editors, *History Museums in the United States*, 174–177.

In some ways, what Disney is attempting with the American Adventure is much more ambitious than the traditional Dis-Historic story. It is attempting to highlight all of American history in 29 minutes or less.[117] Historians might ponder how such an undertaking is even possible (what do you include, what do you exclude), not to mention how do you gauge such a story to an audience that changes constantly from performance to performance. For comparison sake, what Disney is attempting to do is compress two semesters of a U.S. History survey course into less than a half hour. As any professor will tell you, even with the better part of eight months, decisions on what to discuss have to be made. Disney is simply emulating academia.

Critics, not surprisingly, have attacked the American Adventure, just as they have the rest of Dis-History. Despite Disney's attempts to address their concerns, they point out that Nez Perce leader, Chief Joseph, has a speech that is almost entirely fabricated, while suffragist Susan B. Anthony's address is "bland." When discussing America's colonial past, Jamestown is skipped for the Pilgrims, though there is no mention of the larger Puritan Great Migration. Frederick Douglass, the famed anti-slavery leader, is shown on a Tom Sawyer-esque raft, and mentions Harriet Beecher Stowe, with little detail. America's involvement in the First World War is depicted via Eddie Rickenbacker, the famed American fighter pilot ace, with virtually no context (or mention of chemical weapons). The Civil War depiction is more dramatic (with its focus on a family divided) rather than historic. And a film montage, which helps close out the show, relies heavily on professional sports images with little context or substance. Critics argue that the American Adventure celebrates "an America that no longer exists" and showcases "a middlebrow impersonation of an epic story that never took place."[118] Ultimately, the show crafted by Disney, in their opinion, is empty and embarrassing.[119]

While Disney talks a good deal about freedom in the pavilion, wrapping the term in the American flag and swathing it in patriotic music and themes, critics lambast the very idea. As Ramona Fernandez puts it, the American Adventure is a means both "to suppress people of color and women," as well as "suppress anything problematic," no

---

117 Adams, *The American Amusement Park Industry*, 153.

118 Bell, Haas, and Sells, editors, *From Mouse to Mermaid*, 243–244; Adams, *The American Amusement Park Industry*, 154; Smoodin, editor, *Disney Discourse*, 127–128; Lainsbury, *Once Upon an American Dream*, 7–9.

119 James Howard Kunstler, *The Geography of Nowhere: The Rise and Decline of America's Man-Made Landscape* (New York: Touchstone Book, 1993), 227.

matter how important it might be to historical understanding.[120] Talking about freedom, critics argue, is Disney's way of masking the fact that when you are in their parks, you really are not free at all.[121]

But that is not the reaction most guests have. Here, Dis-History is still alive and well. Disney is in the business of edu-tainment after all, and Dis-History is a narrative means to promote a common American culture.[122] In serving those goals, the American Adventure is an unabashed success, as it confirms national identity and inspires its guests to think more than critics give it credit for.[123] Furthermore, it is unclear as to what critics either would or could do better, if given a similar platform, with similar constraints.

As Disney notes in its promotional literature for the pavilion, "Americans have overcome the tragedies of their controversies, which ultimately led to a better way of life. What our show says is that the American Adventure will always be a struggle, but if we can apply ourselves in positive ways and deal with reality, we can move forward to a better future."[124] Critics have become so accustomed to bashing Disney and Dis-History that they often fail to see that it has evolved and does some things quite well. Dis-History may have changed since its creation by Walt, but it remained a viable approach as Disney and the world entered into the twenty-first century.

---

120 Bell, Haas, and Sells, editors, *From Mouse to Mermaid*, 238.

121 Kuenz, Klugman, Waldrep, and Willis, editors, *Inside the Mouse*, 68; T.D. Allman, *Finding Florida: The True History of the Sunshine State* (New York: Atlantic Monthly Press, 2013), 426.

122 Stephen Wanhill, "Creating Themed Entertainment Attractions: A Nordic Perspective," *Scandinavian Journal of Hospitality and Tourism*, published on line, 5 November 2010.

123 Kuenz, Klugman, Waldrep, and Willis, editors, *Inside the Mouse*, 66; Benedict Anderson, *Imagined Communities: Reflections on the Origin and Spread of Nationalism* (New York: Verso Press, 1998), 3. The painting that caught my daughter's eye in the summer of 2014 while we waited for the show was the depiction of immigrants entering New York's harbor. The "huddled masses" approach a land where the sun is rising, not just on a new day, but on a new dawn breaking for them as the Statue of Liberty bids them welcome. With this, as with most of Dis-History, the affect can be inspiring—in this case it prompted a discussion about our own family's arrival in the United States.

124 "American Adventure: 1982," American Adventure Attraction file, Walt Disney Studio Archives, Burbank, California.

HAPPILY EVER AFTER

A Dis-Historic Conclusion

Experience Fireworks over the World

We return one last time to Cinderella Castle. As evening sets in and the park prepares to close, guests begin to gather in groups to watch the final parade, buy one last piece of merchandise, or do one more ride. And they linger a bit longer before leaving to view Disney's closing act: fireworks. At Magic Kingdom, each night ends with a stunning display of fireworks. At times the castle looks as though it is under assault (perhaps by Maleficent herself) and is shrouded in smoke from spent rockets. The display outlines Main Street and lights up the buildings, while casting colorful glows upon the guests below.

Fireworks loom large at the Disney parks. The shows are impressive and they vary depending on location. For the sixtieth anniversary of Disneyland, Sleeping Beauty Castle received an all-new fireworks program, with reverberations from the blasts so strong they rattled hotel windows across the street. At Epcot, the evening ends with Illuminations, a fireworks show around the World Showcase. Fantasmic (at Disneyland and Hollywood Studios) mixes pyrotechnics and characters in a captivating story. The World of Color (at California Adventure) has fireworks and video images projected onto large water fans. Even Animal Kingdom now has a night spectacular, just as Hollywood Studios boasts a Star Wars fireworks show as part of its daily activities. And that does not count special fireworks themed around holidays like the Fourth of July, Halloween, and Christmas. If you are a guest at a Disney park, in addition to shows, attractions, and merchandise, you will witness fireworks displays that make all others pale in comparison.

However, these displays never start until after sunset. And yet like the Victorian-era British Empire, the sun never sets on Disney's empire.[1] The chief reason for that in the twenty-first century remains

---

1 Benjamin R. Barber, *Jihad vs. McWorld* (New York: Ballantine Books, 1996), 134.

Dis-History, and its ability, as an organizing principle, to entertain, educate, and invoke a nostalgic sense of "home" for Disney's guests.

To the Twenty-First Century and Beyond

Magicians will often tell their audience that in order for an illusion to work, those seated need to believe that it will. In the case of Disney, the magic created—whether in the parks, or its films, books, songs, or products—is done by a corporation, and it too requires guests to believe.[2] For much of its life, Dis-History has been a guiding principle for the corporation, in both its drive for standardization of well-known stories and in the creation of their narrative to make dreams into reality. The question that looms before the company today (and for us as well) is, can it last? We have seen Dis-History evolve. But can it continue to do so and still remain Dis-History?

Walt knew that both his work and plans would outlive him. The spirit of optimism that he imbued into his first park, and that was used in subsequent incarnations, is attractive. Ray Bradbury believed what Walt had accomplished in creating a park narrative that merged the fantastic, myths, legends, and history that came to life would be studied for centuries.[3] Christopher Finch argued that prior to Disney, Americans had little tradition with the world of fantasy, and that by creating parks where fantasy comes alive, by making fantasy normal, Walt had given the nation (and the world) a stunning gift.[4] By transforming fairy tales, by standardizing them (taking a variety of myths, with variations and contradictions, and making one coherent story) into (yes) commodities, but also (and more importantly) stories that he could tell,[5] Walt helped standardize Western civilization (including, of course, its American component). Dis-History gave the United States a role in the wider Western culture it was already a part and product of.

As we have seen, Walt was able to translate "ancient myth" to the screen. He borrowed from many sources to make American stories and

---

2   James B. Stewart, *Disney War* (New York: Simon and Schuster, 2005), 6; Janet Wasko, *Understanding Disney: The Manufacture of Fantasy* (Cambridge: Polity Press, 2001), 1.

3   Stephen F. Fjellman, *Vinyl Leaves: Walt Disney World and America* (Boulder: Westview Press, 1992), 117; Kathy Merlock Jackson and Mark I. West, editors, *Disneyland and Culture: Essays on the Parks and Their Influence* (Jefferson, NC: McFarland and Company, 2011), 220; Bob Thomas, *Walt Disney: An American Original* (New York: Disney Editions, 1994), 359.

4   Christopher Finch, *Walt Disney's America* (New York: Abbeville Press, 1978), 199.

5   Fjellman, *Vinyl Leaves*, 259-260.

showcase what he believed to be American values (enshrined now in the American Experience at Epcot). Dis-History became the means to create edutainment, a vehicle to instruct the young and remind the old of lessons that were important for the modern world and necessary to the survival of democracy.[6] Walt believed you could educate people, but only by not telling them you were.[7] As one guest noted of Walt Disney World, "It's teeming with history, geography, culture, science, math, economics ... and more!" The key to making it so is on the guests themselves. Disney has simply provided all the components, like a good teacher who gives their students the materials needed to achieve success on their own.[8] In a very real sense, Walt's Dis-History re-created what Lawrence W. Levine described as "a rich shared public culture that once characterized the United States" during the nineteenth century.[9]

Those who assumed control of the company after Walt's death were there to "perpetuate Walt's dream."[10] Roy Disney, in his opening-day speech at Walt Disney World, said that the Magic Kingdom would be a place "where the young at heart of all ages can laugh and play and learn—together."[11] Dis-History even survived two secession crises, but it also changed as the twentieth century gave way to the twenty-first. It has become a means to tell Disney's history, including its relation to wider popular culture. And yet, the metamorphosis was not without tension. Walt's vision remained at Dis-History's heart and always below the new version's veneer.

The man heading Walt's studio today understands this Dis-Historic dichotomy. Born in Long Island, New York, Robert (Bob) Iger joined ABC in 1974, shortly after graduating from college. By the early 1990s,

---

6 Benedict Anderson, *Imagined Communities: Reflections on the Origin and Spread of Nationalism* (New York: Verso Press, 1998), 116; Alexis de Tocqueville, *Democracy in America* (New York: Mentor, 1984), 298.

7 Marty Sklar, *Dream It! Do It!: My Half-Century Creating Disney's Magic Kingdoms* (New York: Disney Editions, 2013), 324.

8 Joe Flower, *Prince of the Magic Kingdom: Michael Eisner and the Re-Making of Disney* (New York: John Wiley and Sons, Inc., 1991), 263; Neal Gabler, *Walt Disney: The Triumph of the American Imagination* (New York: Vintage Books, 2007), xiii; Jackson and West, editors, *Disneyland and Culture*, 226; Magical Mousecapades's Blog, "Walt Disney World Educational? Of Course It Is!," http://magicalmousecapades.wordpress.com/2009/08/30/walt-disney-world-educational-of-course-it-is/, 14 Maye 2014.

9 Lawrence W. Levine, *Highbrow/Lowbrow: The Emergence of Cultural Hierarchy in America* (Cambridge: Harvard University Press, 1990), 9.

10 Sklar, *Dream It! Do It!*, xv.

11 Sklar, *Dream It! Do It!*, 159.

he was running the network, a position he continued in after Disney bought it in 1996. In 1999, as the Comcast-Eisner drama was unfolding, Iger was named the head of Walt Disney International, with the responsibility of overseeing Disney's ventures outside of the United States. In 2000, he became president and chief operating officer, five years later becoming CEO, and in 2006 became chairman and CEO of Walt Disney. Iger brought a new vitality to the company's various components—including taking risks, spending money on expansion and new parks, and being watchful of the Disney brand. It was Iger who worked to buy Pixar (or bring it back into the Disney fold). It was Iger who engineered Disney's purchase of Marvel. It was Iger who worked to purchase LucasFilm. And it was Iger who put together the planning necessary for the Shanghai Disney park. He even brought Oswald the Rabbit home.[12] The moves guaranteed that Disney would have a large stable of new stories and characters to develop for decades to come, increasing revenue streams and undoing some of the bad feelings associated with the final few years of Michael Eisner's time leading the company.[13] Disney, perhaps now more than ever, stands as a giant in the formation of popular American (and global) culture.

Iger's arrival was a relief to many Disney fans. A backlash against Eisner had emerged, not just within the Disney family and many stockholders, but on the streets as well. Even as they continued to see Disney movies, buy Disney products, and see Disney shows, there was growing resentment at how the company was being run—there were the real and near failures in Disneyland Paris, Disney's America, and California Adventure, a decline in the quality of the company's animated films, as well as confusion (thanks to the purchase of ABC) as to what the mission of Disney was.[14] Iger had the blessing and support of Roy E. Disney. The two agreed on many things. Roy, who died in 2009, believed that the company was in good hands with Iger, and was pleased that John Lasseter, trained as a Disney animator before leaving to join Pixar, was now heading a revitalized Disney Animation division.[15]

---

12 "Robert A. Iger," http://thewaltdisneycompany.com/about-disney/leadership/ceo/robert-iger, 19 August 2014; "Bob Iger: Disney's Fun King," http://fortune.com/2012/05/09/bob-iger-disneys-fun-king/, 19 August 2014; Andi Stein, *Why We Love Disney: The Power of the Disney Brand* (New York: Peter Lang, 2011), 41-46; "Disney CEO Iger's Empire of Tech," http://fortune.com/2014/12/29/disney-ceo-bob-iger-empire-of-tech/, 12 January 2015.

13 *The Economist*, 19 December 2015.

14 Janet Wasko, *Understanding Disney: The Manufacture of Fantasy* (Cambridge: Polity Press, 2001), 209.

15 David A. Bossert, *Remembering Roy E. Disney: Memories and Photos of a*

One of Iger's first jobs was to reorganize the company around the synergy that had long held it together. Movies, for example, needed to be thought of in ways that could most easily fit into what Disney did with parks and merchandising—including new attractions for the parks. Iger also invested in technology to make guest experiences at the parks more user friendly. This is perhaps best seen in the MagicBands system, which are in place at Walt Disney World. The bands, which can be bought at the park or shipped to guests' homes before their arrival, act as keys to Disney hotels, credit cards for merchandise purchases, and for downloading pictures taken at the parks. These wrist-size memory makers not only make life easier for guests (you no longer have to carry a wallet or camera with you), but also allow Disney to track and accentuate guests and their experiences, while also helping them to spend more money. Iger's current contract runs until 2019, guaranteeing a continued steady presence for the company and a central role for Dis-History in the twenty-first century.[16]

Disney has achieved a sort of universal understanding and acceptance. No other company is as well known.[17] Even when they claim to have "out grown it," Disney remains a positive memory for many Americans, and a company (and place) that those same people plan on introducing to the next generation.[18] Much of this has to do with Dis-History. According to Janet Wasko, the values Walt tapped into when creating the concept include that work will bring success, a belief in progress, the ability of the individual to achieve great things, a fun-loving innocence, optimism, and a "sense of fair play and what is right."[19] Disney might know how to market itself to consumers, but it

---

Storied Life (New York: Disney Editions, 2013), 149–151, 190; Andi Stein, *Why We Love Disney: The Power of the Disney Brand* (New York: Peter Lang, 2011), 84–85.

16 Stein, *Why We Love Disney*, 86-87 ; "3 Mind-Blowing Things that Future Theme Parks Will Do," http://orlandoinformer.com/topic/3446-3-mind-blowing-things-that-future-theme-parks-will-do/, 31 January 2015; "Disney CEO Iger's Empire of Tech," http://fortune.com/2014/12/29/disney-ceo-bob-iger-empire-of-tech/, 12 January 2015; "Disney Extends Iger's Contract through 2018," http://fornue.com/2014/10/02/disney-iger-extend-through-2018, 20 October 2014; Future of Disney World: Hollywood Studios," http://orlandoinformer.com/page/articles.html/_/blog/central-florida/future-disney-world-hollywood-studios, 15 February 2015.

17 Flower, *Prince of the Magic Kingdom*, 2–4.

18 Janet Wasko, *Understanding Disney: The Manufacture of Fantasy* (Cambridge: Polity Press, 2001), 3, 191, 221–222.

19 Wasko, *Understanding Disney*, 224.

is not dominant because it is ubiquitous. Rather, much of its success has to do because Dis-History helps make it unique. This is especially true when it comes to the parks.[20] The consumed nostalgia that it portrays taps into a fear that the modern world moves so fast that referentials are being lost, but that recapturing the past is worth the effort.[21]

And while Dis-History has survived critical attacks and has evolved, it now finds itself in jeopardy from external forces. Benjamin Barber argued that while conflict generates headlines, corporations have increasing amounts of control over information, communication, and entertainment, and thus the potential to create a homogenized (largely conflict-free) consumer ethos on a global scale. Global consumerism, in turn, can be seen as undercutting national identity, citizenship, and even democracy itself, because personal worldviews and loyalties are now shaped by corporate agendas.[22] Dis-History then becomes anachronistic (in terms of its focus on American history and ideals) and corporate propaganda (undercutting that history and those ideals) all at the same time. But that is only if the critics are correct, and as Walt often showed, that is not always the case.

Part of this academic debate concerns the park system. The Disney parks are destinations unto themselves. Unlike cultural attractions, which can add something to a vacation, Disney is an all-encompassing destination. And though some academics argue that Disney is only about Disney,[23] as our exploration of the parks has shown, there is much more going on. Disney has both become an advocate for and taps into the heritage industry and helps define what a cultural institution can be.[24] We should not be surprised, nor expect, that Dis-History gives the parks a voice, nor that said voice has the Midwestern accent of the man behind Mickey Mouse even today. After all, we do not expect museums to be value-free. Nor, according to Stephen E. Weil,

---

20 Ken Roberts, *The Leisure Industries* (New York: Palgrave Macmillan, 2004), 158–159.

21 Gary Cross, *Consumed Nostalgia: Memory in the Age of Fast Capitalism* (New York: Columbia University Press, 2015), 10–11.

22 Barber, *Jihad vs. McWorld*, 8, 20, 297; James Howard Kunstler, *The Geography of Nowhere: The Rise and Decline of America's Man-Made Landscape* (New York: Touchstone Book, 1993), 221; Wasko, *Understanding Disney*, 178; Eric Smoodin, editor, *Disney Discourse: Producing the Magic Kingdom* (New York: Routledge, 1994), 182–183, 191; Sharon Zukin, *Landscapes of Power: From Detroit to Disney World* (Los Angeles: University of California Press, 1993), 12.

23 Ken Roberts, *The Leisure Industries* (New York: Palgrave Macmillan, 2004), 70.

24 Roberts, *The Leisure Industries*, 72–73.

should we want them to be. They are places where information, values, experience, stimulation, and empowerment can and do take place.[25] Dis-Historic venues and attractions are the means by which Disney enters into this kind of discussion.

Dis-History in Its Second Century

While Walt's values remain at its center, Dis-History's longevity is due to its embrace of popular culture as a means to craft a common culture for all Americans. Walt believed popular culture could serve as a bridge between "high" and "low" forms of culture. With Dis-History, he hoped to "translate" larger truths "into terms that struck a popular chord."[26] The creation of Disneyland gave Walt a platform to become the main arbiter "of American popular culture."[27] Walt's vision for Dis-History survives because it is being supported by his company's own success at creating its own history and myths and its embrace of popular culture, rather than just its use, as ultimately something that many critics fail to understand and appreciate. As Karal Marling noted, "In a pluralistic society, where experiences of church, school, and ethnicity were not universally shared, Disney motifs constituted a common culture, a kind of civil religion of happy endings, worry-free consumption, technological optimism, and nostalgia for the good old days."[28]

It is not just popular culture that Disney helps to craft for Americans, as a means to help them (and increasingly, others globally) to navigate the modern world.[29] The company is also an advocate of its guests feeling as though they are "agents" in making history. While

---

25 Stephen E. Weil, *Rethinking the Museum and Other Meditations* (Washington: Smithsonian Institution Press, 1990), 52–53, 166; Beth Dunlop, *Building a Dream: The Art of Disney Architecture* (New York: Harry N. Abrams, 1996), 9; Christian Moran, *Great Big Beautiful Tomorrow: Walt Disney and Technology* (Theme Park Press, 2015).

26 Virginia A. Salamone and Frank A. Salamone, "Images of Main Street: Disney World and the American Adventure," electronic version, 91.

27 Paul Jerome Croce, "A Clean and Separate Space: Walt Disney in Person and Production," *The Journal of Popular Culture*, 25 (Winter 1991), 91; Neal Gabler, *Walt Disney: The Triumph of the American Imagination* (New York: Vintage Books, 2007), 566; Douglas Brode, *Multiculturalism and the Mouse: Race and Sex in Disney Entertainment* (Austin: University of Texas Press, 2005), 14–15, 268-269; Steven Watts, *The Magic Kingdom: Walt Disney and the America Way of Life* (New York: Houghton Mifflin Company, 1997), 23.

28 Karal Ann Marling, "Disneyland, 1955: Just Take the Santa Ana Freeway to the American Dream," *American Art*, 5(Winter-Spring, 1991), 201.

29 Michael R. Real, *Mass-Mediated Culture* (Englewood Cliffs, New Jersey:

this is personal history (the stuff of memories), to be sure, it is history all the same.[30] While critics might be troubled that a corporation is facilitating popular history, there is little doubt of its potential not just to enhance the lives of individuals, but also academic history as well. If there is any doubt as to the power of this personal history to influence professional history, one need only consider the holdings of the Wolfson Archives. Among their digital holdings are over fifty home movies, donated for posterity, depicting average Americans and their trips to Disney's parks. For the historian, these films are snapshots in time, of the parks, of fashion, of family dynamics. They are a treasure trove in re-creating the past, not just for the families involved, but for all those who ponder them.[31] And they remind us that Disney has had and continues to have real impacts on those who visit the parks and the places where their parks have found a home. Few would doubt, for example, that Disney did not alter the history of Orlando by its decision to buy land there for Project X.[32] But the personal histories, the memories created by guests, are also an important part of Dis-History.

Some theorists, when considering these legacies of Dis-History, might be tempted to argue that what Disney has actually been engaged in is the ultimate form of postmodernism. Since Disney has always mixed "the real and the fantastic," and as a simulacrum of actual society, postmodernist thinkers argue that we should question the reality and the validity of what is presented as "the real" at every opportunity—even in the parks and the experiences they create.[33] At a time when cultural institutions have embraced consumerism, and cities themselves have become versions of shopping malls (where people also live), such an argument raises the question of how we really should understand Disney's parks and Dis-History in fundamental ways.[34]

Prentice-Hall, 1977), 84–85.

30   Henry A. Giroux, *The Mouse that Roared: Disney and the End of Innocence* (New York: Rowman and Littlefield, 1999), 126-127.

31   Wolfson Archives, "Disney," http://www.wolfsonarchives.info/, 15 October 2015.

32   T.D. Allman, "The Theme-Parking, Megachurching, Franchising, Exurbing, McMansioning of America," *National Geographic* 211 (March 2007), 96–115.

33   Fjellman, *Vinyl Leaves*, 254–255.

34   Fjellman, *Vinyl Leaves*, 299, 319; Stacy Warren, "Popular Cultural Practices in the "Postmodern City," *Urban Geography*, published online 15 May 2013; "Luis Marin: Disneyland as Degenerate Utopia," http://lmc.gatech.edu/~broglio/1101/marin.html, 23 September 2014; Theodor W. Adorno, *The Culture Industry: Selected Essays on Mass Culture* (New York: Routledge, 1991), 184;

Disney's embrace of both popular and consumer culture, in this postmodernist light, can thus be viewed as key components of what Theodor Adorno described as mass-culture industry. A product of capitalistic societies like the United States, mass culture creates superficial cultural products with little redeeming value, but that are eagerly consumed nevertheless. According to Adorno, mass culture, wedded to middle-class expectations and driven by mass tourism, is based upon the manipulation of time, both the past (what people once did, or nostalgia/history) and the present (what people are doing now). That means that any free time consumers find themselves with should be used "productively," creating an entire leisure industry (Disney) that is based around getting people to plan (via advertising) and experience their free time in a structured environment (the parks). Consumers believe, according to Adorno, that they have a choice in the matter, but they actually do not.[35]

However, people are not as passive as social scientists sometimes like to suggest. They have agency that is rarely subsumed by corporations. As Cher Krause Knight notes, "The anxiety over Disneyfication engulfing our culture is both oversimplified and overstated."[36] True, most people are consumers not producers of culture, and so they gravitate toward what is commercially available to them, and Disney does a good deal of work creating an image that they are a good place to spend money at. However, enjoying entertainment and even taking part in it does not mean people have lost the ability of reflect on what they are seeing and doing.[37] There is a good deal of evidence (in large part, thanks to the internet) that consumers today are increasingly savvy about what they buy, and research large purchases rather than making impulse buys. What that means is that despite the messaging, branding, and advertising, consumers ultimately do choose where they spend their money.[38]

Andrew Lainsbury, *Once Upon an American Dream: The Story of Euro Disneyland* (Lawrence: University of Kansas Press, 2000), 172.

35 Adorno, *The Culture Industry*, 75, 85, 98, 117, 102, 126, 160, 163, 181, 191–194; Roberts, *The Leisure Industries*, 128, 156; Wasko, *Understanding Disney*, 183; David Nicholson-Lord, "The Politics of Travel: Is Tourism Just Colonialism in Another Guise?," http://www.emily.net/~schiller/pol_trvl.html, 26 August 2014.

36 Cher Krause Knight, *Power and Paradise in Walt Disney's World* (Gainesville: University Press of Florida, 2014), 150–152.

37 Roberts, *The Leisure Industries*, 192; Adorno, *The Culture Industry*, 12.

38 Andrew Benett and Ann O'Reilly, *Consumed: Rethinking Business in the Era of Mindful Spending* (New York: Palgrave MacMillan, 2010), 127, 171.

There is a danger in "commodifying the past. Few would want Disney to copyright history (as they were accused of doing with Disney's America).[39] Likewise, there is a danger in the merging of culture and history into "heritage," especially if that is the only way people are exposed to what underlies a park attraction's design.[40] But none of that means history cannot be entertaining, or that organizations, even corporations, like Disney cannot use the past to help people (or consumers) appreciate and enjoy the present. Guests are smart enough to know that Dis-History is not the same as visiting an historic home, battle site, or museum. It is something else—it is the employment of the past not solely to education but to entertain. And just as Walt had hoped, people remain drawn to it.[41]

To be fair to the critics, though, there is little doubt that Disney could do more with their use of history as part of Dis-History. As Michael Wallace pointed out, the company could do more with educational outreach (lesson plans, even web links). They could do more with partnered outreach (the various presidential libraries, for example). They could sell more scholarly books in their gift shops. They could even confront the past in a compelling way (such as talking about the Disney studio during World War II) and still attract crowds.[42] Because of their place within American culture, anything that Disney opted to do is sure to have an impact on what guests take away from the park.[43] And it might even prove a powerful critique of their postmodern critics, by showcasing that there really is such a thing as history to begin with.[44]

But none of those academic arguments should detract from what Dis-History actually does accomplish. Whether as an introduction to a classic story (how many people have started with the Disney version

---

39 Michael Wallace, *Mickey Mouse History and Other Essays on American Memory* (Philadelphia: Temple University Press, 1996), 171.

40 William A. Covino, "Walt Disney Meets Mary Daly: Invention, Imagination, and the Construction of Community," *JAC* 20(Winter 2000), 161.

41 "Luis Marin: Disneyland as Degenerate Utopia," http://lmc.gatech.edu/~broglio/1101/marin.html, 23 September 2014; Warren Leon and Roy Rosenzweig, editors, *History Museums in the United States: A Critical Assessment* (Chicago: University of Illinois Press, 1989), 178.

42 Michael Wallace, *Mickey Mouse History and Other Essays on American Memory* (Philadelphia: Temple University Press, 1996), 170–171.

43 Giroux, *The Mouse that Roared*, 29-30; Michael R. Real, *Mass-Mediated Culture* (Englewood Cliffs, New Jersey: Prentice-Hall, 1977), 81, 248–249; Eric Avila, *Popular Culture in the Age of White Flight: Fear and Fantasy in Suburban Los Angeles* (Los Angeles: University of California Press, 2004), 238–239.

44 Richard J. Evans, *In Defense of History* (New York: W.W. Norton, 1999).

of, say, *Cinderella*, but eventually found their way to the Brothers Grimm?) or sought out more information on an American president (after having viewed the Hall of Presidents), or decided to one day visit the real Eiffel Tower (after visiting Epcot), Dis-History has very real power. It gives the world a vision of the past in which fantasy meets reality, where past and future meet. Dis-History assures guests that history can be fixed and the future will astonish. And while it may not showcase much conflict, or even be a place where conflict drives the historical narrative, it also offers those who experience it an alternative to what can be a more difficult reality. But Dis-History also offers hope that perhaps conflict should not be at the center of how we define ourselves or the past. The real world is held at bay by the boundaries of the park. It will still be there, but perhaps the hope is that guests will take some of that Dis-Historic optimism back with them.[45]

Disney is likely to continue employing Dis-History. They will continue to help influence, for good and bad, heritage sites like Colonial Williamsburg and Conner Prairie.[46] Disney is likely to continue to employ, at least as consultants, historians. What they create will not be history in its purest form, but a medium by which guests are exposed to at least a portion of the past. In that respect, they will continue to influence future generations of historians (even before they know that history is calling to them) as well as the general public.[47] Part of the attraction is that Disney is also honest about what it is and does, much more so than some tourist-based experiences at actual historic areas, which introduce themed experiences that do not fit with the narrative focus of the site, merely to attract guests and generate revenue.[48]

Postmodern assumptions aside, perhaps the largest conceptual problem with Dis-History, according to its critics, is that Walt's plan for utilizing the past leaves very little room for contemplating the present. The present is forgotten, with the past merely showcased as prologue

---

45 Fjellman, *Vinyl Leaves*, 399–400; Giroux, *The Mouse that Roared*, 148-149; Michael R. Real, *Mass-Mediated Culture* (Englewood Cliffs, New Jersey: Prentice-Hall, 1977), 86.

46 Gary Cross, *Consumed Nostalgia: Memory in the Age of Fast Capitalism* (New York: Columbia University Press, 2015), 181, 194–195.

47 Cary Carson, "Mirror, Mirror, on the Wall, Whose History is the Fairest of Them All?" *The Public Historian*, 17(Autumn 1995), 66–67; Richard Francaviglia, "History after Disney: The Significance of 'Imagineered' Historical Places," *The Public Historian*, 17(Autumn 1995), 71; Harrison Price, *Walt's Revolution! By the Numbers* (Orlando: Ripley Entertainment Incorporated, 2004), 175.

48 Salamone and Salamone, "Images of Main Street," 91; *Richmond Times-Dispatch*, 13 March 2016.

to the future.⁴⁹ As historian E. H. Carr noted, "The present has no more than a notional existence as an imaginary dividing line between the past and the future," with "past, present and future are linked together in the endless chain of history."⁵⁰ Of course such criticisms, that the present is ignored, miss one salient point. Disney is worried about the present. It wants guests' time at their parks to be filled with fun. The present experience is what matters because it creates memories and nostalgia in its own right that benefit the guests and Disney itself.⁵¹

Virtually all the criticisms leveled at Dis-History have the same problem: Disney is an easy target but also one that its critics cannot meet on even ground. Unlike in academic discourse, while they can write books and articles condemning this or that facet of the Dis-History (or the company in general), they cannot build a park system (let alone a media empire) of their own to test their theories or prove their points conclusively. Indeed, the problems with trying to outdo Disney by being "more Disney than Disney" is that you will inevitably face not just comparisons but critics of your own. Perhaps Disney's largest competitor, Universal Studios, sidestepped this issue by not even trying to replicate Dis-History. Its parks have content with rides and theming (even on a large scale like Harry Potter) based off of movies. Their thrill rides appeal to youth and make no claim to promoting any heritage or culture. As a result, Universal's parks have few critics.⁵²

For Disney though, Dis-History remains. And even in its evolved, current form, the company seems unlikely to jettison it completely. Not only would it face a backlash for altering Walt's vision, but there would also be the danger of disrupting the nostalgia and memories, those personal history facets, that have helped make the parks so successful. Disney has seen what can happen when attractions are changed or erased from the map (due to new construction or re-Imagineering). How many times has Tomorrowland been altered? What happened, in the Magic Kingdom, to the 20,000 Leagues Under the Sea attraction, or where guests could visit Mickey and Minnie's houses in Fantasyland? More recently, it has been the transformation of Maelstrom in Epcot's Norway pavilion into Frozen Ever After, a ride built to create more

---

49 Alan Bryman, *Disney and His Worlds* (New York: Routledge, 1995—ebook version), 136 ; "Luis Marin: Disneyland as Degenerate Utopia," http://lmc.gatech.edu/~broglio/1101/marin.html, 23 September 2014; Tzvetan Todorov, *The Fantastic: A Structural Approach to a Literary Genre* (Cleveland: The Press of Case Western Reserve University, 1973), 42.

50 E. H. Carr, *What is History?* (New York: Alfred A. Knopf, 1962), 142, 179.

51 Sklar, *Dream It! Do It!*, 308.

52 Sklar, *Dream It! Do It!*, 306; Cross, *Consumed Nostalgia*, 202, 217.

synergy with the film *Frozen*.⁵³ This latter example does raise an issue for Dis-History and its new evolution. Each time the park is altered, guests and fans complain and worry. It is not that people do not embrace the new creations, but it is that Dis-History helps craft nostalgia, and that causes angst as things change. In the parks, unlike outside of them, things are not supposed to change (except for the better). In the case of Frozen Ever After, the very fabric of Norway, of the edutainment behind Epcot, is endangered, even if the ride itself is wildly popular, expertly Imangineered, and (largely) fits in its new location.⁵⁴ And of course the addition of the Muppets presenting Great Moments in American History in Liberty Square, or the complete transformation of Hollywood Studios away from the largely fictional backstory that it was a working studio guests were visiting into a park where guests can "ride" their favorite movies (once Star Wars Land and Toy Story Land are complete) further show the way Dis-History is being changed and challenged in the twenty-first century.⁵⁵

One of the most powerful aspects about Dis-History is that its nostalgia can be seen as a critique of the modern world. Here, on the "Disney side" of life, things are done differently. At Disney parks, while a guest can use some modern (even futuristic) transportation, most movement is done on foot. Eating is part of the experience, not just a necessity, and it is done as a family. Indeed, the family is more relaxed here, with regular roles and daily expectations of what "has to be done" somewhat subverted by the overall object of having fun together. The parks, then, are not just about consumerism, they are about offering a different perspective on life—as Walt wanted, a place for people to come together.⁵⁶ Here, his vision of what the world could be is made manifest.⁵⁷

---

53 "Frozen Getting Its Own Disney World Attraction," http://www.foxnews.com/travel/2014/09/16/frozen-getting-its-own-disney-world-attraction/, 16 September 2014.

54 "Frozen Ever After," https://disneyworld.disney.go.com/attractions/epcot/frozen-ever-after/, 4 November 2016.

55 "The Muppets Present...Great Moments in American History," https://disneyworld.disney.go.com/entertainment/magic-kingdom/muppets-present-great-moments-in-american-history/, 3 October 2016. While the transformation of Hollywood Studios is far from complete, when it comes to the Muppets, based on our 2016 trip, not only was it edutainment (with a comedic flair) but the show did seem to pull guests into the Hall of Presidents as well.

56 Mark Gottdiener, *The Theming of America: Dreams, Visions, and Commercial Spaces* (New York: Westview Press, 1997), 28–29, 112–114; Paul Marx, *Jim Rouse: Capitalist/Idealist* (New York: University Press of America, 2008), vii.

57 Andrew Lainsbury, *Once Upon an American Dream: The Story of Euro*

As dominant mainstream cultural institutions of the past lose their power or market share, what is amazing is the degree to which Disney has not. And much of that success can be attributed to the power of Dis-Historic nostalgia. One of the hallmarks of the Disney parks is the belief within the company that they are not about escapism, but rather reassurance. John Hench argued that they were "a public place where you can talk to a stranger and let your children play without fear. We are proof that a public place can be clean and things can work. We reassure people that the world can be okay!"[58] Hench's analysis is not just about the future or the present, it is about the past as well. Dis-History tells us that our story is "okay." And it ensures that generations of Americans can learn and have fun together. "Family fun," Walt argued, "is as necessary to modern living as a kitchen refrigerator." It was "no longer a dispensable luxury."[59] And that is why most of the rides are designed for families—not just kids.[60] Walt's goal was for all of this happen, together.

In the end, Walt Disney was quite successful at forging a variant of public history, Dis-History, and his successors have worked hard to keep that story alive. Perhaps it is fitting if we let Walt himself have the last words when it comes to Dis-History. When Disneyland opened, a portion of his speech read: "Disneyland is dedicated to the ideals, the dreams, and hard facts that have created America ... with the hope that it will be a source of joy and inspiration to all the world."[61] He believed there was "enough ugliness and cynicism in the world," and felt no need to add more.[62] Perhaps that should be enough for us as well. Maybe we can have some fun and learn a few things along the way.

Disneyland (Lawrence: University Press of Kansas, 2000), 197; "Elie Wiesel Visits Disneyland," http://www.tabletmag.com/jewish-arts-and-culture/books/206125/elie-wiesel-visits-disneyland, 27 June 2016.

58 Sklar, *Dream It! Do It!*, 345.

59 Dave Smith, *The Quotable Walt Disney* (New York: Disney Editions, 2001), 147.

60 Bushman, Bruce. Interview, Lectures and Transcripts, Walt Disney Studio Archives, Burbank, California.

61 Karal Ann Marling, "Disneyland, 1955: Just Take the Santa Ana Freeway to the American Dream," *American Art*, 5(Winter-Spring, 1991), 170.

62 Andrew Lainsbury, *Once Upon an American Dream: The Story of Euro Disneyland* (Lawrence: University Press of Kansas, 2000), 13.

About the Author

When he is not at a Disney theme park, Jason Lantzer is the assistant director of the Butler University Honors Program. He is an historian of American history and the author of several books. A native Hoosier, he lives outside of Indianapolis with his wife, two children, and two dogs.

About Theme Park Press

Theme Park Press publishes books primarily about the Disney company, its history, culture, films, animation, and theme parks, as well as theme parks in general.

Our authors include noted historians, animators, Imagineers, and experts in the theme park industry.

We also publish many books by first-time authors, with topics ranging from fiction to theme park guides.

And we're always looking for new talent. If you'd like to write for us, or if you're interested in the many other titles in our catalog, please visit:

www.ThemeParkPress.com

• •

Theme Park Press Newsletter

Subscribe to our free email newsletter and enjoy:

- ⬥ Free book downloads and giveaways
- ⬥ Access to excerpts from our many books
- ⬥ Announcements of forthcoming releases
- ⬥ Exclusive additional content and chapters
- ⬥ And more good stuff available nowhere else

To subscribe, visit www.ThemeParkPress.com, or send email to newsletter@themeparkpress.com.

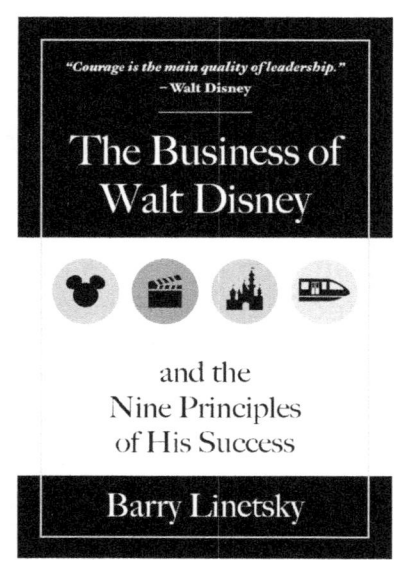

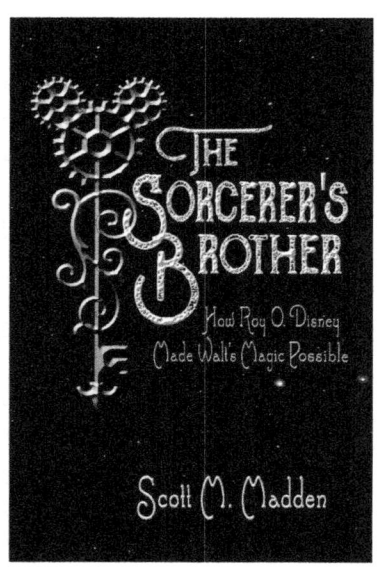

Read more about these books and our many other titles at:

www.ThemeParkPress.com

Made in United States
North Haven, CT
22 August 2022